war on the
Eastern Front

James Lucas

war on the
Eastern Front
1941-1945

The German soldier in Russia

Bonanza Books
New York

This 1982 edition is published by Bonanza Books,
distributed by Crown Publishers, Inc., by arrange-
ment with Stein and Day Incorporated.

Manufactured in the United States of America

**Library of Congress Cataloging in Publication
Data**

Lucas, James Sidney.
  War on the eastern front, 1941-1945.
  Bibliography: p.
  Includes index.
  1. World War, 1939-1945—Campaigns—Soviet
Union. 2. Germany. Heer—History—World War,
1939-1945 3. Soviet Union—History—German
occupation, 1941-1944. I. Title.
D764.L78   1982   940.54'21   82-4228
                                     AACR2

ISBN: 0-517-382857

h g f e d c b a

Contents

Illustrations

Maps

Photographs follow pages 6, 38, 134, 166 and 198

Introduction and acknowledgements

"The imposing vastness of the space in which our troops are now assembling cannot fail to strike a deep impression . . ."

THE CHIEF OF THE GENERAL STAFF JUNE 1941

At 03.30hrs on the dawn of Sunday 22 June 1941 seven German infantry armies, their advance spearheaded by four panzer groups, attacked the Soviet Union and opened, thereby, the greatest struggle in the history of military operations.

A commander when planning a campaign must have always in mind certain factors which will determine its successful outcome. Chief among these are the limitations of time and space, the strength of his own army as well as that of the enemy and the considerations of terrain and climate.

The war which the German Army undertook against the Soviet Union was the struggle of Titans; a war of superlatives both for the area it covered and for the numbers involved. The frontier at the opening of hostilities was nearly 1,600 kilometres long, excluding the 100 kilometre-long border between Finland and Russia. Then, as the German Army moved eastwards and entered Russia proper the Front expanded like a fan, so that the battle line eventually reached from northern Finland to the Caucasus, a distance of nearly 3,000 kilometres. The depth of the fighting area was 960 kilometres. Within these vast areas of longitude and latitude there marched and manoeuvred the German Army on its way, or so it thought, to a new, short and victorious war. Three million German soldiers, 600,000 vehicles, 3,580 panzers and 7,184 guns, covered by a Luftwaffe umbrella of 1,830 aircraft, rolled across the frontier in the first offensives. Propaganda had led the world to believe that the German Army was a vast mechanised, all-motorised force, but this belief was false. Pulling the guns and the carts of the supply columns or working as pack animals went nearly three quarters of a million horses – more than had entered the Kaiser's war in 1914. The imposing half-tracked troop carriers were few in number and the German infantry foot-marched vast distances, often covering seventy kilometres per day for periods of several weeks together.

The army which contested the German invasion was the Red Army of Workers and Peasants – an unknown factor and an army which Hitler had dismissed as being a clay colossus without a head. It was known to be mighty in numbers with a huge field force backed by a vast reservoir of reservists. It was thought to be poorly commanded and badly armed but, unknown to the OKW

(Oberkommando der Wehrmacht, Supreme Command of the German Armed Forces) planners, was the fact that the Russian host was equipped with some weapons, particularly tanks, which were qualitatively superior to those on issue to their own divisions. These shocks were yet to come.

The country into which the armies were advancing was a vast land mass made up of every type of terrain. From the pine-forested emptiness of northern Finland the line ran through the wide expanses of Russia's western border zone. Much of that region was covered by almost impenetrable swamps, the greatest of which extended for a distance equivalent to that between London and Carlisle. South of this and crossing the wide and monotonous steppes of the Ukraine the land changed and was succeeded in the extreme southern part of the battle front by the sub-tropical climate and terrain of Georgia and the Caucasus. Across whole regions of the line from Finland to the Caucasus were great forests of such density that they were almost jungle. The presence of the natural obstacles of mountain, desert, marsh and jungle forced the German armies into predictable routes of advance and it was to break through these passages, defended by the Red Army, that many of the bloodiest battles were fought.

The appreciation of terrain which von Greiffenburg, at one time Chief of Staff of the 12th Army, wrote, can be applied to regions other than the one about which he was reporting. "East of the Bug–San line in Poland[he wrote] terrain conditions and the shortage of roads restrict movement . . . the rivers often overflow and cause widespread flooding. This disadvantage becomes more pronounced the farther east one penetrates, particularly in the marshy, heavily-forested regions of the Pripet marshes and the Beresina river . . .".

The terrain was usually bad, the river obstacles were wide, the roads few in number and poor in construction and the main railway lines could be counted on the fingers of one hand. The German Army which was armed for, and had prepared for a short and tactical war, was expected to use the equipment designed for operations in western Europe, in all the types of terrain which were contained within the Soviet Union.

Three of the four military considerations had been considered. Only that of climate needed to be added to the calculation and this factor, OKW was confident, could be disregarded, for it was planned to finish the war with Russia before the onset of bad weather. All things considered there seemed to have been no impediment which might cause Hitler to shrink back from that decision which Josef Goebbels was to declare had caused the whole world to hold its breath. At dawn on the day following Midsummer-Day and preceding that day on which Napoleon had invaded Russia, the guns spoke and their voice was to remain unstilled for forty-six months of battle during which tens of millions were to die. The greatest war in recorded history had begun.

This book sets out to describe only certain features of the Russo-German war of 1941–1945 – those as seen by the Germans and their allies. It is not a history of that war, neither is it a chronology of its battles, nor a potted description of the progress of the campaigns. Rather it is a random selection of experiences and events which serve to illustrate the peculiarities of life on the Russian Front. It is a compilation of experiences which were unique to war on that Front, of conditions which were first encountered there or which impressed their own stamp upon the fighting there.

That it has to be a random selection of personal experiences is unavoidable. In all more than ten million men served on the Axis side during the years of war. Each of these had personal reminiscences. Each division which fought there should be accorded the mention of its service. Each battle, the tactics and the weapons used in it, should be adjudged, weighed and analysed. Conclusions should be drawn from this gallimaufry but this book is not the one to draw them.

It will also be seen that there is a heavier emphasis on the first two years of the war. The principal reason for this is that by 1943 the weapons, tactics and experiences which had made the Russian Front unique had become commonplace. A secondary reason for this imbalance is that the German Army had begun to lose the war by 1943, and its death at the hands of the Red Army was only a matter of time. Diaries and letters written in later years seldom reveal a writer's true thoughts for in retreat or defeat the principal consideration is survival. Writers of letters home resort to clichés and to circumspection so that they do not worry those at home and diary entries, in so far as these exist, usually record only the distances marched, the names of fallen comrades or the number of 'kills' made.

All wars are concerned with aggression and it can be seen that often this aggression recoils and strikes the aggressor. Some wars follow a pattern in which the victim emerges victorious, after having suffered bitter reverses, while the attacker, after brilliant initial successes, crashes down into defeat. The Russo-German war followed that pattern. There was, however, one difference which set it apart from any other campaign of the Second World War: the hatred with which it was fought. The reasons for this are dealt with in the opening chapter. This mutual animosity produced on both sides acts of so terrible a nature that I have deliberately excluded them, except in those places where their inclusion sets the seal upon some particular tragedy.

It is not my intention to weigh the political and moral attitudes of the protagonists. That their policies and methods were alien to us does not need to be stressed and I have attempted no judgements.

For the text of this book I have drawn upon interviews with former soldiers, upon diaries, letters and similar unpublished material. To supplement these personal narratives recourse has been made to war-diaries, hand books, reports and to official histories. For much of the research that was carried on I am indebted to a number of very good friends: Terry Charman, Phillip Reed and George Clout, all of the Imperial War Museum, and particularly to Matthew Cooper for the work which he carried out on many of the unpublished documents.

To all those other gentlemen with whom I corresponded or whom I interviewed go my grateful thanks. These range in rank from a former SS General Officer down to private soldiers; from a Hungarian Field Officer to an Alpini rifleman who fought with Army Group South. My thanks go also to the institutions and museums in Great Britain and on the Continent whose archives were consulted.

At a deeply personal level my thanks go, as always, to those who have supported and encouraged me: to Traude, my wife, to Barbara Shaw, to Mary Harris and to Sheila Watson, as well as to the staff of Macdonald and Jane's. Particularly I should like to mention the expert advice and assistance given by my friends in that company: Judy Tuke, Isobel Smythe-Wood, Michael Stevens and Alex Vanags.

1

'Operation Barbarossa'

*"Since the early hours of this morning there
has been fighting along the
Soviet Russian frontier . . ."*

OKW COMMUNIQUÉ, 22 JUNE 1941

At the end of the summer of 1940, Adolf Hitler was the master of continental Europe. The armed forces of the Third Reich, whose Supreme Commander he was, had conquered an Empire which ran from the Channel coast to the river Bug in Poland and from the North Cape to the Alps. Surveying the situation at the end of that victorious summer Hitler could be pleased. Taking as a starting point March 1938, the month in which German troops occupied Austria, a country outside of Germany proper, he had gained much through diplomacy, bluff and short campaigns. He had taken Czechoslovakia in two bites, between September 1938 and March 1939; Memel, that city emotive to the German mind, had been absorbed in the autumn of 1939 and then had come the invasion of Poland.

Within a month Poland had been destroyed. Two short campaigns had captured the Scandinavian countries of Denmark and Norway and had reduced to the status of vassals the Empires of France, Belgium and Holland. Only two countries stood outside the influence of Greater Germany. The one was Great Britain, now bereft of allies on the mainland of Europe, and the other the Soviet Union, an ally of Germany through a non-aggression pact signed in 1939.

There was a partial demobilisation of older age groups of servicemen, but at the same time on the western coasts of France Army divisions were practising embarkation into and debarkation from barges in which they expected to cross the Channel and invade England.

Luftwaffe squadrons had begun the 'softening-up' process of bombing airfields from which the RAF might attack any German sea-borne landing upon the coasts of Sussex or Kent. All seemed set for 'Operation Sea Lion', the invasion of the United Kingdom, but the Führer lacked enthusiasm for the enterprise. Indeed he retired to Berchtesgaden for a holiday at the end of which he announced that the projected invasion would not take place. His mind was made up. He had decided upon his next move which would make Germany's the only voice in Europe. He would destroy Russia.

THE BATTLE AREA ACROSS WHICH THE
RUSSO-GERMAN WAR WAS FOUGHT

BALTIC SEA

Archangel

R. Severnaya Dvina

L Onega

Kronstadt

L Ladoga

Leningrad

L Peipus

L Ilmen

Pskov

Valday
Hills

Riga

Dünaburg

R Dvina

Gorki

R Volga

Königsberg

Vitebsk

Moscow

Smolensk

Warsaw

Mogilev

Tula

Lublin

R Pripet

Gomel

Orel

Voronezh

Saratov

Kiev

R Dnieper

Kharkov

R Volga

CARPATHIAN MTS

Stalingrad

R Don

Odessa

Ploesti

Bucharest

Maikop

Grosny

BLACK SEA

CAUCASUS MTS

Istambul

0   200 Km

0   200 Miles

In a speech on 21 July 1940 to the heads of his armed forces he announced his intention, made necessary, he claimed, by Stalin's flirtation with Britain and, during the discussion which followed, the strategic outline of the new war was drawn. The notes made by Halder for his war diary and dated 22 July 1940 record that the intention was "... the defeat of the Russian Army, or the capture of at least as much Russian territory as necessary to prevent enemy attacks against Berlin and the Silesian industrial areas ... strength required: at most 100 divisions." This last sentence is significant, for such was the confidence of the German military commanders in the ability of their own army and such was the low opinion of the fighting qualities of the Red Army, that they considered one hundred German divisions to be more than enough to win the war.

When a comparison is made between the campaign in France during 1940 and the plan for the assault upon Russia, the astonishing fact emerges that for the new war it was proposed to commit only a handful of divisions more than were used during the second stage of the war in the west. In terms of area the German Army was to be deployed in about a million square miles of Russia, whereas the area of western Europe in which victory had been gained in 1940 with slightly fewer divisions had been approximately 50,000 square miles.

By any standards the plans of OKH (Oberkommando des Heeres, Army High Command) were optimistic but a reason lay behind the enthusiasm with which they began planning. It was not that they were keen to attack the Soviet Union. The generals all realised the menace to Germany which that nation represented but there were considerations of grand strategy which suggested to the Army Command that there were more urgent priorities than the attack upon Russia. As they saw it, there was a far greater need to reduce Great Britain and her Empire. The defeat of the Italian Army in North Africa by the British Army under Wavell convinced OKH that, necessary though a war against Russia might one day be, the first priority had to be to destroy Britain.

The principal reason for the Army's keen acceptance of the Führer's directive for a new war lay in the desire of the General Staff to make Hitler realise that he needed their professional skills. In the past the attitude of the generals vis-à-vis Hitler had fluctuated between unenthusiastic acceptance of his orders and hostility to them. They had opposed almost all of his pre-war political adventures, but these had won the Rhineland, Austria, Sudetenland and Czechoslovakia. With the outbreak of war the Führer had taken an increasingly more dominant role in the making of military decisions. His plan for the main effort of the attack upon western Europe to be launched through the Ardennes had been reluctantly accepted by the generals but had proved to be the move which brought victory. The attitude of the Army commanders had perforce changed from that of being pessimistic opponents of Hitler's policies to men who attempted to anticipate what these might in future be and to plan for them, in order to show their loyalty to their Supreme Commander. It was with this attitude in mind that von Brauchitsch, Commander-in-Chief of the German Army, had ordered his Chief of Staff to prepare a plan for the invasion of Russia, in order that "...OKH would not be unprepared..." Thus, when Hitler announced his intention of turning eastwards the Army General Staff could tell the Führer with pride they had already undertaken active planning.

As a result of the information which had already been gained from that planning the Army Commanders were able to convince Hitler that his original intention to open the new operation in the autumn of 1940 was impossible to realise and this was thereupon postponed to the spring of 1941.

The new campaign was predicated upon the ability of the German Army to destroy the Red Army west of the Dnieper river. If the Russian Army did not give battle but withdrew into the vastnesses of the Soviet Union, then the Germans would be sucked into a long drawn-out war for which they did not have the resources. The writer, A.J.P. Taylor, underlined the last point when he wrote "...while his potential opponents [the other Great Powers] were rearming for a great 'war in depth', Hitler rearmed Germany 'in breadth' – everything for the front line and no reserves for a second campaign...".

With the benefit of hindsight we can encapsulate not only the situation which confronted Germany's military planners but also the way in which it developed. Their armies, weaker in strength than those of their opponents, were expected to destroy the enemy in so short a time that the problems of winter warfare could be avoided and the greatest terrain problem of western Russia – the Pripet Marsh ignored.

As it happened the Red Army was not destroyed west of the Dnieper. True, a host equal to the number of divisions which OKH had estimated to constitute the Soviet field force had been killed or captured by the end of autumn, but always there were more Russian divisions to contest the German advance. Such was the nature of that opposition put up by the Red Army and such was the effect of terrain upon the speed of the drive that the war did drag on, producing in the first winter a defeat for the Germans, despair among the soldiers and a growing belief that victory was not possible.

The factor of the Pripet Marsh, its influence upon the course of operations and its subsequent use as a base for partisan operations was to prove an ulcer in the German body.

We have been able to encapsulate the problems and their development. We can, in like fashion, summarise the principal faults of which the German Command were guilty. For the war against Russia, the General Staff had overestimated their own Army's

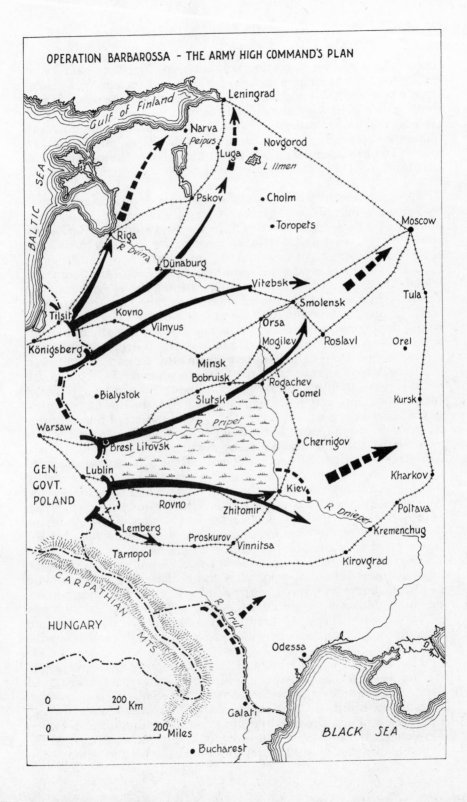

OPERATION BARBAROSSA - THE ARMY HIGH COMMAND'S PLAN

Gulf of Finland

BALTIC SEA

Leningrad

Narva

L Peipus

Luga

Novgorod

L Ilmen

Pskov

Cholm

Toropets

Moscow

Riga

R Dvina

Dünaburg

Vitebsk

Smolensk

Tula

Tilsit

Kovno

Orsa

Roslavl

Orel

Königsberg

Vilnyus

Mogilev

Minsk

Bobruisk

Rogachev

Gomel

Kursk

Bialystok

Slutsk

Warsaw

R Pripet

Chernigov

Brest Litovsk

GEN.
GOVT.
POLAND

Lublin

Kiev

Kharkov

Rovno

Zhitomir

R Dnieper

Poltava

Lemberg

Proskurov

Vinnitsa

Kremenchug

Tarnopol

Kirovgrad

CARPATHIAN MTS

R Prut

HUNGARY

Odessa

0   200 Km

0   200 Miles

Galati

BLACK SEA

Bucharest

potential, they had underestimated that of the Red Army and Soviet ability to lead and to equip that Army. They had ignored the factor of terrain and had left unconsidered that of climate. The sum of these faults was a plan for disaster and the war did end disastrously for Germany. What is surprising is that the German war machine won important strategic victories right up to the middle of 1943, and a great number of tactical ones thereafter. Such was the measure of its capabilities.

The active planning for the new war was based upon plans drawn up by various senior officers. Marcks, Chief of Staff of the 18th Army, envisaged a two-phase campaign. In the first stage the Red Army would be encircled and destroyed close to the frontier. During the second the German Army would then go on to occupy the valuable industrial areas of western Russia and at the end of the campaign would have reached a general line running from Archangel to Rostov. The two groups of forces needed to carry out Marcks' plan would at first be separated by the obstacle of the Pripet Marsh but would then combine on its eastern edge to carry the all-out assault towards Moscow, while a small holding group detached from the main body prevented the Red Army from attacking the Roumanian oil-fields, which were vital to the German economy.

In a revision of his plan Marcks advanced the logical, but as it turned out completely inaccurate premise, "... the Russians cannot avoid a decision as they did in 1812. Modern armed forces of one hundred divisions cannot abandon their sources of supply. It is anticipated that the Russian Army will stand to do battle in a defensive position protecting Great Russia and the Eastern Ukraine."

Marcks was not to know that the Soviets had developed other sources of supply than those in Western Russia and that a relocation of Soviet heavy industry was under way which would place the factories east of the Ural mountains. Those two facts negated the whole premise of the Marcks plan.

That put forward by von Paulus, Deputy Chief of General Staff, amended parts of the Marcks' plan and proposed that there should be not two but three Army Groups, each with a specific objective. He, too, made Moscow the prime target and according to Halder's war diary "... the capture of Leningrad and the Don basin beyond Kharkov would depend upon the progress of the general offensive against Moscow ...".

Plans drawn up by Chiefs of Staff of each of the three Army Groups foresaw the importance of Moscow as the target. Two agreed on its importance as the prime target. Von Sodenstern, however, doubted the ability of the German Army to bring the Red Army to battle west of the Dnieper and proposed lightning advances upon Moscow, Leningrad and Kharkov with the aim of crippling the Soviet leadership. The plan presented to Hitler by the Commander-in-Chief of the Army and his Chief of Staff on 5 December 1940, produced the response from Hitler that Moscow was of no great importance. This was a complete reversal of the principle upon which the Army's plan was based.

The Führer's directive stated: "The main weight ... will be delivered in the northern area ... The more southerly of the two army groups [of this northern grouping], will have the task of advancing ... and routing the enemy forces in White Russia ... [and will help] to destroy the enemy forces operating in the Baltic area. Only after the fulfilment of this essential task [including the occupation of Leningrad] will the attack be continued with the intention of occupying Moscow."

By March 1941, there were fears at OKW on whether the German forces were sufficient in number. In view of Hitler's reluctance to use troops of nations allied to Germany, the southern thrust had to be weakened and the Führer also claimed the Pripet marshes presented no serious obstacle to a linear advance. The arguments of his senior commander notwithstanding, the final plan for 'Operation Barbarossa' was as follows: Army Group North would attack from East Prussia in the general direction of Leningrad, Army Group Centre would advance from Poland to force a break through towards Smolensk. These two groups would then join to destroy the enemy formations in the Baltic area. Meanwhile Army Group South would move from southern Poland and through Kiev to the great bend of the lower Dnieper.

There then followed a vague statement that once the northern objectives had been attained freedom of movement for further tasks was assured. This implied a co-operation with Army Group South, presumably to assist that Army Group to complete its tasks. Thereafter, there would come the advance towards Moscow.

The German dispositions

Army Group North, commanded by von Leeb, had two armies on its establishment. Busch's 16th with eight divisions and the 18th Army, under Küchler, with seven. To lead these infantry forces there was a Panzer Group, Hoepner's 4th, made up of three panzer, three motorised and two infantry divisions. There were six other divisions (three infantry and three security) in Army Group reserve and two more infantry divisions in the OKH reserve, held behind Army Group's front.

The strongest of the Army Groups was that of the centre under von Bock. The 4th Army (von Kluge) had fourteen divisions while that of Strauss (9th Army) had nine. With this Army Group there were two panzer groups: Guderian's 2nd with fifteen divisions (five panzer, three motorised, a cavalry and six infantry) and Hoth's 3rd with eleven divisions (including four panzer and three motorised).

Army Group Centre had one infantry division in reserve and a further six in OKH reserve.

Von Rundstedt's Army Group South disposed three armies. The 17th, under Stulpnagel, had thirteen divisions, the 6th, commanded by von Reichenau had six and the 11th Army with seven divisions was commanded by von Schobert. The 1st Panzer Group (von Kleist) with Army Group South had fourteen divisions, of which five were panzer and three motorised infantry. Army Group South reserve was one infantry division and the OKH reserve was made up of six divisions.

Thus, on 22 June 1941 a host made up of seven armies and four panzer groups was ready to move across the frontier. The whole force consisted of one hundred and thirty-four divisions, of which seventeen were panzer, thirteen armoured infantry, the only cavalry division in the German Army, four mountain divisions and nine security. The remainder were infantry.

To this purely German force must be added the armies of her allies, of which there were fourteen Roumanian and twenty-one Finnish divisions. Later these would be joined by Hungarian forces, a Spanish division, a whole Italian Army together with a number of smaller contingents from other European nations. Later still the number of foreign units would include regiments and divisions of the Waffen SS raised from French, Belgian, Dutch and Scandinavian volunteers. The presence of those men in the war against Russia is dealt with in another chapter.

Although the number of armoured divisions available for 'Barbarossa' had more than doubled (fifteen in May 1940; thirty-two in June 1941) the number of vehicles had increased by only a third (2,574/3,332). Hitler, aware of the importance of the armoured thrust to the new campaign had raised the number of panzer divisions by the simple expedient of cutting in half the establishment of existing divisions and thus creating two divisions out of one. It will be appreciated that, of course, the regular formations retained the best of the equipment and parcelled out the remainder to the new units as these were formed. Those who were among the last to be raised were issued equipment of the most diverse nature. The 18th Panzer Division, for example, had no vehicles at all until June 1941, when French trucks were supplied. With no delay the troops were then carried straight from the 18th division's concentration area to the form up zone, east of Warsaw, and put into action. When the division entered the fighting it did so with 162 different types of soft skin vehicle, among the twenty-one major groupings of which it was composed. One of those groupings had seventeen different types of lorry within a unit establishment of thirty-three vehicles. The artillery regiment had 445 vehicles on establishment and there were sixty-nine different types of lorry. The problem of spares for these many, and often unusual, different types of machine can best be imagined. There was, however, one vehicle which was not included on the war establishment and which was yet to be found in every unit.

This was the Russian *panje* cart, a horse-drawn waggon, robustly constructed, light and extremely mobile. One transport officer was to remark bitterly, "The *panje* cart was the only standardised transport we had, and that was not even an official issue."

Three million German soldiers went into 'Operation Barbarossa' supported by more than seven thousand artillery pieces and with their advances led by 3,332 tanks. When this mighty force moved forward on the dawn of 22 June 1941 a turning point was reached in the Second World War. Britain, which for a whole year had stood alone and unconquered against Hitler, once more had an ally and the spectre of a two-front war arose again to haunt the German General Staff. All that they had feared was coming true.

The Red Army's dispositions

The Soviets, conscious of the threat imposed by the growing power of Hitler's Germany, had deployed the Red Army in four special military districts along the common frontier. In the belief that Germany's aim would be to seize economic prizes and, in particular, the oil and wheat of southern Russia, the Red Army's High Command had concentrated the greatest number of its armies in the districts which covered the Ukraine.

The Soviet line of battle, starting in the south and working northwards, had at its most southerly point the Odessa Special Military District with 9th Army under command. This Army controlled twelve infantry and two armoured divisions which were deployed in the area between the rivers Pruth and Dniester, covering a front which ran from the Black Sea and along the whole length of Moldavia.

The next Special Military District was that of Kiev and this disposed four main armies. These were, running from south to north, 12th, 26th, 6th, and 5th. Behind those front line armies a new one had been raised, 28th, whose task it would be to act as a deep reserve. The Kiev district had forty infantry and sixteen armoured divisions in its command; excluding the divisions of the newly formed 28th Army, and the line which the district held stood along the Carpathian mountains and continued northwards conforming to the line of the lower Bug.

Of the four districts the next, the Western, was in the most exposed position for it projected strongly into Poland as it followed the river Bug, which formed the frontier between Germany and Russia.

One of the Western District's armies, the 10th grouped around Bialystok, was outflanked both to the north and south by two German panzer groups. The Kiev district had three armies in the line: 4th, 10th and 3rd, with the newly-raised 13th Army in reserve. Of the thirty-six divisions under command, excluding those of 13th Army, twenty-six were infantry and ten armoured.

The most northerly of the four Special Military Districts facing the German Army was the Baltic, with 11th and 8th Armies under Command. Like the Kiev and Western district the Baltic had a newly formed Army, the 27th, in reserve. In the Baltic district there were twenty infantry and six armoured divisions disposed along the East Prussian frontier and extending northwards to touch the Baltic Sea in the area of the republic of Latvia.

Thus, ten Russian armies were in the line with a further three in reserve. A force of ninety-eight infantry or motorised divisions and thirty-four armoured divisions was in the field together with a number of cavalry and other divisions. The German appreciation of Russian strength was based on summaries completed during 1938 and 1940 and, therefore, grossly underestimated the forces which the Soviets could produce. The frustration which was felt at the outpouring of men can be seen in Halder's war diary. During mid-August there is an entry which admits: "we reckoned with two hundred divisions, but now we have already identified three hundred and sixty".

The Germans found that the fighting quality of the Red Army units varied considerably and one reason for the poor showing of the early days was that there was no great unifying force, no emotional object with which the soldiers could identify themselves and for which they would fight.

Not until the declaration of the war as being that fought for the Fatherland did the attitudes of the ordinary Russian soldiers change and their resistance to the invader become more fierce. This is not to say that there was no heroism shown by the Red Army in the early days of the campaign, nor does it mean that there were not units which even in 1945 did not collapse and retreat in panic. There were such units, of course, but the Red Army after 1942 was an entirely different one in spirit from that of the days of June 1941.

The concept of the 'Great Patriotic War' was also responsible for the growth of the Russian partisan movement from small and scattered bands into an unseen army which worked against the rear echelons and supplies of the German forces. The feeling of omnipresent danger was expressed by an officer of the SS *Leibstandarte Adolf Hitler*, 'Panzer' Meyer, when he remarked "The Front is everywhere."

The greatest blunder committed by the German Supreme Command was that of underestimating Russia's capacity to put vast numbers of men into the field armies and into the partisan movement and to supply them with weapons. Of much less significance were the problems of climate and terrain. Both of those factors can be met and mastered. But to have considered an enemy to be a powerless rabble and then to be made aware that it is none of those things but a powerful, well-armed and aggressive force was the experience of the German General Staff when it first became clear that the intelligence appreciations upon which they had based their plans for conquest had been totally false.

For the ordinary soldier the unending battle against an enemy which his generals had told him had been defeated produced a peculiar depression. Particularly when he contrasted the dwindling numbers of his own companies with the flood of men whom the Red Army could put into action and of whom there seemed to be no end.

But all this was in the future, in the years of struggle which lay ahead. Let us instead go back in time to the early hours of the morning of 22 June. No order came to cancel the operation. The minutes ticked away and then at 03.15hrs the die was cast. The Führer, whose decision it was that Russia be destroyed, sent his armies pouring across the frontier. The statistics with which he had been supplied had led him to believe that the war machine which he had constructed would win another short war. It had to be short for Germany could not risk a long one.

The summer night was warm. The woods along the frontier were full of troops resting, waiting, sleeping. The concentration areas were full of men who had arrived, many after long journeys from France, eager to be in on this new enterprise. One officer recorded how his comrades had brought with them from France bottles of vintage champagne and that they stood, as the slow minutes ticked away, ready to drink to the success of the new war. As the first greyness of a summer dawn was seen in the east the dark western sky was lit by muzzle flashes of German guns as they fired upon selected targets on the eastern bank of the Bug river. 'Operation Barbarossa' had begun.

Using a very simple analogy the course of the German–Russian war of 1941–45 can be said to have resembled the action of a pendulum. In the summer of 1941 it had swung eastwards to bring the German armies to the gates of Moscow. The Russian winter offensive had then returned the swing from east to west as it drove back the German forces. During the summer of 1942 and the period of the second German summer offensive the pendulum swung eastwards once more and at the farthest extent of its swing reached the Volga at Stalingrad. The Russian offensive during the second winter of the war then forced the movement back again. Another German attempt, launched during the summer of 1943, failed and this time, without waiting for the onset of winter, the Red Army flowed westwards on a long and continuous swing which was maintained with halts of only short durations until the war's end.

The German Army entered upon the campaign with the full confidence of winning victory within months. Because of this falsely-engendered belief there had been no forethought, no proper planning to equip the armed forces with modern, strategic weapons, and even to hint at the possibility of a need for winter clothing was tantamount to doubting Hitler's word that the war would be quickly won. Thus the Wehrmacht, and particularly the Army, went into a war which had not been strategically thought through, was too hastily planned and subject to too much interference from a Supreme Headquarters hundreds, sometimes thousands, of kilometres removed from the battle front. No wonder then that the regiments bled almost to death in that first bitter winter. The realisation of the scale of the sacrifices which had been made by the ordinary fighting man was so strong in the mind of Model that he rounded on Hitler who had dared to remark that the men of 1943 were not of the same calibre as those of 1941. "Of course they are not, my Führer" retorted the fiery General. "The men of 1941 are dead, scattered in graves all over Russia."

At the end of the year 1942, and by the time that winter had come again, the Army had learned how to overcome the difficulties of the cold weather season and how to convert its disadvantages into advantages.

The ad hoc improvisations of that first year had been regularised. The Army had come to terms with one of the unique features of warfare on the Eastern Front; only the Supreme Commander was still incapable of making a decision and sticking to it. Also he was beginning to show signs that the strain upon him had become too great and that his mind was becoming deranged.

By the middle of 1943 the pattern of the war had become established and with very few exceptions all the weapons and tactics that had once been peculiar to the Russian front were in use in other theatres of operations.

It is, therefore, principally the Russian campaign in its first two years that this book deals with and the few references to events, battles or tactics of other and later years serve only to illustrate a particular point.

One should at this juncture, state that the war on the Eastern Front was fought with a particular savagery. Neither side saw it as a mere struggle between nations, nor did they view it as a contest between ideologies: National Socialist Germany against Communist Russia. It was to many Germans and Russians a resumption of that conflict for domination between East and West, between Slav and Teuton, which had marked the progress of European history for over a millenium. It is as well to remember this for only then do the sacrifice and effort, the atrocities and the brutalities of the forty-six months of war become comprehensible.

To this folk memory of genocidal battles fought in centuries past must be added a religious aspect of a crusade against godlessness which caused many young men in western Europe to enlist with the German forces. This idealistic, almost romantic concept of being a crusader may have been but brief, nevertheless it cannot be denied that it existed and was reinforced in the early days of the campaign by the action of villagers in the Ukraine who blessed the men in the vehicles marked with the black cross and who saw the German soldiers as a liberating, Christian host.

Crusading idealism vanished in the cannon's roar but even those who quickly lost this religious/ideological surcoat, or those who had never been covered by it, were soon convinced as a result of their experiences on the Eastern Front of the need to fight on until Germany won the war. They had seen the way in which the lives of Russian soldiers were casually wasted in repeated and hopeless attacks.

And this Oriental contempt for the individual convinced most of the German soldiers that if the Russians held the lives of their own men so cheap, how much cheaper would they hold those of their enemies. Other soldiers, from the recollection of sights seen in recaptured hospitals or retaken trenches, were convinced that to surrender might well be the prelude to death or torture, or else to long years of hard labour in the mines of some Soviet slave camp. To prevent that nightmare from becoming a reality every sacrifice must be made, every demand met, no effort left undone to ensure total victory. Western civilisation had to be saved. Germany had to win or else she would be destroyed.

There is no doubt that many Germans and many of those Europeans who fought in the ranks of the Waffen SS, really did see themselves as bastions of western European civilisation. Equally, of course, there were millions in Germany who had not supported Hitler in 1933 and who had viewed his policies with repugnance just as they viewed Germany's future with despair. Yet, when Hitler invaded Russia, many of these political opponents accepted that he had been right to attack the eastern barbarians before they moved westwards and destroyed the German fatherland.

For their part the leaders of the Soviet Union soon realised that if their country was to be saved from this new invasion of Teutonic knights then it was not sufficient to call upon the masses to rally around Marx and Lenin. The Communist leaders, too, appealed to the deep instincts of patriotism which lay within the soul of the Russian people and converted the war into a struggle to defend Russia the Motherland; the Soviet Motherland.

In a paper which he wrote on experiences gained in combat against the Russians SS General Max Simon stated "A *national* concept had not at this time (summer and autumn 1941) penetrated the minds of the Russian Front-line troops; it was not proclaimed by Stalin until late autumn ..." From that time on the tenacity with which the Red Army fought changed to become a fanatical determination to drive the invaders from their homeland. It was with this bitterness in their hearts that Soviet troops fought their way westwards across Europe, destroying their enemies and capturing the capital city of Berlin which sheltered the man who had brought about the war. The Red Army men had seen their country invaded and had witnessed the results of that war and its effects upon the Russian people. Their vengeance was terrible.

The war on the Eastern Front was unique not least for the sheer size of the battlefield and of the numbers which fought there. On no other Front did such masses of men and materials move across so great an area. The scale of losses is unbelievable. The German Army lost nearly one thousand horses per day for every day of the war. Red Army tank groupings in the last year of the war numbered thousands of machines massed on quite small sectors of the Front. The size of the battle area, the vast expanse of the Pripet Marsh and the factors of terrain had as great an influence on the strategy of the Russian war as SP guns and rocket weapons had on the tactical. The climate with its harsh winters, scouring dust in summer and clinging mud for much of the rest of the year were other factors peculiar to the campaign in Russia.

To open this book the first chapters accompany the German Army in the early days and weeks of the campaign. These rely very heavily upon the stories of Germany infantry as they experienced the sights of this strange, closed land which ran halfway round the world from Poland to Alaska. Then the Red Army is dealt with, as are some of the principal weapons used by both sides: the rocket artillery of the Germans and the development of self-propelled guns. Turning to the factors of climate and terrain, the terrors of the winter season and the frustrations of the tenacious mud of Russia are handled as well as the influence of ground on the development of the first campaign. Finally, the book deals with a military phenomenon which developed in Russia: the deliberate acceptance by German forces of being encircled.

This is a book solely about the Army; the Luftwaffe and the Navy have no place in it. It is about soldiers and the tragedy of war.

2

The German Army

"At the beginning of the campaign . . . we German soldiers, generally speaking knew little about our adversary . . ."

Max Simon
LIEUTENANT GENERAL OF THE WAFFEN SS

To the German soldier who waited upon the opening of 'Operation Barbarossa' his new enemy, the Soviet Union, was a complete enigma for since the Revolution little positive and accurate information on conditions there had been published in his country, or in the world in general. There had been propaganda put out by the supporters and the detractors of the Communist state and somewhere between the two extremes of falsification lay the truth. That the system was a dictatorship had never been denied and, therefore, the government was certain to be rigid, autocratic and unyielding. The standard of life was believed to be lower than that enjoyed in the West and it was believed that the Russian people were prisoners of a ruthlessly-governed, economically-underprivileged society.

The Germans saw the Communist political and economic system as more restrictive than that under which they themselves lived and to this was added a racial element in that many of them held it to be self-evident that the Slav peoples were an inferior race. Since all Slavs were inferior it followed that conditions in Russia, the mother Slav country, must be even more primitive than in those other Slav nations which had had contact with the West. The standard of life in Poland, which the German Army had defeated two years earlier, had been filmed and commented upon by the German propaganda machine to prove conclusively, to any who still questioned the master race dogma, that the Slavs were inferior and that they subsisted in backward conditions, simply because they were inferior.

A rigid Red dictatorship and grinding poverty for the masses were the accepted ideas of conditions in the Soviet Union. But what of the power of the Red Army? Thousands of Germans had fought as soldiers on the Eastern Front during the First World War and later on, during the 1920s and early 'thirties, German officers also served in the Soviet Union when the Communist government granted those facilities which enabled the German High Command to evade the limitations of the Versailles Treaty and to test the theories of contemporary warfare and modern military techniques. The men who had trained in Russia were fewer in number than those who had

fought as combatants on the Eastern Front but they had been, in
those Weimar days, the most promising candidates for high position
in the German General Staff and they should have acquired a first-
hand knowledge of the country, its people and its Army. This
knowledge must have been laid before the section of Intelligence
dealing with foreign armies in the East. If anyone in Germany
should have known about Soviet capability it should have been
them.

Nevertheless, most Germans, like most people everywhere, were
generally ignorant of the Soviet Union. They knew that
geographically it was a vast territory covering nearly one sixth of
the land surface of the globe, but in Russia they were unprepared for
the depression which was engendered by the realisation of its
terrible vastness. They were unprepared for fields of sunflowers
which went on for kilometre after kilometre after weary kilometre;
solid blocks of colour stretching forward to the distant horizons. In
the summer a sea of upraised heads, gold and yellow, stood erect,
while in the searing heat of late autumn this pride had been brought
down and the flowers stood with bent heads burnt to a deep brown by
the fierce sun.

There were maize fields of unimaginable size and immense
forests which were like jungles in the density of their tangled
undergrowth. There were woods of such impenetrability that most
German troops could advance scant hundreds of metres into them.
The soldiers were unprepared for marshes which form one of the outstanding natural obstacles of the central and north-western republic
of Byelo-Russia; marshes so great in extent as to be as large as two
provinces of their German homeland. They found rivers unembankmented and prone to flood with waters which swept across the flat,
monotonous landscape, increasing for months at a time the already
vast marsh area. Thus far the terrain.

They had, in their naivety, those German troops, perhaps
thought of Russia as having the same road and rail system as their
own. Of course, they reasoned, the primitive Slavs would not have an
autobahn like Hitler's Germany, but a first-class road system, or so
they thought, must certainly exist. Instead of a vast network they
found that the number of all-weather roads in western Russia could
be counted on the fingers of one hand and that these roads converged
upon Moscow, the Soviet capital: the heart and power house of the
Red Empire. They then discovered that most roads, excepting only
the few main highways, were turned into impassable mud tracks
following only moderate rain fall; that surfaces became deeply
rutted through the weight of traffic, that they were completely
impassable in winter and were sandy, engine-scouring dust traps in
the summer. The railway, the only other main source of
communication, was just as inadequate. Not only were the main
lines few in number and the branch line system poor, but the whole
railway network used a broader gauge than that of western Europe,

a difference which brought about a tremendous strain upon the small amount of rolling stock which the Army was able either to seize or to adapt.

Even the maps used in the early days had little information on them that was correct. Rundstedt's statement, "Everything was false", was the heart cry of an officer to whom the topographical details on a map were as sacred as the law and who found it incomprehensible that cartographers could fill maps with false details. "Where main roads were marked," Rundstedt went on to complain, "none existed. On the other hand, where a country track was indicated this frequently turned out to be a main highway. Maps would show an industrial area and we would find nothing but a swamp or a forest. Then where steppe was marked we would suddenly be confronted by a modern industrial region. Little or nothing on the maps with which we were issued was true."

It was, however, in the attitude of the masses of the Soviet peoples that the ordinary soldier of the German Army found such a contrast between his own country and that in which he was fighting. The great mass of the population was made up of peasants and these *Moujiks* were passive. In bad weather or in the periods of the greatest mud, after having laid in sufficient stock of fuel and food, they went into a form of human hibernation emerging only rarely and then just to feed the cattle or to draw water. To attempt to work in such conditions was unheard of. As a peasant one retired indoors and waited for the bad time to pass by. A dumb submission, a humble acceptance of fate's blows, whether it was drought or flood, a Party ukase, a German occupation or the destruction of his primitive house: all were accepted without demur. The eternal *Moujik* remained unmoved. He knew that basic things mattered and remained. The soil mattered and would still be there whether Tsar or commissar ruled. For the rest, if the hut burnt down or blew away it would not take long to build another. If the cow died either the *Kolkhoz* would supply another or it would not, and if it did not then one went without milk - *Nichevo*.

The passive Slav acceptance was annoying to the more agile and questioning Teuton mind and the ordinary soldiers could not comprehend how human beings could be so lacking in human dignity or spirit that they would accept to live in the primitive conditions which were encountered throughout the conquered regions. They had known that Russia must be less well endowed with the good things of life than was their own German homeland, but they were shocked to find that the ordinary peasant lived little better than the animals with whom he shared his quarters. In letters, diaries and reports the German word *Sauberkeit* (cleanliness) was the most frequently recurring one when the writer dealt with the living conditions of the Russian peasant.

Another great contrast between Germany and Russia lay in the climatic conditions. In Germany there were certainly cold winters and hot summers but not the extreme differences in temperature encountered in the Soviet Union; the bitter cold of thirty or forty degrees below zero, the searing heat of summer when temperatures rose to unbearable levels, both were strange phenomena. One question posed in post-war years was whether the appalling hardships suffered by the German Army during the first frightful winter might have been avoided or at least minimised had the Russian road and rail system been more widespread and able to overcome the climatic conditions. If OKH had had the ability to bring fresh troops into the line or to withdraw those exhausted by the privations then this mobility might have gone a long way to sustain the German Army. It might have been able, perhaps, to have held in check the great Soviet winter offensive. Climate may be, as the opening statement of one chapter says, "a series of natural disasters", but these might have been less disastrous had a competent road and rail system existed, or had the German engineers built them.

Lacking efficient channels to support their life system, the regiments on the open steppes were the victims of every catastrophe from frostbite to pneumonia and typhus. These ranged from long marches retreating through waist high snow where progress could be as little as five kilometres in a day to enduring attacks by wave after wave of well-equipped and warmly-clad Siberian riflemen who, completely at home in the sub-zero temperatures, swept out of the blinding snowstorm to harry and to kill.

The presence of such élite troops leads, inevitably, to the German opinions of the Red Army. Those who had fought the Russians in the years of the Great War were very much aware of the tremendous courage of the ordinary Russian soldier and his ability to suffer great privations, but they had little belief in his ability to think for himself or to act upon his own initiative. Those senior German officers who, as young soldiers in the days of Weimar, had practised and manoeuvred on the steppes around Kazan thought of the leaders of the Red Army as competent to command corps but felt that they lacked the stature to command Armies or Army Groups. The poor showing of the Soviet forces in the war against Finland, the primitive equipment of the infantrymen of the Red Army met at the end of the Polish campaign, all were signs which reinforced the German belief that the great strength of the Red Army lay in its historic role as a steamroller, operating without subtlety and unwieldy in manoeuvre as it rolled blindly onwards crushing the enemy into the ground.

It was widely believed that the great blood-letting of 1937, when Stalin had executed his marshals, his general officers and many of his field officers, had led to a weakening of resolution in the highest échelons of the Soviet military structure. The known presence of the political officer or commissar at every level of command in the Red Army, and the power of these officials to revoke a plan with which they did not agree, also helped to convince the German Command that sound military decisions might well be reversed and the success of any plan jeopardised by the interference of men who may have been politically astute but who were very often militarily incompetent. By a fateful paradox senior German officers were eventually to see the policies and decisions of their own warlord, and another military amateur, compelling them to carry out plans which went against all military logic but which were insisted upon by him since he, as a politician, was convinced that propaganda was more important than the lives of his soldiers.

To begin this section of the book which deals with the German soldiers' experience of Russia it must be stated that much has been compressed, that a great part is a consensus of experience, that the sources chosen are random ones and that the chapter is one full of generalisations. Nevertheless, they are incidents as the participants saw them and, therefore, a picture of service in the line. To many the descriptive style may be naive, full of schoolboy heroics and senseless posturing, but, and this must be appreciated and accepted, these were the attitudes current at the time, these were the held opinions and those were the postures taken.

There can be no doubt that so far as the German Army was concerned it was chiefly upon the infantry that the main burden of battle fell and that it was they who suffered the heaviest losses. It was their incredible marching ability which set the seal of victory upon those battles which the armoured forces had initiated. As the writer of the account which opens this section has stated, it was the foot-soldier who had to fight his way through village and forests and across vast areas of steppe. He had to do all this and still maintain a marching rate of up to seventy kilometres per day.

It is, therefore, the experiences of the infantry which have been selected to represent, at this point, the story of the German Army in the East although other chapters will deal with SPs and rocket artillery. Both arms of service were important but ever and always it is the foot-soldier, with a light and mobile personal weapon, who secures the ground, captures it, defends it and holds it and who is the irreplaceable factor. He is irreplaceable because he is physically present upon the ground and dominates it in a way that no machine ever can.

This then, to begin the story, is the war of infantry: the way in which they coped with problems, overcame difficulties and dealt with the myriad things, both natural and unnatural, normal and abnormal, which dominated their lives. It is the story of men along a 2000-kilometre battle-front fighting against a tenacious enemy, and the vagaries of terrain and difference in climate.

The first of the narratives which make up this section of the book is an abbreviated excerpt recounting the opening stages of 'Barbarossa'. Then follows an account which records the last days of an SS tank-busting unit in the province of Brandenburg during the final weeks of the war. These accounts have been selected for the contrast they show between the attitude of an infantryman in 1941 and the bitter despair of an ad hoc, bicycle-mounted team in 1945.

With tired eyes smarting from the sun, with dry and crusted lips, with faces bedewed with sweat they were marching. They had been marching for seven hours and it was still not midday. Clouds of dust enfolded them. In long, endless columns they pushed eastwards. In the dawn hours of this day their widespread companies had thrust forward and had crossed the frontier. It was the bark of a PAK, the rattle of the heavy machine gun which drove them forward. The fires of excitement which they felt in their hearts were damped down somewhat by the debilitating heat.

Their thoughts went back to the start. The eastern campaign had begun. At last the fearful waiting for an unknown something was past. Seven hours ago it had started – it – that important, special, 'it' – war against the Soviets.

After short, bitter fire fights with the surprised but determined frontier troops they were now advancing more quickly. In front of them the assault guns, behind them their own heavy artillery firing deep into the enemy's lines. German bombers cruised overhead weaving silver trails across a sky in which hung only the glowing, pitiless silver disc of the sun. They went on. Feet sank into dust and puffed it from soles of boots so that it rose to lay a crust upon them. Kilometre after kilometre the feet marched. Horses coughing in the dust clouds gave off a pungent odour. A cloud of silent tiredness hung above the marching men. After the fight in the frontier area they had had to bury their first dead comrades. This had all occurred so suddenly that it seemed as if it had never happened. And yet it had – only a few short hours earlier.

The hands of the watches had shown 3.05 and they had rushed forward springing in quick steps to reach the Soviet frontier pill-boxes. A few short bursts had been sufficient to beat down the resisting enemy who were dressed only in vest and pants. Only a few were killed. In the short minutes of the first contact they knew what had now come, inescapable and unbelievable – war. Then they had moved on into the first villages.

This picture was repeated everywhere along the battle line from the Baltic to the Black Sea. Strange huts, wooden walls, some fitted with tiles but most covered with mossy green straw. Foreign people who stared with inquisitive eyes, shocked by the force of the explosion, by the burning, crackling houses set alight by artillery shells. There lay the first dead. Earth-brown uniforms, pale faces, pointed and white; thin noses projected from dead faces. It was war . . .

Everywhere on the long frontier they had been the first . . . the infantry. Certainly they had been accompanied by engineers and anti-tank teams but the first shots were fired from their machine guns and theirs were the first prisoners: Red Army men brought out of the houses and swept into captivity as an arm sweeps clear the table. The sun was pitiless in its intensity.

There was no water, only sweat that burned in the eyes and made the shirt flap wetly against the skin. The companies, battalions, regiments had regrouped after the breakthrough and now they were on the march again. Fast reconnaissance groups from the motorised elements of the division and regiments set out along the deeply-rutted roads, through patches of loose sand and clouds of dust, heading always eastwards. Securing the flanks were squadrons of cyclists, cavalry and armoured cars. All were seeking an enemy who had pulled back to high ground and to the field fortifications on river banks where he would offer resistance. The scene repeated itself along the whole front from Tilsit to the mouth of the Danube.

The infantry advanced through the sticky, hot woods, through small villages dozing in the sunlight or along the side of the great road to the east. On the few main highways the advancing armour was followed by the motorised units. Behind the virile panzer thrusts the infantry marched and there where resistance was met they went in to destroy it.

At Memel, at Brest Litovsk, at Przemysl and in front of Lemberg there had been fighting and the end result had been the defeat and destruction of the enemy. The first days passed.

In between the fighting the infantry had marched, sometimes seventy kilometres each day and this they had achieved in enemy territory, where waving cornfields hid the crafty *Kalmuk*, where trees carried not only the heavy fruits of summer but the wily sniper. Burning villages, staring bodies of fallen Soviet soldiers, swollen carcasses of dead horses, rusting, blackened and burnt out tanks were the signposts of the march. Soviet cavalry, enemy tanks, dive-bombing aircraft and *Rata* fighters skimming low, fast and straight as arrow flight; all tried to halt the advance but none succeeded. More tired now were the feet, more dry the throats and the lips of those who marched and marched were long since silent. The sun stayed in the sky for hours and only slowly did night approach. The heat, however, did not die.The head of the marching columns halted, the battalions closed up and took up all round defence positions. Even when that was done patrols still had to go out, moving on tired and painful feet to seek out the enemy. Rapid, heavy firing betrayed the Soviet positions and showed how watchful they were. At last the column bivouacked for the night and lukewarm coffee cleansed the lips. The soldiers began to chew on their rations and the first words were spoken.

The soldiers forced their tired bodies to wield entrenching tools and dig shallow slit trenches in which they could take cover, but not in which they could rest, for during the night there would be no rest for them. They lay waiting for the enemy who lurked out there in the darkness. The Soviets attacked. In the treacherous light between dusk and total darkness the Reds either made infantry assaults or called down a rain of artillery shells which fell around the German positions. The Soviets had collected reserves of shells for months past and the fire from their guns seemed unending.

A new day dawned.

It was the same as those which had preceded it. The same, fiendishly the same, except that the enemy had now pulled himself together and lay at the edge of the great woods, concealed in well prepared positions. At point-blank range fire was opened upon the men of the German infantry advance guard and even though their numbers were reinforced Soviet resistance, too, continued to grow. The enemy was fighting for time to withdraw their heavy weapons but there were some Red Army units which scorned to pull theirs back to safety and fought them to the death. They expected no mercy as they knew none. And now they lay across the machine guns, across their mortars, their bodies torn by hand grenades or stabbed by bayonet thrusts.

But it was hot, so mercilessly hot. There was no water but there was blood and that ran in streams.

From cornfields machine gun fire rattled, well-aimed shots came from trees. The riflemen were baffled and bombarded snipers' posts with anti-tank gun fire. Bodies hung down. They did not fall from the branches for many Red Army men had bound themselves to these in order to achieve a more stable platform from which to fire. The German infantry continued its march to the east. Here a platoon or a company would move out of the main column to search through half a dozen houses or barns. There a battalion would be detached to comb out a forest. Shots broke the afternoon quiet. The rattle of machine gun fire, the whoom-whoom of mortar bombs and the gargling sounds of artillery shells in flight disturbed the silence of those hot June days. The hammer of war was striking relentlessly and accurately.

The German infantry had the handle of the hammer in their hands. They were the strong arm of their commanders. Within days they had reached Mitau, Kovno, Grodno, Brest Litovsk and Lemberg.

The armour thrust through. It overran the enemy but took no heed of flank protection, no contact with the rear. The cry was "At, through and follow-up". But then what? The panzer sat in a town like Dunaburg and were forced to laager. Halted and impotent they fired at an enemy who bombarded them with artillery or they were attacked by his aircraft, drawn like flies to a honey-pot. It was only when the infantry gained touch that the tanks were safe. The armour may have made its name with the capture of great towns: Minsk, Bialystok, Dunaburg, Vilna, but who was it who had to comb the woods and the death-dealing cornfields? Who cleared the hundreds of villages, who cleared the barns and outhouses? The infantry.

Thus it was and thus it will remain for as long as the campaign in the east lasts. Infantry are the constant factor. They strike the killing blow, they carry out the deciding orders, those millions of infantrymen who, nameless and brave, marched eastwards, conquered, died or were killed in action and who now lie out there under slender birchwood crosses.

The infantry pays the highest price of battle – they decide the outcome of battles. The armour may fasten to its colours the name of places and accompany these with loud fanfares, but it is the infantry which covered the distances between the towns and it is they who made the river crossings: the Memel, the Bug, Prush, Narev, Pripet, Stry and Dneister. These they crossed. Often swimming stark naked with only light weapons in their hands to open the path for those who come behind. In the hectic fire of Soviet pill-boxes, across field fortifications they fight. They reach the river, cross it, gain the other side and rush the Soviet positions there with only entrenching tools to split the heads of those of their opponents who will not surrender. Together with men of the assault pioneers the infantry crossed the broad rivers in assault craft either behind a roaring engine noisily or else with stealth as they paddled quietly through the deepening twilight to make a silent crossing.

Thus is the picture formed of those first weeks of fighting. The feet continued to march.

Men and horses of a cavalry regiment cross the Russo-German frontier; 22 June 1941.

The morning of 22 June 1941. A Propaganda Company photographer takes pictures of troops as they cross the frontier.

A young lieutenant and his platoon take leave of three of their comrades who fell in action during the first weeks.

Men of a machine gun company passing a statue of Lenin as they advance towards Leningrad in late summer 1941.

In Byelo-Russia the sand roads were as tiring for the horses as the mud was later to be. Men of infantry units were often used as auxiliary motive power.

The road to the front: German infantry unit marching up the line in the first summer. It was their marching ability in the opening offensives which led to the successes in the great encirclement battles in the southern sectors.

German troops enter Kharkov in autumn 1941.

Top right: A soldier of a machine gun group, exhausted in the summer heat, makes his way across Byelo-Russia during the fighting of autumn 1941.

The eternal infantryman. A heavily burdened soldier of the Eastern Front; the man on whom the main brunt of the fighting fell, whether he was German or Russian.

In Russia, during the war, two worlds – East and West – met.

The infantry gun company of an infantry regiment in action on the northern front in the late summer of 1941.

Digging in. The infantryman's first task. Here an NCO digs a slit trench in a railway embankment. Kiev front, August 1941.

A German half-track vehicle passing the debris and destruction caused by German bombers during the great encirclement battles of autumn 1941.

Assault engineers of the German Army crossing the Dnieper river.

A German supply column in difficulties in the Ukraine in the rainy season of 1941.

Reconnaissance vehicles of a panzer division advancing through a Russian village during the first weeks of the war.

3

The last days of tank destruction unit DORA II in Brandenburg during April 1945

It was in the last weeks of the War, in April 1945, that one small detachment, Commando Unit DORA II of the SS 500th Bewahrungs Battalion, fought its last and most memorable battle.

To overcome the shortage of trained infantrymen and of adequate weapons in the months and weeks of Germany's military decline more and more use was made of small groups of dedicated, hard and skilful men who were prepared to undertake operations of the most hopeless sort to help save their native country. The name of one of these men, Otto Skorzeny, was, to his contemporaries in the German Army, synonymous with cool bravery and daring. This account, however, is not Skorzeny's but that of an SS company which had formerly been part of his commando battalion. This had been split up to form a closely woven network of small groups charged with the task of blocking the advance by the Red Army, as it made that great thrust towards Berlin which STAVKA intended would end the war in Europe. Separated from the parent SS commando, the next step had been the conversion of this assault company into a para-commando and then into an anti-tank company. These were not, however, conventional gunners with conventional anti-tank guns but a group of determined tank hunters, individual destroyers of enemy machines who went out with hollow charges and other close combat weapons to launch themselves at the Soviet vehicles, to clamber onto the moving machines and to plant their explosive charge firmly so that it exploded and destroyed its victim. There were other methods of killing the Red armour of which a favourite one was to rise from the ground, to stand in a wave of tanks, to select a victim and then to smash it with the missile from a single-shot rocket launcher.

The soldiers who, in this particular account, carried out this type of dangerous mission were men of long experience and years of combat on the Eastern Front. They were led by Untersturmführer Porsch. Born in 1924, he had joined the Waffen SS in 1941 and before he was nineteen years of age was a Company Commander who had been awarded the Iron Cross First Class. The actions which are here recounted won for him the Knight's Cross of the Iron Cross to add to the other visible emblems of his bravery. On his upper left breast glittered the assault badge in gold and on his right breast pocket was the German cross in gold. Then there was the golden badge for close combat, a mention in the Army's book of honour and no fewer than four tank destruction badges.

In the fighting which marked the last days of April 1945 in Brandenburg the heights of Seelow were lost to the Germans, and the Russian forces, following the classic Blitzkrieg tactics, had probed for and found a gap through which their tanks had driven and had by-passed the few remaining pockets of German resistance in and around the town of Seelow. One of those pockets was that which held the DORA II and soon it had become clear from the volume of Russian fire as well as from its direction that the SS unit was outflanked and in a salient. The Soviet spearheads were now far to the west and to destroy this remaining opposition in Seelow part of an armoured regiment of JS tanks and T 34s was sent in.

A Red tank squadron charged with the tanks fanned out, and far beyond the range of DORA II's close quarter weapons opened fire upon the SS detachment. The commander and his grenadiers accepted the losses which the Soviet tank gun and machine gun fire inflicted upon them, holding themselves ready for the time when the great machines would approach to within killing distance. Porsch named his men, allotted to them the tank they were to destroy and then the two groups of combatants met in battle. On the one side the human with his explosive charge or rocket launcher, whose only defence was mobility, against, on the other side, an opponent heavily armoured and strongly armed.

One JS tank which rolled towards the small group of men who made up the company headquarters suddenly swung on its tracks, halted and began to burn. A Panzerfaust had torn into its vitals and fire consumed the vehicle so quickly that none of the crew escaped. This first 'kill' was the signal for a general mêlée as the men within the tanks and the men outside them fought to destroy each other.

A sudden change of direction was made by the Russian commanders aiming to take DORA II in flank but this failed when their machines were caught and destroyed by Skorzeny's group holding position on Porsch's right. Vehicle after vehicle stopped, 'brewed up' or blew up. In Porsch's company area six were on fire and the remainder pulled back to allow waves of Red Army infantry to storm forward, hoping to achieve the victory which the tanks had been unable to gain.

The MG 42s whose rate of fire had been increased to over 2,000rpm came into action, swinging backwards and forwards along the brown-coated files, smashing the cohesion of the attack and destroying it before the assaulting Russian regiment had had time to shake out into tactical formation. The killing was prodigious and the survivors of the crumpled Red battalions pulled back and withdrew out of range of this small group of determined defenders.

For the outflanked German groups in the salient there was only one course of action and the exhausted detachments were pulled back, but not to rest. DORA II was ordered to move on Lebus and there to attack a Soviet tank group which was concentrating around the town. The road forward was choked with retreating troops and columns of refugees who hindered the advance so that it was not until just before dawn that the small SS column of men and machines reached the objective; they had arrived too late. The town had fallen and under the relentless pressure of massed Soviet tank assaults DORA II and its flank detachments were pushed further and further back. But there were successes even on that black day.

The company scored its 100th kill and Porsch his twelfth and thirteenth victims.

At nightfall the detachment rested in a farm set some 300 metres behind the main German firing line which was held by men of a dozen, mixed sub-units separated from their parent bodies. At some time during the night the front line was driven or taken back and Porsch was awakened to the news that his unit was now almost alone, was unprotected and that the farm courtyard was full of Russians. These were killed and then a cautious reconnaissance showed the village to be empty of all German troops except for a detachment of about eighty assault engineers who joined forces with Porsch's 100-strong company. This mixed group filled the gap and formed a temporary battle line. Later again during the night a group of grenadiers from the Dutch SS Division *Nederland* came up as reinforcements and with this increase in strength the German commander felt his group strong enough and they struck forward in a counter attack.

The company continued to score victories. The 125th victim was gained and Porsch destroyed his seventeenth. Other attacks by the German group pushed back the Russians in the Neu Zittau area and during one thrust on 20 April Porsch and his men, mounted on bicycles, smashed through the Soviet line held by a whole battalion, reached and then captured its headquarters staff of fourteen officers and some women.

On 26 April Porsch was informed that he had been awarded the Knight's Cross of the Iron Cross and as if to set a seal upon this decoration he destroyed with Panzerfaust and machine pistol fire a pair of Russian anti-tank guns which had sought to halt his company's advance. Later during that day his bicycle-mounted troops, accompanied by a handful of men from the SS Division *Frundsberg* made a swift assault upon a battery of mortars whose fire was particularly destructive and wiped out most of the Soviet battery. Eight mortars were captured.

The very success of the advance which the SS group had made was its downfall, for then it once again formed a small salient which was under constant and heavy bombardment. Then Soviet troops cut the neck of the salient. By this stroke the German force became a pocket, cut off from the main body and surrounded on all sides by the Soviet enemy. The defiance which it still maintained attracted to it soldiers from every type of German front-line unit and of every rank: men who had been cut off from their own formations. Women and children, old and young entered into this tiny enclave of German-held territory, enduring the bombardments, the aerial assaults, the privations and shortages and often sharing with the soldiers the common end of death. The civilians would endure anything just as long as they could stay with the pocket now trying to fight its way through line after successive line of Soviet defences. Death and wounds continually reduced the number of fighting men. The dead were hastily buried and then the pocket rolled on to meet and overcome in fierce fire fights some new Russian obstacle between it and the main German line.

Pressure built up as the Red Army closed its fist around Porsch's little SS group, reduced now to only forty-eight men. Between Markisch-Buchholz and Töpchin the last act was played out when a Soviet infantry battalion invested the group. In such a hopeless situation surrender was the only logical military decision and the officers of army units in Porsch's sector decided to capitulate. The SS commander put the situation very cogently to his men: "We can none of us expect to emerge alive from this situation and to be taken prisoner is the only way out. If any man wishes to surrender along with the army group he is free to do so and I shall not condemn him as a coward." No man of DORA II made a move to join the Army soldiers and the young commander, deeply affected by this display of loyalty, went from man to man shaking each warmly by the hand.

The soldiers of the Army unit moved off waving their white flags; the civilians had already been dispersed and now on the stricken field of Töpchin only the SS remained. Seven of them fell in the first of a series of attacks which the Red battalion then launched. At the end of the second Soviet assault eighteen of the group had been killed. All day the noise of battle echoed across the open fields of Brandenburg but by last light the Red infantry and artillery had still not subdued the defiant SS.

First light on 28 April opened with a mortar barrage and at 09.00hrs the Soviets, considering that the time had come to administer the *coup de grâce* to DORA II, sent in their battalion, only to have it driven back once again. But no success against the Soviet battalion, no Russians drawing back from the fury of German gunfire could disguise the fact that the end was now very near. One SS man, his legs shattered by bomb blast, bade his comrades goodbye and blew his life away with a hand grenade. A mortar bomb destroyed three more of the little group and, in another shell hole, two more badly-wounded men ended their lives by committing suicide.

The Soviet battalion was re-organised and under a mortar barrage came in again to the assault. A quick check among the SS men showed that only one round of ammunition remained. Its owner shook hands with the survivors of the little group for the last time, raised a pistol to his temple and fired. Although there was no more ammunition left Porsch still chose to attack. Not for nothing had he gained the nickname of 'Old man forwards', and he led his last eleven men into their final assault, to meet oncoming Red infantry.

The SS men followed Porsch's upraised Volkov staff as they had done for so many years and then the struggle was hand to hand as the last eleven closed with the Russians. Porsch's staff rose and fell as it smashed the heads of his opponents and he cut a path through the Red Army men. Then he was down. It was all over but there still remained one last defiant gesture. Porsch and those of his group who still remained alive secured from the Soviet commander permission to bury their dead. In a final act of comradeship these were laid, in SS fashion, side by side; their faces to the rising sun and with their weapons at their side. To conclude the little ceremony the final few of DORA II sang the SS anthem, and then, turning, they trudged off into the grey anonymity of a prisoner-of-war camp.

4

The foreignness of it all

*"Few western Europeans have any idea of the
actual habits and mode of life
of the Russians ..."*

Max Simon
LIEUTENANT GENERAL OF THE WAFFEN SS

SS General Max Simon, whose report is quoted elsewhere in this book, has stated that war with the Soviet Union brought home to the ordinary German soldier the realisation that he was embarking upon a journey into an unknown and alien world. How unusual can be seen in the attitude of the civilians whose country the German Army had invaded.

Excepting always the determined, usually bitter and frequently fanatical resistance of the Red Army, most German troops found that they were met with warmth and acclamation by the population of the extreme western provinces of Russia whose native inhabitants had been citizens of the once free and independent states of Poland, Latvia, Lithuania and Estonia. Those nations had lost their freedom as a result of Soviet occupation in 1939 and many of their peoples considered Soviet rule to be harsh, repressive and brutal. Accordingly, when the first columns of German infantry and armour swept through their lands, there were many Balts and Poles who welcomed them as liberators. Nor was this welcome restricted to just those countries. In certain regions of the Soviet Union proper, notably in the Ukraine, Georgia and the Caucasus, the same situation obtained and from all those republics volunteers came forward in large numbers to make common cause with the Germans against the tyranny of the Communist system.

It was this expression of revolt against the central and elected government which the German soldiers found hard to accept even though they believed the story that the great mass of the Soviet peoples were yearning to be free. The simple soldiers could not conceive of such a situation arising in Germany, under which the peoples of German provinces could welcome an alien invasion because they rejected the Reich government. They could not understand the acclamation which they received, even though they did welcome it. It was after all better than having to fight every step of the way.

This then was the time of flowers thrown to passing German vehicles, of buckets of water or milk placed outside houses to refresh the men in the dusty, sweating columns on their march. Those were the heady days when villagers stood along road sides holding high their family bibles, their religious pictures and their household crucifixes to bless the German troops as they passed en route, or so the locals considered it, to undertake a crusade against atheistic Communism. Many were the simple, bare-footed peasants who pointed to or stroked the black crosses on German lorries, convincing themselves that the men whose army carried this holy symbol on their vehicles were their allies in Christ. Where halts were made by the German columns to billet for the night local dignitaries would come out to meet the commander of the troops. Pretty girls, usually dressed in national costume, would bring gifts of bread and salt, the traditional offering to welcome honoured guests. Vodka would be drunk; there might even be singing and dancing.

"Those were the days." With high optimism, the young-hearted infantry, fit in body and convinced of their ability, marched eastwards to carry out their Führer's directives. Seeing the great mass of guns and tanks which were accompanying them, the fleets of aircraft flying silver overhead ready to smash the enemy host where it lay, the soldiers asked themselves: how could an enterprise backed by such power ever fail? The record of successes which their army had gained in former campaigns gave reason for optimism and the welcome from the local populations was convincing proof that these people were yearning to break free from the Communist yoke.

It was this civilian fervour which was most frequently commented upon by German soldiers, who found it hard to reconcile the fact that although they had been welcomed by the civilians as liberators, Red Army rearguards would fight to the last man and that behind the German line in those regions in which they had been welcomed civilian-supported partisan activity would spring up and produce actions of so bitter a nature that any act of clemency could almost be construed as aiding and abetting the enemy. Many commanders, officers and men, being faced with situations for which no solutions had been given, no firm guidelines laid down and who needed immediate results decided on the seemingly easy option of execution and repression.

Repression begets resistance. Terror produces a counter-terror. Fanaticism brings forth a greater fanaticism. Thus it was that those who fought as front-line infantry, and who, in the opening months and years of war on the Eastern Front had marched forward to the cheers of the peasant peoples, found on their bitter road of retreat westward that the same civilians were prepared to attack them, to kill them, to torture them if they were captured alive and to collaborate wholeheartedly with that regime from which they had hoped to be freed.

In this section of the book, which deals with infantry, it is neither apposite nor indeed fitting that the actions of those Nazi Party officials who filled the senior administrative positions in the occupied territories of Russia should be recorded. These were the 'Golden pheasants', the brown and gold uniformed ones, whose greed, lust for power and brutality, as well as their contempt for the Slav and Balt peoples, converted those who would have been prepared to help construct Hitler's New Order in Europe into some of its most bitter and hate-filled opponents.

Because of the hate and desire for vengeance it was the infantry rearguards who suffered most as the German Army was driven out of Russia, out of Poland, from eastern, south-eastern and central Europe. When the last German heavy tanks and artillery had rumbled through the villages and towns of occupied Europe heading westwards towards the Fatherland, partisan groups emerged and waited to attack the trudging infantry. Now marching, now turning at bay to fight off a persistent and pressing Soviet group, the grenadiers, who represented to the civilians the bitter years of war, would come under attack. The peasants had old scores to settle and they killed as they themselves had been killed, terrorising as they themselves had been terrorised. The road back was a Calvary for the German infantry.

Files of grenadiers would come into sight, moving as the infantrymen move, with economy of effort, swaying with the weight of the equipment, feet sliding forward without excessive movement, each man wrapped in a cocoon of thoughts or memories, silently cursing the weather, the poor food, the shortage of cigarettes and the few peasants whom they saw; the flat, expressionless Slav eyes which watched them pass and which held no hint of emotion. Then from out of the trees there would be a burst of firing. Grenadiers would fall and the sections would move out across the sodden fields or through the dripping forests, taking casualties from snipers as they advanced. "The worst things in Russia", had written one man, "are lice and snipers", and here the sharpshooters were indistinguishable from harmless civilians.

The guerrillas would usually avoid pitched battles, preferring to weaken, to slow down, to tire out the retreating German troops and thus make them easy prey to the Red Army. At other times the grenadiers would find the mutilated bodies of German soldiers hanging obscenely from the trees. Men – drivers perhaps of ration trucks or else motor cycle despatch riders, captured by the partisans, tortured and then hanged. Their bodies swinging in the wind would warn the trudging grenadiers that they could expect no other treatment if they, too, fell alive into the clutches of those who had betimes cheered them on into the new campaign against Russia.

For the great mass of the infantry life on the Eastern Front was a series of constant reminders of the foreignness of the place. It was not merely the architecture, nor the people alone, for those of western Russia looked European enough. Nor was it the landscape, depressing though this was, No, it was an indefinable, intangible but always present feeling of being lost. Many of the men had the feeling that they were living somehow in the past, in former centuries and needed the comforting presence of their own engines of war to remind them that they were indeed living in modern times and were from a technological civilisation.

They were all aware, as infantrymen of all armies are aware, that High Command frequently, indeed usually, sent them into attacks, allotted them targets or fixed for them objectives which were beyond their capacity to attain or to overcome. Nothing had prepared them, however much they had experienced in the first years of the war, for the casual contempt for the life of their soldiers shown by the commanders of the Red Army.

Soviet infantry were often sent forward in human waves that extended from horizon to horizon and whose ranks were cut to pieces without their having gained a single metre of trench line. Attacks were sent in at precisely timed intervals; lack of co-ordination between rival arms of service resulted in heavy loss to the unsupported Russian infantry. The German soldiers observed the rigid, almost robot-like advances, the unbelievable spectacle of Red Army men clambering over a wall of bodies of their own comrades killed in earlier assaults, or tearing away those bodies in order to advance without impediment. These sights shocked the German soldier and frightened him.

During the autumn of 1941, an infantry division of the 6th Army was ordered forward to drive-in a salient left in the German line. The strategic moves which were to lead to the Kiev encirclement were under way on sectors nearly 100 kilometres eastwards and this was merely a tidying-up operation, a mere straightening of the line. Opposition to this little operation and carried out chiefly by the 37th Red Army was at first strong, then determined and finally fanatical. Nevertheless the German division eventually captured its second bound objective, the high ground above the Kiev road. The reaction of the Soviet Command was to counter-attack repeatedly and it is how these assaults came in which is described in the following account.

> I can never forget the first mass attack by Russian infantry which I experienced just after we came into the line during August 1941. I could not believe that in the Second World War the tactics of the First Great War could still be used by any one of the major combatants.
>
> The whole assault was so ineptly handled that I found it difficult to believe that it was being carried out by a professional Army and this incompetence reinforced the belief held at that time by many German officers, that the Red Army was being handled no differently to the Tzarist Army. It was the same old steamroller.
>
> My regiment had been counter-attacked many times during the campaign in France during 1940, and one of these assaults, which took place south of the Somme, had really been exceptionally well done. The co-operation between arms, the use of ground and the tactics chosen for the ground had been impressive, particularly since our French attackers had been numerically inferior to us.

The Soviet assaults on the other hand were carried out by masses of men who made no real attempt at concealment but trusted in sheer weight of numbers to overwhelm us. Our regiment had occupied high ground to the right of a village and thus we dominated not only the Kiev road but also the country in front of us for a distance of several kilometres. The terrain was fairly open being without extensive forests but covered in part by high-standing crops. Immediately to our front there was no cover except for dead ground and we had good fields of fire for more than 600 metres.

The indications of imminent attack opened with a short bombardment by enemy field artillery, but this fell behind us. It was clear that Ivan's forward observation officers thought that we were much higher up the slope and nearer to the crest than we actually were. Both our battalions were up together with the machine gun companies for our CO brought every automatic weapon into the line once he realised what were the Soviet intentions. The Soviet artillery barrage stopped – started – stopped abruptly once again and then, after a fifteen-minute interval crashed down again, but this time on the slope behind the crest. The Russian gunners expected us to have our main body on the reverse slope and had hoped to catch our rifle companies as they moved forward.

Then quite a long distance from our positions there were lines of brown uniformed men tramping forward. The first of these crossed a small river and was followed at about 200 metres distance by a second line. Then there rose out of the grass – literally from out of the ground – a third wave, then a fourth and a fifth.

The lines of men stretched to the right and left of our regimental front overlapping it completely and the whole mass of Russian troops came tramping solidly and relentlessly forward. It was an unbelievable sight, a machine gunner's dream target. It was rumoured that the commissars worked out the number of machine guns which we had, multiplied that number by the number of rounds per minute that we could fire, calculated how many minutes it would take a body of soldiers to cross the area and added to the final total a couple of thousand men. Thus some men would get through our line; the others could expect to be killed or wounded. The execution of this particular attack certainly seemed to have been carried out according to such calculations.

At 600 metres we opened fire and whole sections of the first wave just vanished leaving here and there an odd survivor still walking stolidly forward. It was uncanny, unbelievable, inhuman. No soldier of ours would have continued to advance alone. The second wave had also taken losses but closed up towards the centre, round and across the bodies of their comrades who had fallen with the first wave. Then, as if on a signal, the lines of men began running forward. As they advanced there was a low rumbling 'Hoooooraaay' which they kept up for some time. That they could run and shout at the same time surprised me.

The first three waves had been destroyed by our fire, but not all of the men in them had been killed. Some who dropped were snipers who worked their way forward through the grass to open fire upon our officers and machine gun posts.

The rush by the fourth wave came on more slowly for the men had to pick their way through a great carpet of bodies and as the Soviets moved towards us some of our men, forgetful of the danger, stood on the parapets of their slit trenches to fire at the oncoming Russians. The machine guns became hot from continual firing and there were frequent stoppages to change barrels. Some of the enemy were mounted. These were Field Officers, I suspect, and one of them rode backwards and forwards along the lines of his men waving his arms and obviously urging them on. He was too good a target to miss and he fell in the way which he must have hoped to have been killed, at the head of his men, leading them in a charge.

The great mass of the Soviet troops was now storming up the slope towards us but our fire was too great and they broke. About an hour later a further five lines of men came on in a second attack. We smashed this and then crushed a third and fourth assault. The numbers of the enemy seemed endless and the new waves of men advanced across their own dead without hesitation. I cannot remember ever seeing in that series of assaults, a Russian stretcher bearer; all the waves were made up of armed men. The Ivans kept up their attacks for three days and sometimes even during the night. Suddenly they stopped and withdrew for some considerable distance and our subsequent advance on that sector was uncontested for nearly two days.

The number, duration and fury of those attacks had exhausted and numbed us completely. Not to hide the truth they had frightened us. Our advance had been no great strategic drive but an ordinary move on a fairly narrow sector and yet they had contested it for day after day and with masses of men. If the Soviets could waste men on our small move and there was no doubt that these men had been sacrificed, how often, we asked ourselves, would they attack and in what numbers if the objective was really a supremely important one? I think that on that autumn day in 1941 some of us began to realise for the first time that the war against the Soviet Union was going to be bigger than we had thought it would be and a sense of depression, brought about by a fear of the unknown, settled upon us. That we would win, we had no doubt, but what we were now engaged in would be a long, bitter and hard fought war.

The history of Panzer Corps *Grossdeutschland*, too, records how very early in the first campaign many men of the regiment, as it then was, were overcome with depression at the immensity of the task involved in subduing the Soviet Union and of the war which they were committed to fighting.

The same thought occurred to many: that extending from the German front line and reaching to as far as Vladivostock there existed a vast area of enemy territory wherein they, their regiments, indeed the whole German Army, could vanish without trace. The German Supreme Command might choose to ignore the great size of Soviet Russia when they constructed their battle plans but those men whose feet walked every metre from the Bug to the Volga and back again, were well aware of its immensity. They could see for themselves that the absence of roads and railways would make the supply position difficult. Appreciating the poverty of the local inhabitants upon whom they were billeted they could realise that the order to live off the land, which had been given to Guderian's panzer group as early as 14 September 1941, would bring in little to feed the Army but that it would make the peasants suspicious, hostile and dangerous. Although this order to live off the land expressly forbade requisitioning by individuals or by small units, it was difficult to detect or to stop, particularly if the soldiers were prepared to back their criminal robbery with force of arms.

As in all similar circumstances a black market was born and flourished. Authority again forbade soldiers to barter soap or cigarettes for food and issued regulations laying down the official prices for honey, fruit and eggs, seemingly the only comestibles in adequate supply. What peasant, however, would hand over scarce foodstuffs for paper money and what soldier would forgo the chance of swapping a handful of cigarettes for a dish of fried eggs? The ordinary soldier and the Russian peasant established a *modus vivendi* that was at variance with all the teachings of Soviet or National Socialist dogma. This is not to say that there was not at any time friction nor harshness, nor contempt, nor injustice. These things there certainly were, but there was also, strangely, a mutual feeling of compassion. From the civilians for those strange, alien young men, with young men's eyes and young men's bodies who were being sent out to fight and die. The German infantry, by comparison, had compassion for the primitive and miserable existence which the civilians endured, for the hopelessness of their position and for the limited horizons of their pitiful ambitions.

The standard of life in the East was so incredibly low. Illumination in houses in the country was by paraffin lamp, and that only in the better off rural areas for in the most primitive regions it was the light of the sun which controlled the length of the working day. Before dawn and after sunset there was a total blackness. Moonlight or even starlight were then the only poor sources of illumination and thus reliance upon the sun for light was absolute. In those particular regions even the headquarters building of the local Communist Party, invariably the best constructed and furnished building in the area, would have at best a paraffin lamp- a source of wonder and envy to the primitive peoples, an example of unbelievable luxury and a reminder of how good life was under the aegis of the Party.

To many German soldiers this meeting with the Workers' Paradise was a shattering revelation. Many of them, particularly those over thirty years of age, had perhaps been Socialists or even members of the German Communist Party before the Nazis had come to power. They had carried in their hearts a picture of the fine life which the fortunate Soviet peoples were enjoying. The reality when it was encountered was devastating. The following account by a soldier of Army Group South is the Soviet Union as seen by an ordinary German working-class soldier:

> We were quartered in a house outside the town. The town itself was unimpressive but at least the houses were of something other than wood. But they were ugly, square, concrete boxes of varying sizes. The only decent looking places dated back to the days of the Tsar.
> Our dwelling for the night was a wooden house already occupied by a Russian family consisting as we later found out of five children and

an old grandmother. We were bitten all night by vermin. Next morning
we were able to see the place properly [the unit had arrived at night:
translator's note]. It was poorly furnished. A huge stove served to
warm the family and they slept on or near it at night. A sort of swing
affair on ropes suspended from the ceiling was a cradle holding the
youngest child, a girl about a year old. There was a table, a few chairs
and a box which served as a small cupboard.

The inside walls of this hovel were wall-papered with pages from
newspapers and there were the usual pictures of Stalin and Lenin who
have taken over as the guardian angels of this workers' and peasants'
paradise. We opened our tins of food and made coffee, sharing what we
had with the children and the old woman.

The man of the house was a soldier and the mother, so far as we
could make it out, had been taken away to dig trenches, probably an
anti-tank ditch, and had not come back to the family. The children all
had the protruding bellies of long-term malnutrition and this was the
Ukraine, the great wheat-growing region of the Soviet Union, that
region whose fruitful black earth supposedly filled a horn of plenty.
This horn of plenty gave to this family a diet of potatoes, kasha, salt
cucumbers, sunflower seed oil in place of butter and an occasional salt
herring. The satirical joke which I had heard in a Berlin night club
years ago but had never really believed had become true. 'The first
communists were Adam and Eve. They had no clothes to wear, had to
steal apples for food, could not escape from the place in which they
lived and still they thought that they were in paradise.' The reality of
the situation is that in twenty-two years of Communism a salted fish
occasionally is for this family upon whom we are billeted, the height of
luxury. How this country depresses me.

The remark in that account of the mother's unexplained absence
and the fatalistic resignation with which it was accepted
represented another aspect of conditions which the ordinary soldiers
found hard to comprehend. Back in Germany there was no
conscription of women. Industry was not really on a war footing.
Even the enthusiastic response given to Josef Goebbels' famous, if
rhetorical question in a speech made in 1943, "Do you want total
war?" did not change conditions very much and the German nation
was not geared to war in a sense that we in Great Britain knew it, nor
the total involvement in the sense in which the citizens of the Soviet
Union understood it.

The ad hoc, impersonal, unfeeling attitudes and methods of the
Communist Party when applied to the peoples of the Soviet Union
brought home to the German soldier, and quite forcibly too, the
degree of control which was exercised upon the Russian masses by
their masters. One letter home recorded the way in which human
beings were being used to create lanes through uncharted minefields
so that the armoured regiments of the Red Army could advance.

One feature of Soviet attacks was the numbers involved. One day
during the retreat [from Kursk in 1943: translator's note], we found out
how these were obtained. Apparently as we withdraw the Red Army re-
occupies the area and rounds up all adult civilians, men and women
alike. These are formed into makeshift workers' battalions and then
sent into attacks to make up weight and numbers. It does not matter
that these conscripts are untrained, that many are without boots of

any kind and that most of them have no arms. Prisoners whom we took told us that those without weapons are expected to take up those from the fallen. These unarmed civilians forced to accompany the assault had been suspected of collaboration with us and were paying, in many cases quite literally, with their lives because of this suspicion.

I saw other attacks which were preceded by solid blocks of people marching shoulder to shoulder across the minefields which we had laid. Civilians and Army punishment battalions alike advanced like automata, their ranks broken only when a mine exploded killing and wounding those around it. The people seemed never to flinch nor to quail and we noticed that some who fell were then shot by a smaller wave of commissars or officers who followed very closely behind the blocks of punishment victims. What these people had done to deserve this sort of treatment is unknown but we found among prisoners whom we took officers who had failed to gain a given objective, NCOs who had lost a machine gun in action and men whose crime had been to fall out on the line of march. These stragglers, swept up by flying columns of OGPU troops, were given a hasty court-martial and then sentenced to unbelievably long terms of imprisonment. Some of them had to serve part of their sentence clearing mines and in these cases this was carried out by blocks of men tramping forward across our gardens of death.

And yet none, or very few, ever complained at their treatment. Life was hard, they said, and if you failed to achieve a target you paid for your failure. None was prepared to accept that the given objective might be unattainable or that their sentences were unjust. A given task had to be accomplished or dire punishment was the expected and the accepted result.

5

The Waffen SS on the Eastern Front

"Meine Ehre heisst Treue" (Loyalty is my honour)

Any account of the war with Russia must include that German military organisation which, starting from small beginnings at the outbreak of the campaign, rose to become a force with thirty-eight or thirty-nine different divisional names. That force was the Waffen SS and its development is bound up with the war in the East.

At the outset let it be said that there was no such thing as a single SS organisation but rather a collection of various bodies loosely grouped round the Nazi party and directly subordinate through Heinrich Himmler to Adolf Hitler.

This section of the book deals only with the Waffen SS – the SS in arms – in Russia during the Second World War and it is well that at this point certain matters are dealt with so that there is no misunderstanding of the soldiers or of the organisation which is described here. One of the most important points, when the Waffen SS is under discussion, is to bear in mind that nearly a million men fought in its ranks and that among any such numbers there are men of sterling character as well as those of a criminal nature. Survivors of the Waffen SS claim that few of them ever saw a concentration camp or guarded one. They say they are condemned as the protagonists of Himmler's racial purity and yet among their divisions were men who, supposedly, were of 'inferior race'.

There had been SS (Schütz Staffeln or defence squads) in the Nazi Party's organisation from the very earliest days, originally formed to defend the person of Adolf Hitler. After 1934 and the destruction in that same year of the power of the S.A. (Sturm Abteilung or Assault Units), the other Nazi Party para-military body, the SS, rose in number and influence within the Party. Within a year the SS organisation, out of which the Waffen SS developed, was made up of three independent infantry regiments or Standarten formed from full-time cadres of barracked units which were stationed in the larger cities of Germany. From those cadres *Deutschland* and *Germania* Standarten were formed while in Berlin the *Leibstandarte SS Adolf Hitler* was garrisoned. Later, with the annexation of Austria into Greater Germany, a fourth Standarte, *Der Führer*, came into establishment.

There were difficulties in obtaining sufficient officers for the newly raised Standarten and the great majority had been former NCOs of the German Army. These were regular soldiers, discharged on pension after twelve years' service: hard bitten men with backgrounds that were predominantly working-class. Their thorough knowledge of service techniques and the vast experience which they were to gain during the war brought many of these men to high command, firstly as company commanders, then as battalion commanders, and as general officers commanding divisions. To ensure a flow of regular officers Junker schools were then founded and these graduates too were mainly of working-class origins. Indeed, no man could be commissioned who had not served as a simple soldier in the ranks.

The few professional officers who did join the SS brought with them new ideas of tactics which had been considered revolutionary by the Army commanders. One of the most successful innovators was Felix Steiner who abolished barrack square drill and replaced it with training using live ammunition. His regiment *Deutschland* astounded Hitler in the spring of 1939 when the new tactics which he had designed were demonstrated. Hitler, who had been searching the ground with his binoculars, asked when the attack was about to begin, only to be told by Steiner that it had been in progress for twenty minutes. Then there appeared within storming range of the objective small groups of assault troops moving rapidly and easily forward, almost undetected, not pausing or allowing themselves to be pinned down by fire. This demonstration group of *Deutschland* Standarte had advanced a distance of three kilometres in less than twenty minutes, but had still arrived at the objective so fresh that they could fight a close quarter battle using hand grenades, demolition charges and machine pistols in place of rifles.

This was a time when expansion of the force should have taken place but recruitment lay in the hands of the Army authorities who deliberately withheld men from the SS. After the Polish campaign a fresh look was taken at the problems of replacements and expansion. One solution was to obtain men from the German police forces and the *Totenkopf* units and to form these into the SS Police Division. Three of the peace-time Standarten, *Deutschland*, *Germania* and *Der Führer*, were combined to form what eventually became known as *Das Reich* division. Not until 1942 did *Leibstandarte* reach divisional status. These original Standarten were made up of Germans or men of what Himmler defined as Germanic or Nordic stock. Upon those foundations was built an organisation drawn from all the nations of conquered Europe and including men from non-Nordic races.

Those foreigners had joined the SS because they could not join the German Army. There were divisions and armies of foreign nationals fighting alongside the German units but these were major groupings of organised bodies for there was no apparatus, in the early days, for accepting individual recruits. Realising the potential that existed and being themselves starved of recruits the SS set out on a vast recruiting drive. At the end of this chapter is appended the full list of those units which formed the Waffen SS, together with their national composition. A great number were composed of foreign personnel stiffened either with Reichsdeutsche (Germans from Germany proper) or Volksdeutsche (Germans living outside Germany and living in colonies in other lands).

The purely Germanic divisions formed the élite of the Waffen SS in so far as the scale and type of equipment issued was concerned. The fighting spirit of all the units of the Waffen SS was high but there were some which fought with a desperate courage that made them noteworthy. That is certainly true of the *Charlemagne* Legion of the French Waffen SS which fought in Berlin and whose devotion to death has been remarked upon by every writer who has dealt objectively with the fighting for the German capital city. One of the most interesting features of the war against the Soviet Union was the enthusiasm with which this was taken up by certain European peoples as a crusade against Communism. It might have been expected that the extremely Catholic countries would have sent contingents but the enlistment of men of such widely diverse cultures as Scandinavians and Muslims was an unusual feature. They and the other men who fought, whether they were Dutch, Norwegians, Christians or Muslims as well as those who accepted some mystic Nordic belief, all fought together and for any one of a number of reasons, some for political beliefs, some for racial, some for sheer adventure, others for the sake of Western civilisation, for that vaguely-felt struggle of West against East which has been alluded to in earlier pages. The reasons are not important; rather more interesting is the fact that they fought and, according to the SS, as a supra-national European army.

The losses suffered by the SS were enormous. After the first winter in Russia, during which *Der Führer* regiment had been fighting without reinforcement around the strategically important town of Rzhev, it was eventually relieved and moved out of the line. The commander of the 9th Army, Model, visited the unit and asked *Der Führer's* commander for the combat strength of his unit. Obersturmbannführer Kumm pointed out of the window to the thirty-five men standing in the snow. The Standarte had gone into the line over 2,000-strong; the strength of half a platoon – the survivors – were on parade. Nor was this scale of losses remarkable in later days. It became usual for SS units to hold the line, to be a fire brigade or else used to spearhead new and desperate assaults.

Within the first year of the war with Russia it had become clear that between the SS Front soldiers and the political organisation back in the Reich there were differences that could not be met. The men in the trenches became more and more disillusioned with the senseless and peremptory demands from the Führer's headquarters. During the battle for Kharkov in the early months of 1943, Hitler's direct order was that the SS should hold the town, but the SS corps commander realised that to obey such an order would destroy his divisions. The SS had all sworn personal loyalty to Hitler. Indeed their belt buckles were inscribed with the legend "Loyalty is my

honour" and it was this loyalty to their sworn commander that was
their *raison d'être*. The field commander, Hausser, chose to save his
men and to disobey Hitler's order and ordered the city to be given up.

This was the first major instance of SS commanders refusing to
obey orders. Faced with the bizarre orders from SS Main Office they
felt that their men were being deliberately sacrificed. Then too there
was the feeling that the Army High Command was making them
bear a heavier burden of the fighting so as to wipe them out as rivals
to the army's monopoly of military power. It is hardly surprising,
therefore, that the SS, men and officers alike, trod a narrow,
introspective and bitter path. True, there were many instances of
glowing Orders of the Day praising the SS for its ability in battle of
which Guderian's "the longer the war lasted the more they became
part of us [the army]" is the most famous, but the feeling was always
present that they were the victims of any order which was issued
ordering some senseless attack. The refusal by Steiner to attack with
his Army and to relieve Berlin was the last and, arguably, the best
known of all the stories of a commander's loyalty to his men
superseding his oath of fidelity to a Head of State.

There grew up within the SS itself a sense of comradeship among
men who knew that they were condemend to death and who realised
that it was in their loyalty to each other that their strength lay. To
maintain that sense of comradeship any sacrifice had to be made:
wounded would not be left behind; those too badly wounded to be
moved would not be left to fall alive into the hands of the enemy and
every effort would be made to rescue trapped and encircled units.

The history of the war in Russia is full of such stories and not
merely loyalty to other SS units but also to those comrades in the
Army. In 1943 the *Leibstandarte* was asked to help the 302nd
Infantry Division which was withdrawing under Soviet pressure
and which was burdened with more than a thousand wounded. At
the time that the request for help was made the *Leibstandarte* was
fighting to hold the line of the Donets river and was itself under the
most severe assault. Without hesitation Dietrich, the divisional
commander, withdrew Jochen Peiper's Panzer Grenadier battalion
and sent it in. It crossed the Donets, smashed through the advancing
Red Army and crushed their furious counter attacks, pushing on
until it had located the surrounded infantry division. It then formed
a protective ring and held off the Soviet assaults till the whole
division had been safely conveyed across the river. It was then seen
that the river ice was too thin to bear the weight of Peiper's half
tracks so he swung his unit round, back and through the Red Army's
assault, carving its way until it had reached a bridge near a German
bridgehead capable of bearing the vehicles.

To fill the ranks emptied by the blood-letting of the first winter
recourse was made to recruit more of the European volunteers
already mentioned and as an inducement promises were made
regarding the independence of their homelands in a National

Socialist Europe – promises, in fact, which would not have been kept. These men formed the great bulk of the Waffen SS divisions so that by the end of 1944 there were thirty-eight names of units which, on paper, had divisional status. Many were nothing more than battle groups in regimental strength which, with poor armament and insufficient training, were expected to carry out tasks which would have taxed a division at full fighting strength.

By this stage of the war the SS had formed its own higher military organisation. Individual divisions had formed corps; some of these had also been formed into an Army, the 6th Panzer, which fought as the spearhead unit in the 1944 Ardennes offensive and in the battle to relieve Budapest during the spring of 1945. There were other less orthodox units. Some legions or battalions which were raised were as unusual and diverse as the ideas of the SS Central Office. Among these colourful detachments was an Indian Legion, made up of prisoners of war captured in the desert and whose men never fired a shot in anger, at least not as an SS unit. Hitler apparently had been kept in ignorance of what unusual units SS Headquarters in Berlin was forming and of the Indian Legion said, "If they were given the task of turning prayer wheels then they would be the most tireless soldiers in the world." The battle performance of other legions was seldom of a very high standard and even the 310,000 Volksdeutsche in the Waffen SS were not considered altogether reliable. Steiner wrote of them that they malingered because they pretended not to understand orders given to them in German. There was a bitter rule of thumb in the SS that the more Volksdeutsche there were in a unit then the lower was its military capacity – a generalisation which was in fact fallacious.

By the end of the war the SS divisions which had fought with such élan in the bitter years of war on the Eastern Front were but a shadow of their former selves. Of the 6th Panzer Army its commander Dietrich said, "They call us the 6th Panzer Army because we have six tanks left." In the area of Berlin the 4th SS Division had been reduced to having its field kitchens drawn by cows and the armies of SS which Hitler had drawn upon the map in the Führer bunker were only flags on a map. The wheel had come full circle. The SS had entered Russia in 1941 as just a handful of soldiers among the great mass of the army divisions. By 1945 it was once again a handful reduced to that level by a casualty rate which was shocking in its enormity.

Those who survived were condemned *in toto* by the Nuremberg tribunal as war criminals and their sentences, particularly by the courts in those countries east of the Iron Curtain, were in keeping with that total condemnation.

SS Divisions raised during the Second World War

Name	Theatre in which it principally served
1st SS Panzer Division *Leibstandarte Adolf Hitler*	Eastern Front
2nd SS Panzer Division *Das Reich*	Eastern Front
3rd SS Panzer Division *Totenkopf*	Eastern Front
4th SS Polizei Panzer Grenadier Division	Eastern Front
5th SS Panzer Division *Viking*	Eastern Front
6th SS Gebirgsdivision *Nord*	Eastern Front
7th SS Freiwilligen Gebirgsdivision *Prinz Eugen*	Balkans
8th SS Kavallerie Division *Florian Geyer*	Eastern Front
9th SS Panzer Division *Hohenstaufen*	Eastern Front
10th SS Panzer Division *Frundsberg*	Eastern Front
11th SS Freiwilligen Panzer Grenadier Division *Nordland*	Eastern Front
12th SS Panzer Division *Hitlerjugend*	France
13th SS Waffen Gebirgsdivision SS *Handschar* (Kroatische Nr. 1)	Balkans
14th Waffen Grenadier Division der SS (Galizische Nr. 1)	Eastern Front
15th Waffen Grenadier Division der SS (Lettische Nr. 1)	Eastern Front
16th SS Panzer Grenadier Division *Reichsfuhrer SS*	Italy
17th SS Panzer Grenadier Division *Götz von Berlichingen*	West
18th SS Freiwilligen Panzer Grenadier Division *Horst Wessel*	Czechoslovakia
19th Waffen Grenadier Division der SS (Lettische Nr. 2)	Eastern Front
20th Waffen Grenadier Division der SS (Estnische Nr. 1)	Eastern Front
21st Waffen Gebirgsdivision der SS *Skanderbeg* (Albanische Nr. 1)	Balkans
22nd SS Freiwilligen Kavallerie Division	Hungary
23rd SS Freiwilligen Panzer Grenadier Division *Nederland*	Eastern Front
23rd Waffen Gebirgsdivision der SS *Kama* (Kroatische Nr. 2)	Balkans
24th Waffen Gebirgs (Karstjäger) Division der SS	Italy
25th Waffen Grenadier Division der SS *Hunyadi* (Ungarische Nr. 1)	West
26th Waffen Grenadier Division der SS	West
27th SS Freiwilligen Grenadier Division *Langemarck*	Eastern Front
28th SS Freiwilligen Panzer Grenadier Division *Wallonien*	Eastern Front
29th Waffen Grenadier Division der SS (Russische Nr. 1)	Eastern Front
29th Waffen Grenadier Division der SS (Italienische Nr. 1.)	Italy

30th Waffen Grenadier Division der SS (Russische Nr. 2)	Eastern Front
31st SS Freiwilligen Grenadier Division	Hungary
32nd SS Freiwilligen Grenadier Division (30 Januar)	Eastern Germany
33rd Waffen Grenadier Division der SS *Charlemagne* (Französische Nr. 1)	Eastern Front
34th SS Grenadier Division *Landsturm Nederland*	West
35th SS Polizei Grenadier Division	Eastern Front
36th Waffen Grenadier Division der SS	Eastern Front
37th SS Freiwilligen Kavallerie Division *Lützow*	Eastern Front
38th SS Panzer Grenadier Division *Nibelungen*	West

6

The Red Army of Workers and Peasants

The new opponents of Hitler's Wehrmacht were the armed forces of the Soviet Union, represented in this book by the Red Army.

Since its birth in the days of the October revolution in 1917, the Red Army had undergone many changes and by 1941 it was in many ways indistinguishable from the army of the Tsars which it had superseded and which it professed to despise. The epaulettes and titles of officer rank were missing but these, too, were re-introduced late in 1942, together with most of the formerly abolished symbols of authority. Indeed, the officer caste had been re-established and these men extracted obedience from their subordinates, as they themselves were submissive to their superiors, under a code of discipline based on the fear of punishment for failure.

It had not always been so. The contingents raised in 1917 to protect the Soviet system had been volunteers, dedicated Communists whose enthusiasm and courage had helped the Red government to survive the wars brought about by Allied intervention and the battles begun by the White armies in the first difficult years following the seizure of power. The victories won by the fervour of the young Red Army, using cavalry and infantry 'wave' tactics, saddled the Army with two traditions which it found almost impossible to discard. Even as late as 1941 the belief was still current that the revolutionary élan of Soviet soldiers would be sufficient to halt any invader at the frontiers of the Soviet Union, from which he would be driven back into his own country and there defeated by an advance guard 'wave' of cavalry supported by other waves of infantry used as a levée en masse. The idea that victory could be gained by employing human waves of men who were inspired by and devoted to Leninism/Stalinism was held for years, and was then discarded only to be revived once more, this time so strongly as to become a dogma.

Over the decades the young Red Army began to develop along modern lines, a process which was speeded up as the older military leaders were replaced by newer men. Military academies began to devise and teach contemporary principles of warfare and even though it was still almost obligatory for an academy student to have had a working-class background, this qualification was no longer the principal one. The concept that only the working-class men were fit to bear arms in the army of the new Russia was one that had soon to be abolished when it was found that insufficient volunteers were coming forward to maintain the levels of infantry regiments. The Red Army then became a force based upon conscription and an instrument of state policy: that is to say, it was similar in structure and allegiance to the Imperial Army.

It had been the case in the early days that an order given by a military commander had had to be sanctioned by a political officer. Modern warfare with its demand for rapid decisions to be taken and acted upon could not be impeded by this obstruction. The military slowly won freedom of action from political control but all that progress vanished when Stalin challenged those whom he thought to be his military adversaries and defeated them as successfully as he had confronted and smashed, only a handful of years earlier, those who in his opinion opposed him politically.

The blood-letting was enormous and the Red Army cast in the revolutionary mould was shattered. When the military purge had been completed, and it lasted from 1937 to well into 1939, three marshals out of five had been executed, together with thirteen Army commanders, fifty-seven corps commanders, 110 divisional generals and 220 brigadiers. The number of field and subaltern officers shot to death ran into thousands. Those who survived the purge and who had seen comrades vanish into the execution yard or into prison, were a cowed remnant incapable of opposition to Stalin's rule. The whole army was riddled with an extensive system of informers and became a frightened force in which an infringement of regulations by an inferior had to be punished ruthlessly by a commander who might, otherwise, find himself accused of dereliction of duty.

The rule of the commissars and the *Politruks* over the military was restored and to those political officers was given, quite literally, the power of life and death over every man in the unit to which they were attached. Stalin and his Party machinery destroyed an army which had experimented in the use of armour en masse, on the use of armour as an arm of service in its own right, as well as even more advanced techniques of paratroop landings and the air transport of large bodies of men. These pioneering techniques were abandoned and reactionary principles based on the obsolescent 'wave' tactics were once again introduced and enforced.

The Red Army sank into apathy as each hoped to avoid responsibility for fear of making mistakes and thus it became an organisation more concerned with the strict letter of the law, an army of adjutants instead of military innovators. The military shortcomings evidenced by the war against Finland were seen as a need for even closer political control and this resulted in an even tighter Party grip on the army's organisation and personnel; and this, too, was a reinforcement for those officers who supported the 'wave' tactics.

Many of these were old Bolsheviks, Stalin's friends, or the protégés of such commanders, and now theirs was the only military voice. It was their plans which were followed, their ideas of the dominance of cavalry (which had once been swept aside by the adherents of armour) which were reintroduced. With no opposition now from the mechanised school of thought, the strategic armoured force which had been formed was broken up by the cavalry clique and the tank regiments distributed among infantry divisions to support the infantry waves.

The success of the panzer concept in the 1940 campaigns forced the Red Army, late in 1942, to undergo once again a transformation. The commander was given once again the whole responsibility for his men, new field service regulations were issued, based on the lessons learnt from the Finnish campaign and the German successes. The idea of armour en masse was re-introduced and a start made at regrouping those units which had been parcelled out among the infantry divisions. One new suggestion was for the establishment of a tank corps structure based upon two tank divisions and one motorised division.

In artillery structure, too, there was the introduction of new and fruitful ideas of the deployment of guns. Building upon the experience gained by a German gunner officer of the First World War, the Soviet General Voronov proposed that divisions of guns be formed and placed directly under the control of High Command to be employed at a strategic level. During the war these divisions were increased in size until eventually they were of corps strength and included within their establishment all calibres of ordnance ranging from super-heavy cannon to multiple rockets.

Proposals for radical changes require time in which ideas can be evaluated and tested in order that they may be either implemented or rejected. Unknown to the Red Army, the time which remained to them was limited and it might have been better not to have attempted such dramatic conversions or to have started them on a small scale for it was risky to have begun such changes in a force which was numerically the largest army in the world. The annual contingent of conscripts was between six hundred thousand and three quarters of a million men each year. The Field Army had a strength of 151 Infantry Divisions, 32 Cavalry Divisions and 38 Mechanised Brigades and behind that vast array there stood three stages of reservist soldiers and then the reservoir of men in the occupied areas who would, one day, form the partisan armies. The military might of Russia, numbering many millions of men, was given the task of making itself efficient for war and of bringing itself up to modern standards less than a year before the war began with Germany.

Numbers by themself are insufficient. A modern army needs weapons to help it towards victory and behind the Red Army stood an armaments industry with its roots based in a tradition of craftsmanship and excellence of design. The inventive genius of the Russian people had produced, during the years of the great industrialisation programmes, men whose revolutionary weapon designs, once approved and taken into production, brought forth arms and vehicles which were to lead the world. In the field of tank design, for example, there can be no dispute that the T 34 was the finest armoured fighting vehicle of the Second World War and that it was run a close second by the KV, both of which were initially armed with the 7.6cm tank gun. All three were the products of the expansion of industry which took place during the late '20s and early '30s.

To increase the infantryman's fire power it was decided to issue machine pistols which in the 1930s were coming into fashion with Continental armies. The first product, that of V. A. Degtyarev, took the circular, 71-round magazine designed by a Finn, included parts from the German 1928 Schmeisser, and these pieces, together with the products of his own mind, resulted in the PPD34, which was in service until the outbreak of war. The PPD was unsuitable for mass production and was expensive to produce. A cheaper and more reliable weapon, the PPSh, was designed by Shpagin, and this very efficient weapon went into production on such a scale that by the end of the war no fewer than five million had been manufactured. It became, in effect, the Red Army's trade mark.

In the field of artillery one revolutionary concept was that of rocket propulsion and the BM13, designed by Kostikov and battle-tested during July 1941, passed into battle to be known by the Russians as *Katyusha* and by the Germans as the Stalin Organ. Max Simon's report remarks that trucks with this weapon's simple framework had been captured but that the significance of the frames had not been appreciated for some time. In anti-tank artillery Ivanov and Grabin designed the 7.6cm anti-tank gun, without doubt the most efficient tank killer of its time and one that when captured was used by German anti-tank gunners, who preferred it to their own Army's less powerful weapons.

Backed by this arms industry of immense size and unusual flexibility the Red Army was well equipped when war came in the summer of 1941. In armour the figure usually quoted is 20,000 machines, although this figure is qualified by the fact that a great number of these were of the lighter, less well-armed and thinly-armoured types. These had been so long in service that many of them were in workshops or undergoing servicing when the German attack came, so that the front-line strength of the Red Army in armoured fighting vehicles was perhaps less than 12,000 vehicles.

The great mass of the Red Army's divisions was deployed in the western half of the Soviet Union and in special military districts along the common frontier with Germany and the other nations of the West. It cannot be claimed that the deployment was well thought out but it must be conceded that it was an Army in a stage of transition and one whose political leader was determined not to make any move that would give Hitler a reason to attack the Union. In obedience to Stalin's order not to be provocative some divisions were deployed more than forty kilometres from the border, while in

the vital Brest Litovsk sector the armoured divisions attached to the
10th Army were dispersed in training camps in Byelo-Russia.

Thus, in the last remaining weeks of peace the Red Army, while
maintaining an outwardly peaceful and non-provocative stance,
was desperately building itself up. In the Baltic, Western and Kiev
special military districts new armies were formed, the 27th, the 13th,
and the 18th, respectively, whose task it would be to act as long stop
to the front line armies.

Millions of Russian soldiers were under arms, thousands of
tanks, aircraft and guns stood ready to defend Soviet territory. The
Army was strong and well equipped but from an hierarchical point
of view the purges of 1937–39 had removed the most capable officers
from the highest echelons of command and now their offices were
filled with men either unsuited to or untrained for the great
responsibilities which were to be thrust upon them. In contrast to the
old Bolsheviks with their outmoded tactics, there were others who
worked diligently to ensure that their particular arm of service
would be used to its best advantage. These, however, were few in
number and the ranks of the militarily incapable were many. Thus it
was with the belief that fervour could overcome bullets and Party
slogans could win victory that the Red Army went to war. The Party
dictated the strategies and the policies so that the initial deployment
of the field army, following the orders of Josef Stalin, gave to the
attacking Germans the opportunity to encircle, capture and destroy
huge armies of Russian soldiers with only minimal effort.

The great defeats suffered by the Red Army in the first disastrous
campaigns reduced the number of men under arms in western
Russia to less than two and a half million. This brought about a ratio
of forces which was favourable to the Germans, but in succeeding
years, as more and more Russian men entered the Soviet forces, this
ratio was no longer tolerable and placed the German forces under an
increasingly heavy strain.

As early as November 1942 the increase in Red Army strength
was apparent as the number of infantry divisions doubled. The
armoured divisions, which had also increased in number, were
formed into corps and although the Red Army had not yet reached
that degree of proficiency or that superiority in numbers which
would guarantee victory, encouraging progress had been made.
True, the failure of the 1941 winter offensive either to smash the
German Army Groups as STAVKA had planned or to destroy the
Hitlerite armies as the propaganda had claimed that it would,
produced a deep decline in morale in the Red Army, for the dogma of
revolutionary fervour being sufficient to win victories had been
accepted totally by the rank and file.

The reorganisation of the Red Army which took place after the
halting of that offensive produced positive results. Unwieldy
groupings were cut down so that they could be handled more
efficiently by commanders whose grasp was still unsure. Infantry

divisions were reduced in size, armoured divisions given greater independence of action but, above all, the Red Army was no longer tied to the obsolescent concept of holding every foot of Soviet soil to the last. Flexibility became the watchword and a series of local offensives took place to test the new groupings and the new ideas. The Red Army was testing itself for the decisive battles to come; as it grew in strength so, at the same time, did the strength of the German Army decline, so the ratio of forces became more and more unfavourable to the Germans. In the summer of 1942 the number of Axis divisions on the Eastern Front had risen (141 in June 1941; 214 in July 1942) but the greatest number of these additional formations were not German but from countries allied to her. Their scale of equipment was lower, their mobility lower still and their fighting capabilities frequently suspect.

This was shown when in the winter of 1942–43 these materially understrength units guarded the flanks of the 6th Army as it fought in Stalingrad. It was against those satellite forces that the massive blows of the revitalised Red Army came in and when they collapsed in the face of the Soviet assault, not only was the 6th Army doomed but the hopes of a German victory in Russia died too.

This is not to say that the Germans were already defeated. Their greater experience enabled them to seize advantages which were presented to them as a result of the slower reactions of Soviet commanders. By the end of the winter of 1942–43 the Soviet Army had more than doubled in size, from 175 infantry divisions in June 1941, to 442 in 1942 and rising to 513 in 1943. The Red Army was well equipped and had regained the confidence lost in 1941. The size of its force in Western Europe had risen to over five millions and the output from Soviet factories had equipped the armoured and artillery divisions on an unbelievably lavish scale.

During the wet spring of 1943, while the German Army was making good its losses and trying desperately to build up its strength for a major offensive in the Kursk salient, the Red Army was increasing its already massive strength for a final contest. When this came during July 1943, in an operation called 'Citadel', the result set the seal upon the success which had been gained earlier that year at Stalingrad. The Red Army now felt itself strong enough to launch a summer counter-offensive as a riposte to the unsuccessful German blow and the success of this stroke showed conclusively that the German Army no longer had any hope of defeating the Russians in ground combat.

There then followed a number of offensives at separate and often widely spaced sectors of the battle line and almost without interruption until at last the spring thaw of 1944 brought mud which halted all offensive operations. As if to confound Hitler's strategy the autumn rainfall in 1943 had been unusually light and had not produced the barrier of mud upon which the Führer had depended to halt the Soviet advance. Another factor, too, was in part responsible for the Russian offensives being halted; the Red Army had outrun its supplies. Its lines of communication were now running across those areas of the Union which had been devastated by war with the resultant lack of roads and railways to nourish the advance. One American correspondent visiting the Russian front at that time described how the soldiers of the Red Army infantry units passing an artillery ammunition dump on their way up the line were each given a shell to carry, in addition to the equipment with which they were burdened. These they carried for miles before they set them down in readiness for the assault artillery to use in the forthcoming assault.

Early in 1944 the Red Army stood at the peak of its power and the successive blows by the various 'Fronts' first drove back the German armies investing Leningrad. This was the first of what were later to become famous as Stalin's 'ten blows', each of which brought a victory and laid the foundation for the final offensive which was to end the war. The second of the ten blows aimed for the liberation of the Ukraine and drove back the forces of Army Groups Centre and South to the borders of Poland and Roumania. Then the Crimea was reconquered and, once again, striking at the far end of the long battle line, the Finns were attacked. It was the sixth blow which was the decisive one, for this smashed Army Group Centre and destroyed more than thirty of its divisions. To add to the catastrophe Germany's allies were suing for peace and voiding the field one by one.

For the final assault upon Germany every detail was worked out and the most thorough training was given. On 13 January 1945 the Red Armies in Poland struck with the strength of 275 infantry divisions and twenty-two armoured corps. The superiority according to Soviet official sources was 7 : 1 in infantry, 7: 1 in artillery and 4 : 1 in tanks.

The offensive cut off East Prussia and reached the Oder river. There was another short halt to regroup and then on 16 April the final act began. The massive fist of the Red Army closed round Berlin and although military activities continued even after the capital fell they were the death throes of the German Army and by 9 May the war in Europe had ended.

7

Two German views of the Red Army

How did the average German see his new opponent and what were his reactions to the Red Army? In his war-time work *Wiedersehen mit Sowjet-Russland*, the German soldier-poet Erich Dwinger set out to rediscover those factors which had first drawn him to Russia many years before. The description of his feelings as he waited to cross the river upon whose further bank he would once again tread on Russian soil are illuminating for they express that love/hate relationship already referred to between the Teutons and the Slavs. "In a few minutes I shall feel under my feet that secret land which I loved as much as I hated it; which satisfied me as no other country did and yet let me hunger as none had done before . . . in whose hot deserts I had thirsted and in whose icy tundras I had wept because of the cold . . . that[land] which robbed me of five years of my young life but which repaid me ten-fold with a wealth of experiences . . . ."

The long forgotten smells came back: old leather mixed with the odour of sour bread, the stink of coarse Russian tobacco and there was also a new smell, a gamey odour, the sort of smell met with in gypsies and which Dwinger found was most noticeable among the captured Mongolian troops. The chapter then describes the stoicism of the Red Army wounded:

Among the prisoners waiting to be ferried back across the river were wounded, many of whom had been badly burnt by flame-throwers . . . Their faces had no longer any recognisable human features but were simply swollen lumps of meat. One of them also had had his lower jaw torn away by a bullet and this wound he had bandaged roughly. Through the rags his windpipe, laid bare, was visible and the effort it made as his breath snorted through it. Another soldier had been hit by five bullets and his right shoulder and his whole arm was a ragged mass of flesh. He had no bandages and the blood oozed from his wounds as if from a row of tubes . . .

Not one of them was moaning as they sat there in the grass . . . Why did they not moan? But this was not the most tragic picture of that day . . . some of our soldiers brought out barrels of margarine and loaves of Russian bread. They began their distribution more than thirty metres distant from the place where the badly wounded were lying and these rose up, yes, even the dying rose up quickly and in an inexpressible stream of suffering hurried toward the distribution point. The man without a jaw swayed as he stood up; the man with the five bullet wounds raised himself by his good arm . . . and those with burned faces ran . . . but this was not all; a half dozen men who had been lying on the ground also went forward pressing back into their bodies with their left hands the intestines which had burst through the

gaping wounds in their stomach wall. Their right hands were
extended in gestures of supplication ... as they moved down each left
behind a broad smear of blood upon the grass ... and not one of them
cried ... none moaned ... they were all dumb, as dumb as the poorest of
God's creatures.

The prisoners he saw had brutal, close-cropped heads with eyes
deep set and expressionless. Yet he found confidence and optimism
among some prisoners. One such was a young Communist who
claimed that the Soviet Union would win the war because of three
advantages it enjoyed. The first of these was that the sand of the
Soviet Union would ruin the engines of the German vehicles and
render the army immobile. Secondly, the partisans would cut supply
lines and compel the High Command to withdraw front line troops
and to garrison the rear areas with huge armies. The third
advantage was the winter and when that began "... then our war
will start, for until now it has been only your war ..."

Dwinger was not alone in his comments on the incredible ability
of the Russian soldier to bear wounds. Another author described how
the turret of a Soviet tank, which it was believed had been destroyed
during the fighting around the citadel at Brest Litovsk, began to
swing and align its gun on a divisional headquarters set up in the
grounds of the citadel. When the machine was finally disabled three
of the crew were found to be in an advanced state of decomposition
and the fourth man, although badly wounded, had held on without
food or water, medical aid or support and in the stench of the
decaying bodies of his comrades for more than a week. He had
obeyed the teaching to strike one last blow for his country. General of
the Waffen SS Max Simon also remarked on this bravery unto death:
"The Russian infantryman, however, always defended himself to
the last gasp ... even crews in burning tanks kept up fire for as long
as there was breath in their bodies. Wounded or unconscious men
reached for their weapons as soon as they regained consciousness."

And yet the Army was a mass of contrasts and conflicting
experiences. There were soldiers like those described above who
fought to the last, who held out in situations that were hopeless, not
merely for fear of the commissar's bullet but because their resistance
was for Russia. There were instances related of a rear-guard fighting
off massed panzer assaults, attacks by panzer grenadiers and dive-
bombing by waves of Ju 87s and yet cracking under an old-
fashioned charge carried out by Hungarian cavalry.

There were instances of some obscure position being held
tenaciously and once it had been taken no more resistance being
offered for scores of miles; of men who fought to the last and others
who broke at the first assault; of a blinding patriotism by some
peoples to the land and its government, a white hot flame of loyalty
which held the wavering battle line intact; but also of other nations
of the Union who welcomed the Germans with open arms, who
furnished them with soldiers, horses and supplies and who fought

against their own nation and its political system.

It was this land of surprising contrasts that the Germans invaded. A land of unbearably hot summers or abnormally cold winters, of poor roads which could have been kept in good repair by only a small squad of men, only nobody had given the necessary order; a land of frequently proclaimed ideals of freedom and of canals dug by slave labour; a vast Empire in which incredible wealth existed side by side with abject poverty of a sort unknown in Western Europe. It was all a mystery and it is no wonder that Max Simon expressed the conviction that the German troops were entering into an unknown. His report, edited and summarised in parts says:

Opinion in the German Army frequently represented the Russian soldier as being discontented with the Soviet system [but] the Russian infantry defended the Stalin line with great tenacity and the further we penetrated into Russia the greater was our astonishment at their powers of resistance, their sniping ability and excellent defensive tactics. Very soon we had to admit that we were up against a different adversary from the one we had expected and I believe that this under-estimation [of the Russian infantry] was one of the reasons for the unfortunate course which the campaign in Russia took. The reasons did not lie in terrain and space, nor to the opposition put up by the air force or the artillery, nor can mere numbers or weapons have been decisive factors. The ability of the Russian infantry who fanatically contested every foot of our advance was the principal, perhaps only, reason.

In attack we lost heavily from snipers and mortars which were more effective than the field artillery, certainly at the beginning of the campaign. The Soviets did outnumber us in guns but there was a lack of co-operation with the infantry which nullified this superiority. On the other hand Russian tanks were from the outset the breast plates of the infantry. In defence the Red Army infantry was remarkable for the way in which they blended into the terrain and they could dig themselves in in an amazingly short time. Their defensive positions were simple and effective. Trenches were discarded to a very great extent and instead deep, narrow holes were dug which held two or three riflemen. Machine guns were skilfully sited so that dead angles were avoided and snipers, of whom there were often as many as forty or fifty in each company, were given the best positions. Trench mortars were available in all calibres and flame throwers, often fitted with remote control, were used in conjunction with mortars so the attacking troops ran into a sea of flames. Well-concealed tanks stood by to take part in counter-attacks or were dug in at intervals. This was defence in depth protected by wire entanglements and numerous minefields, and was a defensive system applied to all kinds of terrain.

Russian battlefield discipline was most impressive. German patrols were allowed to penetrate Soviet lines and even to withdraw without having seen anything. Spotter aircraft usually saw nothing of the enemy who made no movement in their well camouflaged positions. Experienced German officers driving through a seemingly deserted village would swear that there were neither troops nor inhabitants in the place but other troops following up would find themselves faced with a fortified position, defended by an infantry regiment, reinforced by all arms. The positions had been so well camouflaged and the Soviet soldiers had remained so still that the officers as they drove through had noticed nothing.

However, we soon learnt to detect positions and found that attacks upon the enemy flank or rear were almost always successful for as soon as an attack developed from an unexpected direction the Russian system broke down. At the beginning we were not impressed by their attacks which showed little initiative. They were rule of thumb, co-operation with the heavy weapons was lacking and one could sense the absence of flexible leadership. Attacks against our good infantry regiments still intact and firm in well prepared positions met with virtually no success. Usually the main Russian attack was preceded by an artillery preparation lasting several hours. As soon as the artillery fire lengthened the infantry attack began supported by armour and snipers and to the accompaniment of fighter aircraft. If our infantry held its positions until the enemy artillery fire had passed over it, then it could always beat off the first attack. Our intention was always to separate the infantry from the accompanying tanks. Experienced German troops did not bother much about the enemy armour, leaving this to the anti-tank weapons and the special tank-busting teams. Instead they concentrated on forcing the Russian infantry to go to ground. Red tanks would thereupon halt and open fire to cover the infantry which was digging in. If the armour charged the German positions they offered a good target to the waiting anti-tank units.

Where the Russians effected a penetration a handful of resolute grenadiers accompanied by armour and supported by heavy weapons could destroy the enemy before he had time to exploit his success.

The first attack was certain to be followed by a second, third, fourth, fifth or even more. Never in my experience did these successive assaults differ from the first one. Russian commanders were made responsible for failure and always strove to be able to report that their orders had been carried out. Failure to achieve success in frontal assault forced the Russian commanders to have recourse to infiltration, to penetrate undetected behind our front. We found that no water or swamp was too deep and no forest too thick for them to find a way through. Other examples of infiltration were the appearance in the latter part of the war, of officers in German uniform bringing fictitious orders. It was most important to remain alert against any type of infiltration because a Russian patrol driven off from our line would leave behind a small detachment which could remain concealed for days and be gradually reinforced until at a specified time and place a large body of enemy troops would emerge and cause havoc.

Infantry warfare on the Eastern Front. A machine gun post in a slit trench; northern front, October 1941.

German grenadiers fighting their way through a village on the central front during the winter of 1941/42.

A grenadier from an anti-tank gun detachment watching a Soviet tank burning; Ukraine 1941.

A front line trench during the first winter of the war with Russia. The MG 34 has a cover to protect the action against the effects of cold.

A sentry on guard outside his unit headquarters; Ukraine, winter 1941/42.

Tracer bullets from a German machine gun clearly visible in the evening light of winter; central front, 1941/42.

Above: In a thickly wooded part of the northern front in the winter of 1941/42 Soviet patrols had probed to infiltrate the German line and had set up a listening post. A German fighting patrol was sent out to destroy this. The picture shows the Russian sentry surprised and captured by the grenadiers.

Right: One of the soldiers of the Cholm garrison brings in an air-dropped canister of supplies; winter 1941/42.

Below right: A German reconnaissance patrol in the winter of 1941/42, camouflaged in jackets made from old parachutes, pass the dead body of a Red Army man.

Below: Warmly dressed sentries on guard during the first winter in Russia, 1941/42.

Cholm. One of the anti-tank guns brought in by
Ju 52s during the encirclement.

An infantry group on reconnaissance patrol,
camouflaged in white jackets and white
painted helmets. Central front during the
winter of 1941/42.

A Soviet tank destroyed in the close quarter fighting which took place in and around Cholm during the winter of 1941/42.

An SP gun and grenadiers of von Arnim's force raise the siege of Cholm on 15 May 1942.

A German heavy weapons group, including mortars and tripod mounted machine guns, taking position in the Ukraine to protect a main highway from partisan assault in March 1942.

Conditions on the central front when the thaw began during the spring of 1942.

In close combat hand grenades were often a decisive factor in driving back Soviet attacks. Here a runner brings fresh supplies of the standard stick hand grenade through a communication trench; spring 1942, central front.

Mud. German lorries stranded during the spring rains of 1942.

8

The development of the Red Army

Former chapters of this book have dealt with the Red Army's disposition at the outbreak of war and have seen how that force was viewed by two German officers. Other accounts to be found throughout these pages have shown or will show the stubbornness of the Russian soldiers in defence, their defiance in attack, their ability and their disabilities. But what it was like to have served as a soldier in the ranks of an infantry unit, for example, is not easy to say, for very few objective accounts of life at that level have been produced. A collation made up of experiences recounted by former Soviet soldiers living in the West as well as extracts from combat reports, the few books or articles produced during and immediately after the war, may help to make an assessment of life in the Soviet forces.

To Western beliefs the most sinister aspect of service with the Red Army was the presence of an intricate and all-pervading network of spies and informers. Every soldier was expected, indeed was required, to report any dereliction of duty on the part of his subordinates, equals or superiors. Every man was aware of this system of reporting and few objected – it was, after all, the way in which it had always been and, oddly enough, this constant vigilance produced a certain comfort, the feeling of being protected.

The Red Army also had what was certainly the most savage penal code of any military force in the Western hemisphere and this, backed by the passive Slav mentality and the Communist ethos produced an army whose men had a callous indifference to brutality, to suffering and even to death. The teaching of the Communist Party was that the individual was of little or no significance and this was no casual theory but a deliberate policy which was reinforced and demonstrated at every opportunity. The Party demanded the utmost sacrifices from the Russian people and through the system of informers ensured that these were met in full. According to Party dogma there was an obligation on every Soviet soldier to fight to the death and to surrender under this harsh code was the equivalent of desertion. Quite frequently the family of a man who had surrendered or who had deserted to the enemy was held to be politically unreliable and was imprisoned.

Insubordination on active service could be met, quite legally, by summary execution carried out on the spot by an officer and more formal executions were carried out publicly. The Western concept of the liberty of the individual had no counterpart in the Soviet system of things. The individual had no guarantee of any social, political or moral privileges nor immunity from the worst excesses of repression. But if there was a contempt for the individual and a wide-spread repression there were also splendid parades, glittering medals to be worn and a sense of community which encouraged a real *esprit de corps*.

To ensure that the soldiers of the Red Army were not inactive during those times when they were not actually engaged in combat there were frequent lectures dealing with Soviet history and political indoctrination. In addition to these hours of Marx and Lenin there were drill parades, field training and manoeuvres in which live ammunition was used and a wide variety of duties carried out. Spare time in which the soldier might wander at leisure or alone was almost unknown and such behaviour was, in fact, considered to be anti-social. The object of training was to instil into the peasant mind a sense of pride in achievement and there is no doubt that such pride was in fact produced and that it benefited the whole Army.

In training the hours of duty were long, the duty itself monotonous and the food poor in quality with *Kascha* (maize porridge) for breakfast and *Borscht* for the midday meal. At evening there was bread with perhaps a pickled cucumber. Of course, on active service, the quality of the food improved but the type and scale of rations considered essential by Anglo-Saxon soldiers were undreamed-of luxuries. The Russian soldier was encouraged to forage for food to supplement his rations and needed little, in any case, to keep him active and fighting fit.

It was not only in food that there was a primitive simplicity. The summer uniform was a simple lightweight twill or denim two-piece. Jackboots and a greatcoat together with a cap completed the outfit. The Soviet soldier wore his greatcoat in summer for he carried no blanket and this practice of wearing the greatcoat even on the hottest days identified him completely. His winter clothing, by comparison, was well designed, warm and waterproof and superior to the German in every way, but particularly in the matter of the *Valenki* or felt boots which kept the feet warm in the coldest and deepest snow. The winter overcoat was lined and the winter head-dress was of lambs' wool. All in all, the Red Army man in winter uniform was ready to meet the worst cold-weather conditions.

Aware that the great mass of the army was not familiar with mechanical equipment the weapons were also kept deliberately simple. The standard weapon which was carried until late in 1944 was the M1891/30, a rifle which had been on issue in the army of the Tsar. In the last two years of the war a massive distribution of the M1944 carbine and the Shpagin machine pistol increased the fire power of the Soviet soldier. There were, however, severe gaps in the equipment on issue and many men carried their two hand grenades in a pocket or in the linen haversack. Until the automatic weapons came on issue each man had carried 120 rounds of small arms ammunition but the number of rounds was more than doubled to feed the machine pistol. In full battle order the Soviet soldier carried twenty-eight kilograms of equipment and ammunition in summer and thirty-five kilograms in winter.

This then was 'Ivan', as the Germans called him, a simple, enduring, capable and skilful soldier. Usually from a rural background he tended to lack individual initiative and was capable of bewildering changes of mood, veering erratically between confidence and despair. The winter offensive of 1941, to quote one example, had begun with the wildest belief in victory and the realisation that the war had not been brought to a conclusion by that great assault cast the Red Army into the deepest depression.

The ability of the Soviet force to absorb losses which would have crippled units of other armies has already been touched upon but there came a time in the war when the scale of casualties had been so great that conservation of existing units was vital and new infantry regiments were raised by the most severe recruiting methods. The interrogation of Red Army deserters and prisoners showed that late in 1943 a severe combing out of existing units took place with the object of producing more infantry soldiers. The places vacated by the men drafted into the foot regiments were filled by women soldiers who took over such tasks as signallers, telephone operators, laundry women, ambulance personnel and as drivers. From some interrogation reports it was clear that there were some ladies on establishment who had no greater military task to perform than to be the officers' women. There was conscription of women in the Soviet Union and more than two million served in the forces.

In earlier pages it has been mentioned that out of the revolutionary cadres a new officer caste had been developed in the Red Army. Their rates of pay were, of course, higher than those of the other ranks and officers' supplements for combat pay were fifty per cent of their basic wage. For other ranks it was ten per cent. The following account compares the German and Soviet forces and the changes in outlook which both underwent in the course of the war:

The German Army which entered Russia wore a very smart uniform. Officers and NCOs carried silver lace on their shoulder straps, there were coloured bayonet knots. General officers wore gold and scarlet, everywhere there was colour on our uniforms. During the campaign medals were awarded, all of which added to the decoration on the jacket. There was, for example, the 'frozen meat' Order, the nickname given to the medal which was awarded for having fought on the Eastern Front during that first terrible winter. Then there were infantry combat badges, the close combat award, various arm-shields and, finally, in the last two years of the war silver lace badges on the arm to denote an enemy tank 'killed' at close quarters by a single man.

Despite this lavish bestowal of awards there was a deterioration in the uniform we wore. It was not merely in the quality, although it began with that, nor was it the colour which changed from the

traditional field grey to a green colour. The jack-boots had been a
distinctive mark of the German soldier, even though they were not
only uncomfortable but impractical in wet conditions and particularly
in snow. We eventually wore anklets like the British and then our
tunics changed in cut so that they too, looked rather like the British
battle dress. Throughout the last three years of the war our uniforms
were being simplified and many units, particularly in the SS, took to
wearing camouflage pattern suits as a mark of distinction. All in all we
took on the appearance of mechanics in dungarees and were no longer
soldiers in a distinctive and smart uniform.

While we were thus reducing our uniform to a basic and simple
dress the enemy was embellishing his. Within a year of the opening of
the war with Russia, that cunning devil Stalin had turned the whole
concept of the war from a defence of the Communist system into a fight
for Mother Russia. This spurred the masses but the officer class too,
needed its reward and so Stalin restored to them the old Tsarist
symbols of silver board epaulettes. The soldiers were awarded medals
for each resounding victory and, of course, they wore these complete,
that is to say there were no medal ribbons issued; one wore the whole
thing. As the officers of our Army became more democratic and
comradely, at least in front line units on active service, Ivan's officers
were acting in a way that can only be described as aristocratic.

A report was circulated within our corps to the effect that Russian
officers had reverted to practices current in the old Imperial Army. A
Guards infantry division, so the translation of an original Russian
document said, had established an officers' association which held
courts of honour on fellow officers, had opened an officers' club and
restaurant, entrance to which was restricted to commissioned ranks
only and any officer who appeared in the club or restaurant had to
conform to very strict rules on dress, behaviour and deportment. The
traditions of the old Corps of Officers were reintroduced and an
officer's uniform, so the document said, was like the regimental colour:
an object of honour. All these things would have been unthinkable in
revolutionary days. It was peace-time Potsdam all over again and
then, of course, officers had a higher percentage supplement to their
basic salary when on active service.

If the reports sent to the German police authorities in the last
months of the war can be believed the behaviour of those same
officers differed greatly from the high ideals which the document
had set out. The reports which were collected and then disseminated
to local authorities spoke of acts of criminal violence in the provinces
of Prussia, Silesia and Saxony in the late winter and the early spring
of 1945. In most cases officers, some of them of senior rank,
instigated the acts of rape and pillage which were a feature of the
Soviet occupation of the early days. There were stories of mass rape,
the execution of males, the forcible conscription of women into
labour battalions and the deportation of whole villages.

To see the whole picture and to view it objectively it can be
claimed, for the Red Army, that the forced labour battalions were
drafted to clear the roads so that food convoys could reach the towns
and feed the people. It may also be claimed, and with a high degree of
likelihood, that the deportation may have been the attempt by the
Red Army to remove from the combat zone all civilians who might

otherwise have become casualties in the fighting. These things may well be claimed, and may equally well be true, but to the German civilians, frightened, cold and desperate, those acts which they witnessed were the outrages of a horde of murderers. It was widely believed that outside every uncaptured German village the political officer of a unit would read a declamation by Ilya Ehrenburg inciting the Red Army men to wreak vengeance. Of course there were atrocities, summary executions and outrages. One of the most serious atrocities and remarkable because it was, perhaps, unique, was the murder of the Königsberg Volkssturm – a sort of Home Guard – which was declared by the Soviet authorities to be an illegal organisation made up of partisans. *Francs-tireurs* could be executed, according to the interpretation of Soviet military law, and that was the fate of the Volkssturm of Königsberg.

To conclude this chapter let us reflect that at the end of the Second World War the Red Army was the largest, best-armed and most tightly organised force in the world. The theory of Suvorov, a commander in the campaign against the French, was that the strength of the Russian Army lay not in its handling by its officers, but in its composition based upon a peasant mass. This theory was shown to be inaccurate the longer the war lasted. True, there was a peasant mass to begin with but it was never an unwieldy horde and after 1943 it was seen to be a vast army directed by a highly intelligent leadership supported by an absolutely competent Staff system. The Russian Army was not only the giant which it had always been, but it was a giant with a first-class brain. The steamroller of 1939 and 1941 had become a world shaking influence. The Red Army had come out of the military shadows.

9

Partisans

"For psychological reasons the term partisan is not to be used"
ORDER OF 23.8.1942

It was during the campaign in Russia that there began a series of centrally organised operations in the rear of the German invaders. These were not the undeveloped assaults of uncoordinated groups of patriots but a well organised and skilfully directed national movement, the blows of whose guerrilla bands were intended to integrate with the offensives of the Red Army. This organisation and the men and women who fought in the hidden war were the partisans. Their part in the Great Soviet Fatherland War is remarked on and described by almost every author who writes about the Russo-German conflict and the vital role they played during that war can never be over-stressed.

It would have been interesting to compare the role of the SS in Russia with that of their counterparts in the Soviet politico-military organisation, but this is not possible as no histories of the NKVD have come down to us. There was one Russian force which fought the war as mercilessly as did the SS and since they, the partisans, formed an official part of the Army on the Eastern Front, then they must feature in any account of the operations which were carried out there.

As with the introduction to the section on the SS so with this chapter on guerrilla warfare in the Soviet Union there are certain conceptions about those activities which need to be challenged. Firstly, the claim that the hidden war had a direct and important influence upon the strategic conduct of German military operations. This statement has been shown, in the light of post-war research, to be untrue. There were outstanding successes at tactical level but there was only one offensive, that during the summer of 1944, in which success was achieved by a combination of blows struck by the Red Army and the partisan forces.

Secondly, there was not, as some German writers have claimed, an embryo partisan organisation in existence in the Soviet Union before the outbreak of the war with Germany. No state could form an underground organisation in peace time, to combat a possible occupying army. Such a move would have been defeatist and, in any case there would always be the fear, certainly in dictatorships, that such a clandestine movement could form the basis of a counter-revolution.

Thirdly, the Soviet legend of a great partisan movement

springing immediately and spontaneously into life following the outbreak of war is a total myth. It is true that as early as 7 July 1941 Stalin called upon the inhabitants of areas occupied by the Germans to rise in revolt, but there was little response. This is hardly surprising for at that time the German armies were advancing through those regions of the Soviet Union which had been until quite recently independent countries. In those lands, as this book has already stated, the Germans had been received as men who would bring freedom from Soviet domination and there were few locals in those regions who would have been prepared to engage in partisan warfare against an army that was welcomed by the great mass of their fellow countrymen as liberators.

One can, perhaps, count as partisans those bands of armed men belonging to the Red Army who had been by-passed during the German advance. These were still free behind the German lines and were a menace to the Germans and to the Russian civilians alike. Lacking food supplies, those remnants of Soviet military units terrorised the villagers, forcibly requisitioning food and horses before disappearing into the countryside. To defend their homes and their supplies against such depredations many villagers joined a German-run militia armed with rifles and light machine guns, or else led anti-insurgent sweeps to uncover guerrilla hiding-places. In such operations the German forces were at a disadvantage for the size of the battlefield as well as the nature of the terrain inhibited their efforts although they would not always admit it. The writer of the following letter seems to have realised the full measure of the partisan menace:

> On anti-terrorist patrols smell is as important as sight. The Russians smoke a coarse tobacco - Mahorka - and the stink of it hangs about their positions, particularly at dawn or late evening. Some of the partisan commanders soak themselves in cheap scent - they probably think it keeps down the lice - and this can be smelt down-wind for some distance as can human sweat and the smell of horses. We usually have men at the front of our patrols who are non-smokers for they have a better sense of smell than the rest of us. Those, too, who were foresters or game keepers back home have marvellous powers of observation and look for tell-tale signs of the bandits. Sometimes we take dogs but these are not reliable. I think that these Soviet hounds have anti-German feelings because of the things they do. The best trackers are the local Russians who have enlisted with us.
>
> In the early months of the fighting our General put the fear of death into the locals because they supported the partisans. Since then a great number work for us against them. They have to. The lives of their loved ones, their whole future is bound up with us. They can divine where a Soviet group is hidden in the swamps and can lead us to it. They are not always trustworthy. Some Cossack battalions are said to have gone over to the bandits and HIWIS (Russians who had volunteered to work with the German military) who deserted and went over to the Red Army told us, when they were recaptured, that they had only volunteered to work for us so as to escape and rejoin the Reds.
>
> According to the interrogations the bandits are said to be well

organised and even have an airfield somewhere, deep in the marshes. This is a measure of the menace which has grown up. They kill indiscriminately, Germans and Russian civilians. They blow up railway tracks and lay mines. We never seem to be able to capture them for as soon as we have one area quiet, they start their sabotage in another district.

The German anti-partisan patrols seldom penetrated deep into the dense forests and some reports talk of German units considering anti-guerrilla operations as a sort of relaxation after long periods in the line. This naive attitude and the failure of patrols to make deep penetrations into the forests led to an unnecessarily high casualty rate.

To enlarge upon the qualifications which were made at the opening of this chapter a time-scale shows that from the opening of Barbarossa in June 1941 to the end of the German.summer offensive of 1942, there was little partisan activity. Between the winter offensive of 1942 until the German Army was driven from the Soviet Union late in 1944, there was a sharp increase in such operations and many of them were on a massive scale. With Russian soil freed from German occupation there was no longer any need for a Russian guerrilla movement after the autumn of 1944, but there were in other parts of Eastern Europe local resistance groups, often led by Communists, which harried German lines of retreat or even, in the case of Yugoslavia, had raised partisan armies which went into the field and which scored considerable victories.

In those months of little anti-German activity railway lines were left unguarded and only at such vital points as bridges were there sentries. The German rear was, by and large, untroubled. That this peaceful situation changed radically was due to several reasons, of which a principal one was the attitude and the behaviour of many of the Nazi Party officials administering the occupied territories. The programme of repression which those men carried out against peoples whom they considered to be sub-human forced many otherwise passive Russians into the arms of the partisans. With this increase in its strength the undercover movement became more active.

From the time-scale we have seen that the situation in western Russia until the end of 1942 showed there to have been an ineffectual partisan organisation. This had been directed by the Party from remote Moscow while partisan units in the field had been locally formed. These local leaders resented the arrival of officers from Central Headquarters whose ideas on the action to be taken did not always accord with the tactical situation and who accused the local men of lack of moral fibre. Some of those complaining 'outsiders' did not live long.

The peasants, of course, longed only for the chance to carry on farming and resented supplying food to the partisan groups or the scattered bands of soldiers who dared not return to the Red Army for fear of being punished as deserters and who feared to surrender to the Germans in case they were tried as guerrillas and shot.

As the war progressed, regular and direct contact was established between the Homeland and the bands which had amalgamated to form units of brigade size. Next the partisans sought out the scattered Red Army groups whose men were still living the life of bandits and if argument failed to win over these trained but undirected military units then punitive raids were mounted to destroy them. There was not enough food to supply bandits as well as freedom fighters.

With those marauders eliminated, a victory for which the guerrilla forces could claim all the credit, the peasants were no longer subject to bandit pressures and could supply the partisans. The forests hid the underground army; the peasants fed it and from 'the big country' came the weapons and orders which controlled it. The partisan forces had now become almost as important an arm of service as any of those in the regular forces.

Partisans and their operations can be viewed in two lights. The army under attack sees them as *francs-tireurs*, as the enemies of the native population which has accepted defeat and which wishes only to carry on some sort of life under the occupying forces. The nation which puts the partisans into the field sees these men as freedom fighters and as soldiers of a special type who have no Geneva Convention to protect them. Being thus constantly exposed to danger the partisans have a right to demand anything of the local population, whose obligation it is to meet those demands.

The nature of insurgent operations makes it impossible for either side to fight a 'clean' war. To force a hostile reaction from the occupying forces partisans often carried out attacks in the area of villages whose inhabitants were friendly to the Germans and would then leave the mutilated bodies of German soldiers, whom they had taken prisoner and then murdered, to be found by the counter-attacking German troops. Reprisals would then follow against the villagers and that German reaction would normally prove sufficient incentive to ensure that the locals supported the guerrillas. Those who still did not were subjected to threats and those who actively collaborated with the Germans (as, for example, men who had been elected mayor of a village) would be murdered, quite frequently, together with their entire family. It was indeed a dirty war, for the partisans were absolutely ruthless. There was, of course, no Geneva Convention for civilians and those unfortunates were put under severe pressure from native partisan groups as well as from the occupying forces. The lot of the peasants was a desperate one.

To the German military mind there has always been something abhorrent in partisan warfare. In the Kaiser's war harsh punitive actions against *francs-tireurs* carried out by German troops as they advanced through Belgium and France in the west and through

Poland and Serbia in the south and east aroused international condemnation. The Germans had executed hostages during the First World War, frequently without trial and often upon the flimsiest of evidence. During the Second World War, in addition to a military hatred for a civilian attacker, there was added the Nazi belief that the Slavs were inferior beings.

The German Army had always fought in a traditional fashion and this inability to understand the concept of guerrilla operations may have been the root cause of their lack of absolute success in anti-partisan operations. A reading of war diaries and the reports of anti-partisan operations leads frequently to the belief that many innocent Russian civilians were arrested and shot merely on suspicion of being partisans and also to the realisation that even large-scale anti-partisan operations produced very little positive or long-term results.

For some missions several divisions of infantry were employed and these men fought against the natural obstacles such as swamps and all the time aware that the elusive enemy would seldom come to battle. In the marshes any patch of firm ground was certain to be thickly sown with the little wooden mines which could not be detected by mechanical means but which could blow off a foot. There were pits lined with sharp stakes into which the unwary would fall and be impaled and then there were the snipers whose sudden and unexpected shots would come from a thicket or from the thick undergrowth, killing or maiming. In the history of the 10th Infantry Division is recorded one operation which took place in an area 10,000 square kilometres in extent, of which the greatest part was forest and swamp. A massive force, including two panzer divisions, three German infantry and a Hungarian infantry division, a cavalry detachment, two SS battalions and a number of deserters from the Red Army was put into this sweep. The whole operation lasted nine days and the net result was 150 enemy killed and 1,500 prisoners taken. These latter included women and children.

The scale of partisan and anti-partisan operations is shown by the fact that special security divisions had to be formed and large numbers of soldiers taken from front-line duty to pacify the rear areas. In the summer and autumn of 1942 the Germans fielded twenty-five whole divisions on such operations as well as thirty regiments and more than a hundred battalions of police. By the following year this number had been increased by the addition of nearly half a million auxiliaries of Soviet origin. The scale of the hidden war had grown and with it the forces needed to combat it.

There were neither political nor military guidelines laid down for the German occupying and administrative forces on the treatment of civilians in partisan-infested country. Thus each political official had his own interpretation. The task facing the civil administrators was to make the occupied territory produce the wheat, oil, coal and iron to feed the German war machine and it was the task of the army to ensure that those materials were guarded until they reached Germany. These were difficult tasks to accomplish, for the guerrillas were determined that nothing would reach Germany and being elusive could strike at a cargo and vanish before the military could come into action.

Hitler's viewpoints are interesting for his early opinions soon gave way to a determination to destroy the bandits who would not give in. A military instruction summarised his words and said: "The Führer has issued orders regarding this matter [anti-partisan operations] and in this context has given freedom of action against any evilly-disposed civilian enemy encountered during the course of a military operation. On the other hand individual acts of reprisal against the civil population in pacified areas are wrong. Those guilty of such acts are to be punished and if soldiers act against the persons or property of defenceless civilians are not punished then their superior officers are unsuited for their posts." In contrast to this is the preamble to "Combat procedures for anti-partisan operations in the East", issued on 16 December 1942. This stated: "Basically, anything that leads to success is proper ... the object must be to destroy the bandits and to restore order ..." The document went on: "... the enemy is using in his bandit struggle fanatical, Communist-drilled soldiers who do not hesitate to commit any act of terror. It is more than ever a question of 'to be or not to be'. This struggle has nothing to do with military chivalry or the limitations of the Geneva Convention ... if this battle is not fought using the most brutal means ... then we shall not master the plague."

It is interesting to note that as early as the summer of 1942, the word 'partisan' was discontinued in German official reports. The following document is indicative of the increase in partisan activity which took place about that time.

OKH General Staff of the Army. Operations Section

23.8.1942

Guidelines to bring about a more intensive combat of bandits on the Eastern Front (based on the Führer's Instruction No. 46)

General
(1) For psychological reasons the word PARTISAN is not to be used.
(2) The increase in activity has become a threat to supplies reaching the Front and to the economic utilisation of the country. The bandits must be defeated before the onset of winter ... and to bring this about there must be an intensification of anti-bandit activity and of propaganda.
    (a) In this context it is essential to maintain supplies to the civilian population and there must be no cheating, for this leads to their becoming sympathetic to bandit beliefs.

(b) The support of the local population is essential to combat the bandits. Rewards to those who help us to defeat the bandits must be substantial and reprisals taken against those who support the enemy.
   An intimate relationship with the civilians in German employment is to be avoided for even though the mass of the population is anti-Communist there are still some who will be informers and agents.

The areas of delineation are: The SS is responsible in the Reich's commissariat (the rear areas), while the Army has the responsibility for security in the Operations area. Police units which may be employed in the area of operations will be under Army control. All Party organisations, such as the Reichsarbeitsdienst (The German Labour Corps) will be armed. In bandit-infested areas there must be no German who does not take part actively in the battle against the bandits.

Acting in the belief that they were following Hitler's directive some officers found the simple solution to partisan attack. The province or area was depopulated, all livestock confiscated, the men deported to Germany as prisoners-of-war and the women employed to work in German factories. Any civilians remaining in the region were fed from central food depots so that the partisan forces could not be nourished. Goering's laconic explanation for the fact that such moves would do economic harm to the region was: "It is unnecessary to pay any attention to the point of agricultural production being paralysed, for this has already been halted in the bandit areas." Among more moderate voices was that of von der Bach Zelewski who, in his role as director of anti-partisan operations, wrote that the ruthless destruction of the bandits should not entail the extermination of all human life in infested areas. The concentration of a work force was, according to him, vitally important for German industry and he even offered opportunities for former partisans to work in Germany, thus releasing a German worker for active service with the forces.
   Many of the senior military commanders were also opposed to the total seizure of all food, livestock and essential products from the farmers and they reacted vigorously against offenders through courts martial. German soldiers who had carried out acts of revenge as a result of which Russian civilians had been killed, were tried and sentenced to death. The ideas of such senior commanders were set out in local orders and the GOC of one rear area wrote: "It is important to realise that we need the Russians more than ever to help in the tasks of reconstruction as well as to collaborate with us against the bandits. It is not the Russian people who are our enemy but Bolshevism ... livestock must be handed back ... it is not the duty of our soldiers to plunder the country ... our objective must be to win the trust of the population ..."
   It was one thing to view these considerations objectively in a rear area but it was something else when they were considered from the viewpoint of a man engaged in bitter fighting against the partisans.

Under the frightening conditions of the hidden warfare, the uncertainty of who the enemy was, the lack of sleep, the strain and the fear, it is understandable, if not forgivable, that harsh and sometimes unjust measures were used against the civilians. One operation which had severe repercussions in German military circles was 'Kottbus', an action carried out during the period from the middle of May to 21 June 1943. The intention was to seal off the guerrilla-infested area between Borissow and Lepe and to destroy the so-called Partisan Republic which had been set up there. More than 16,000 German soldiers and Russian civilians were involved in this cordon, search and destroy operation.

The offensive opened badly and closed disastrously. Resistance had been expected, indeed fanatical resistance had been anticipated, but the bitterness of the battle fought against partisans, indistinguishable from the civilians among whom they concealed themselves, led to a chain of atrocities which degenerated into mass executions. The insurgents were particularly active in the laying of mines along supply routes and one of the unlawful measures taken by the German forces to clear those was to drive groups of civilians along and across a suspected area. The numbers of those killed as a result of the explosions were between two and three thousand. After this repressive action a report written by Kube, General Commissar for White Russia, commented that enemy casualties were given as 13,000 and yet only 950 rifles had been taken as booty. His conclusion was that ninety per cent of the enemy dead had been unarmed.

Viewing the development of the Russian partisan movement from its beginning with isolated and uncoordinated bands into a national organisation, it may be claimed that initially this growth had less to do with Party organisation or direction than with the reaction of the Russian population to the repressive acts of the German authorities, such as that described above. When this civilian movement began to swing away from supporting the Germans towards helping the Soviets the Communist Party exploited and led this disaffection so skilfully that by the end of 1942 the guerrillas controlled wide regions and there were 'no-go' areas for the German forces, some of which extended up to 150 kilometres in length and within which partisan bases had been established. An example of how secure the guerrillas considered themselves to be from German attack was that when an operation was mounted by the 6th Infantry Division in the area of Briansk during the summer of 1943, a partisan base was captured which contained more than 300 living quarters, over 200 field fortifications and a hundred pill-boxes.

In areas which the partisan forces held in strength they laid out air strips to land by night the transport machines from Soviet territory bringing in arms, food, medical supplies and advisers. One great morale factor was that badly wounded partisans were no longer given the *coup de grâce* to prevent them falling alive into German hands but were removed by air from the 'little country' and evacuated into Russia proper.

Luftwaffe pilots all carried maps on which were marked in red circles the partisan-held areas. By the middle of 1943 the number and area of those circled regions behind the German lines had increased and many were marked with numbers. These indicated the minimum height at which it was safe to overfly those sectors for some partisan groups had been issued with anti-aircraft guns. It was a long way removed from the early days of the war when Luftwaffe pilots had been given religious pictures or packets of salt to pay the peasants to guide them to safety.

It was stated in the opening paragraph of this section that guerrilla war had no significant effect upon German military operations. This may be true but of more significance was the psychological effect upon every German soldier who fought in Russia: the knowledge that the enemy was everywhere. The German telephone system was tapped and there were many instances reported of officers demanding to speak, for example, with von Kluge who were answered by a voice which said in bad German "Kluge? Kluge kaputt. Germans kaputt. Soon you kaputt." The shock effect of such an interruption can best be imagined. Militarily it may not have won a battle but the knowledge that somewhere nearby was a Russian listening to all conversations was unnerving. The derailment of trains by blowing up the track – one section suffered more than 1,200 explosions – did not seriously affect the flow of supplies to the front but those acts of sabotage served to remind the Germans that although they may have controlled the railway during the day, the night belonged to the partisans.

To combat these acts of sabotage against the railway lines the Germans cleared the ground on either side of the permanent way up to a distance of about 400 metres, cutting down all trees and removing undergrowth. In place of the lonely sentry boxes of 1941 a system of block houses was set up: small forts set on tall towers from whose eminence German sentries could monitor the movement along the railway lines. Sand cars were fitted ahead of the locomotives and were effective until Russian explosive experts laid remote-controlled mines to detonate under the engines. Another means of beating the partisan groups was to send convoys of trains along a sector with one train in sight of another and all heavily escorted by armed troops. German infantry patrols went out by day sweeping the ground on either side of the tracks but returned at night to leave the world to the guerrilla who laid mines, blew up more sections of the track or, if the partisan forces were strong enough, attacked the individual blockhouses.

An interesting fact which emerges from a study of documents dealing with insurgent forces and their opponents is the presence of such partisan groups, not merely in German-occupied Russia but also on Soviet territory. Some of these anti-Soviet groups were made up of men whose regions had been overrun by the Germans and then recaptured by the Red Army. These native bands did not disarm when the Soviet authorities came back but illegally retained their weapons and continued to fight for the freedom of their homelands. A certain number of those anti-Soviet freedom groups were the result of agents sent in by the German 'Brandenburg' regiment, an Abwehr intelligence organisation, to foment revolt but most were local expressions of disaffection. An even stranger fact is that there were more than a hundred anti-Soviet partisan groups in regions which had never been occupied by the Germans.

Despite its use of partisan soldiers and its direction of their operations the central administration in the Soviet Union was never at ease with popular movements, except where these were under its complete and total control at all times. That is to say, where the Party directed every movement from Moscow until such time as the Red Army occcupied the region. The partisans were then immediately disarmed and their men dispersed so that neither their weapons nor their knowledge could be used against the central government. In the Red Army's conquest of former Soviet territory there had been several occasions when the NKVD had had to be brought in to crush separatist movements or local governments set up by the partisans. The actions of the NKVD were as brutal as any operation carried out by the SS in attempting to destroy these centres of resistance; yet for many years after the end of the war reports were still received of guerrilla groups in the wilder regions of Soviet Russia still active in the fight against the Communist government.

The lot of the partisans in Russia during the Second World War was not a happy one. Hated by the villagers from whom they extorted supplies, feared by those who only wanted to carry on living even if under a German occupation, pursued by German forces, invariably badly fed and living in primitive conditions the guerrillas fought on until liberation came. And when it did it brought back with it the secret police, interrogation for some, imprisonment for others and at best a medal. The Party was accorded the honour of having organised and directed the guerrillas; for the partisans themselves the honour lay, so the Party told them, in having fought.

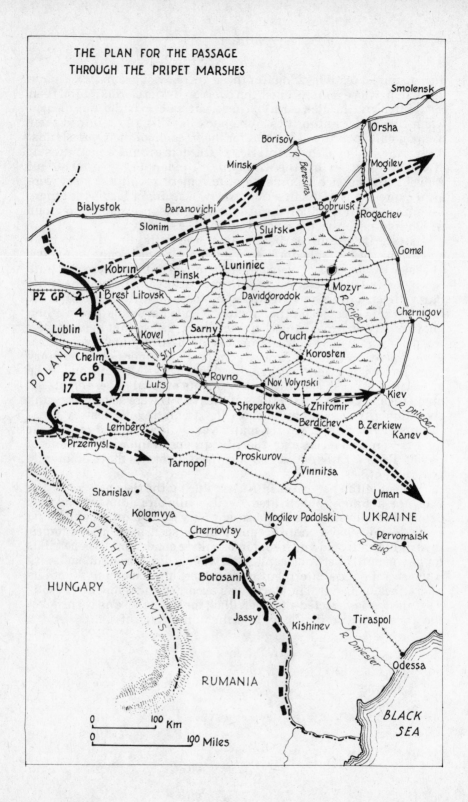

THE PLAN FOR THE PASSAGE
THROUGH THE PRIPET MARSHES

10

The influence of terrain

*"East of the Bug-San line ... terrain conditions
and the shortage of roads restrict movement..."*

General von Greiffenburg
CHIEF OF STAFF TO 12TH ARMY

Terrain has influenced the conduct of military operations throughout the history of warfare. Commanders of the attacking side have always attempted to overcome natural obstacles while the defenders have always sought to exploit these barriers to their best advantage. In bygone days armies, being smaller in number, could generally select the ground on which they would fight, the one side endeavouring to rest its flanks upon features impassable to the attacker, while he sought by manoeuvre to detach the defence from its anchors located in some natural obstacle.

The employment of mass armies in both world wars destroyed the art of manoeuvre. The corps and divisions of those armies moved as a single line in the attempt by the whole force to break the enemy's front and, therefore, some part of the attacking army was compelled to cross that bad terrain which armies of the past would have bypassed.

In the campaign fought in western Russia terrain was an important factor. Russia is a land within whose vast and sprawling territory is to be found every type of terrain. Thus it contains the icy, snowy regions of the polar circle; hot, dry, sandy deserts; fertile steppes as well as swamps, extensive forests, seemingly unending expanses of flat plain and high mountain ranges. This section of the book is concerned not with the terrain in the vast reaches of the Union but only with those regions which were touched by the fury of the Second World War.

It can be seen from the map that the vast area in which the bulk of the fighting took place is well protected by nature to halt an aggressor coming from the west. The main rivers in the combat zone flow on a generally north–south line and each, therefore, constitutes a barrier against an east–west assault. The rivers become wider and deeper the further east one penetrates and most of these are fed by numerous tributaries, each of which is itself a water barrier. The rivers were generally unembankmented and were prone to flooding in spring and autumn.

Great regions of the western and northern provinces of European Russia are heavily forested, while others, through a combination of poor soil, river flooding and heavy precipitations of rain and snow, are extensive marshes. A whole belt of forested swamp protected

Moscow and Leningrad and this defensive belt extended from the White Sea southwards via Leningrad and Vitebsk to a line running through Kolin, Luszk and Kiev. It thus impinged upon the territory of southern Bessarabia, the western Ukraine, southern Volhynia, Galicia, Byelo-Russia, Lithuania and Latvia.

A stretch of that swamp which was located west of the Dnieper river extended for a distance of 600 kilometres and had a width of over 200 kilometres. This was the Pripet, or more correctly the Rokitno marsh. By a bitter twist the Pripet river which traverses the swamp is the only major watercourse in western Russia which flows in a generally east–west direction. The whole area was poor in west–east communications and depended upon a small number of roads, radiating from Warsaw or East Prussia and going through narrow corridors of land to the principal cities of the Soviet Union. South of the great marsh lay eastern Galicia. This was a less heavily forested region but had even fewer roads and, farther south still, lay the open steppe country of the Ukraine.

If terrain was an important factor in the campaign in western Russia then of crucial importance to the success of the whole strategy of the war was the problem of the Pripet Marsh. Planning for the new war was very strongly influenced by the problem which it set for it would not only form a natural obstacle to the eastward movement of the German army, but would divide Army Group Centre from Army Group South for the whole of the first stage of the operation. Not until the Army Groups had advanced more than 600 kilometres into the Soviet Union could they unite and form a single force – on the eastern side of the great marsh.

Accepting that the principal intention of the first offensives was the destruction of the Red Army in a rapid succession of hammer blows, west of the Dnieper river, then some solution must be found which would neutralise the problem of the Pripet Marsh. One question was whether it would be safe for the German Army to bypass the whole area, leaving it to be cleared at leisure after the main body had gone on to fight the decisive battles.

It was accepted at the outset that the marsh would divide the battle line and thus there would have to be fought two uncoordinated battles, one to the north of and the other to the south of the marsh. The Army Group boundary ran along the Pripet river and thus gave to the Army Group South the greater area to clear. Despite this, OKW insisted that the maximum effort to defeat the Red Army would be made to the north of the swamp for the intention was to gain the land bridge from Smolensk, an area which gave access across the tributaries of four of the major river barriers. Jumping-off points would then have been gained from which the second stage of the campaign could begin. High Command was prepared to take a calculated risk in starting the second stage without having cleared the marsh, for it was accepted that weak and bypassed Soviet forces would threaten the supply routes. But, in the interests of the overall plan, these attacks would have to be accepted. The planners appreciated that progress through the swamp would be slower for those corps fighting in that region than for the formations battling towards the jump-off areas but the inner corps would have to keep the advance flowing, for a loss of impetus would mean the loss of the military initiative.

The opening offensives of the new war demonstrated how faulty had been the German staff appreciations of Soviet reactions. Contrary to Hitler's belief, the Pripet Marsh presented an acute problem and the terrain factor, allied to the fanatical defence put up by the 5th Red Army, soon showed that the calculated risk which OKW had taken was not likely to succeed. The enemy in the marshes would have to be dealt with if the assault was to continue. Russian resistance and their counter-attacks caused the German 6th Army to be diverted from its main line of advance towards the Dnieper and this deflection opened a gap between that Army's infantry divisions and the mechanised units of the 1st Panzer Group. Attempts by troops of each force to maintain contact had the effect of slowing the rate of advance of the corps forming the left wing of Army Group South to an average of 11 kilometres per day. Halder's diary entry for 25 June, "Panzer Group 1 and 6th Army are advancing slowly and are suffering considerable losses", shows how, as early as the first week of the campaign, the plan had been confounded. The Pripet Marsh had become a running ulcer in the German side. It was for the early and scattered partisan bands a refuge; a barrier to German anti-insurgent operations in summer but a bridge which the Russians could cross in winter. It was later to become the impregnable guerrilla citadel from whose security the partisan bands could strike and disrupt almost at will.

The Führer Directive No. 33, issued on 19 July hinted that the original intention of 'Operation Barbarossa' had failed; the Red Army had not been defeated west of the Dnieper. Part of this directive stated: "The object of the immediate operation is to prevent the enemy from withdrawing important forces beyond the Dnieper and to destroy these". The words betrayed the failure of the plan and even though it seemed as if the first phase of 'Barbarossa' might have been thought to be completed when some weeks later German armies were menacing Leningrad, Moscow and Kiev, it was all illusion. The problem of the Pripet Marsh remained unsolved and even if great encirclement battles had been fought and Moscow was only 300 kilometres distant the large concentration of Soviet troops in the southern part of the marsh was a problem which remained unsolved and unsolvable. The terrain factor and the effort which had had to be put in during those first weeks had absorbed much of the impetus of 'Operation Barbarossa' and had destroyed the German hope of total victory before the onset of winter.

Another abnormal terrain factor met with in western Russia, and one which was to a large extent ignored in the German army's

invasion manual, were the vast areas of forest. These were not the
tamed and regulated woods and thickets of western Europe but great
expanses of trees set in a tangled undergrowth so dense as to give
them the name of a European jungle. Some tracts of those forests
were at that time untrodden by human foot. German troops who
fought in the first months across the regions covered by these forests
mention that these were seldom penetrated very deeply by their
patrols. It was not merely that the impetus of the assault left no time
for the infantry to comb the woods as carefully as they should have.
Rather it was the sheer impossibility of forcing a way through the
undergrowth and the trees that became closer the deeper one went.

> We do not usually go very far into the forests. You can have no idea
> of what they are like. The trees are mostly deciduous and centuries of
> fallen leaves lie rotting on the forest floor. The stink is indescribable,
> but out of this rich soil spring weeds and bushes to form a barrier
> through which nothing but the smallest woodland creature can go. If
> we do have to move farther into the wood then we look for the spoor of
> larger beasts and follow these trails, but often they pass into low
> tunnels made in the bushes and are not to be negotiated by a soldier in
> battle kit.
> The flies and mosquitoes are a plague and I wonder what these
> blood-sucking pests lived on before we came along. We wear nets over
> our helmets but the beasts work their way up the sleeves and inside the
> collar. To halt is to be covered in a mass of these terrible biting insects
> and the inevitable flies. We are in a swamp but there is little water fit to
> drink. It is all brackish. Even water taken from wells tastes
> unpleasant and we have to boil every drop that we drink.

Fighting in such conditions it is not surprising to learn that the
German Army never completely cleared the woods and that they,
therefore, also failed to destroy the partisans who, although not at
home in the terrible jungle-like conditions, were nevertheless aware
of them and were familiar with them. But even they did not penetrate
deeper than was absolutely necessary. When German patrols
accompanied by armour did make a sweep Russian wood-fighting
tactics were to withdraw deeper into the safety of the trees until the
panzers had passed and then to re-emerge to engage the follow-up
infantry. Inevitably, there was a high casualty rate among the
grenadiers and combats in woods and forests were operations feared
by most German soldiers.

There were only minor difficulties encountered in the terrain of
southern Russia with its open steppes. It was good tank country and
although there were few roads the ground was usually firm enough
in dry weather for it to be used by wheeled or tracked vehicles. One
unusual feature were the *balka*, high and steep-sided, dried-up
watercourses which could obstruct the advance of a tank column
until a bridge had been built or a diversion found. The steppe was
another region notorious for its lack of drinking water and many
letters refer to the melons with which the advancing soldiers tried to
slake their thirst.

It was not until the autumn of 1942 that the German Army was required to fight in mountainous country and an account of a small, morale-raising operation by Gebirgsjäger, which conquered Mount Elbrus, the highest peak of the Caucasus range, completes this section on terrain factors.

As an example of a flamboyant and futile gesture it would be hard to find one in the whole of the war that equalled the raising of the German war flag on that mountain peak. Militarily insignificant though this gesture may have been it is recounted here as an example of how German troops overcame this particular difficulty; how they conquered a mountain range which separates European from Asian Russia.

The background to the operation is interesting. The German Army had as a specialist group of infantry no fewer than six divisions of mountain troops or Gebirgsjäger. These highly trained and specialised troops had had no opportunity to use their skills while fighting on the flat and empty plains, but then in the summer offensive of 1942 their opportunity came.

For that operation the former Army Group South had been divided into two groups of armies, one of which was sent to fight its way to the Volga river and the area of Stalingrad. The second group, Army Group B, was directed southwards to gain the Soviet oilfields of Baku, but barring access to the distant objective lay the Caucasian mountains. An Alpine corps, the 49th, with 1st and 4th Divisions under command was ordered on 28 July to break off the battle in which it was engaged and to proceed with best speed to penetrate the mountain barrier and to reach the Tuapse–Suchum road with their open flank protected by a German Jäger corps and a corps of Italian Alpini. The orders to the German Alpine corps commander were direct and brutal. It was his task to gain the mountain passes before the onset of winter, and the first snows had usually descended to the 4,000-metre line by the end of September. This would have been a difficult task under any circumstances, but 49th Corps was in action more than 300 kilometres from its future start line in the mountains and to reach that point it would have to cross the lines of communication of other corps of Army Group B. Once in position there would be no time for a slow, methodical advance. A single all-out punch must gain the victory before the onset of winter.

By 13 August the divisions had fought their way from the start line to the foothills of the Caucasus region and were preparing to assault the main range. A week later each division had seized a pass and both were preparing to exploit the success. The narrow defiles along which their supplies and reinforcements came were a thin lifeline and it is not surprising that it was against this that the furious assaults of the Red Army defenders came in day after day. The Soviet defenders were not trained Alpinists; Russia had not at that time taken seriously the problem of mountain warfare, but the

Russians were men in superior numbers holding a naturally strong defensive position against the assaults of a numerically inferior foe.

The virile thrusts by these German mountain troops brought the advance slowly forward across the peaks. Using rock climbing techniques and advancing up almost vertical faces their patrols drove in the Soviet outposts and forced the Red troops back almost to the exit passes from the mountains. Each advance was met with a counter-attack and these furious Russian assaults came in day after day against the handful of Gebirgsjäger in the advance guard. Each was repulsed as the slow drive was maintained, but then there was a crisis. Hitler ordered the Italian Alpini corps to Stalingrad. With the loss of such a major group of trained mountain troops the difficult task became an impossibility and 49th Corps was withdrawn to strong defensive positions which it was intended it should hold until spring, by which time OKW calculated the fighting for the city on the Volga would have ended in a German victory.

This was not to be, for the military situation at Stalingrad turned in favour of the Soviets and after only a short occupation of the gateway to the Baku oilfields the Army Group withdrew.

It was in the first days of 'Operation Edelweiss', the drive for the mountain passes, that the 49th Corps commander, Conrad, conceived the idea of repeating that exploit which had crowned the campaign in Greece. But this time the German war flag would not be raised on the summit of Olympus but on the highest peak of the Caucasus. For the assault a detachment would be made up of men from both divisions and, on 8 August, this special High Alpine Group was raised by 1st Division. The men from 4th Division joined the group on 14 August and to each man of the selected group the divisional commander gave an eagle's feather as a mark of special distinction.

On the evening of 17 August the Groth assault group, named after its commander, a captain from 1st Division, began the ascent. By last light the leading roped section had reached the 3,500 metre high Chassen pass and as night came on the temperature fell. The men shivered all night long despite their special alpine equipment, sleeping only fitfully. During the night the rest of the High Alpine Company closed up and passed through them to reach the Chotyo pass where they, too, bivouacked.

On the following morning the next bound was undertaken. The objective for that day was a small hotel which sat on a narrow spit of land between two glacial masses. Close and detailed searching through binoculars showed that the hotel was occupied and a bold plan for its capture was worked out. One group was ordered to climb past the hotel on the left flank and to lie up in a position ready to open fire while the Group Commander intended to walk boldly up to the hotel and demand that it be surrendered. As soon as the covering group was in position Captain Groth's party moved off with him alone and some distance ahead of the main body. He walked past the astonished sentry and demanded that the eleven men standing in the hotel foyer should surrender to him. He convinced them that the hotel was surrounded and with their acceptance of his ultimatum the hotel, a warm and secure base for the forthcoming climb, was in German hands.

In the misty morning of 19 August the hundred-man strong group climbed through the thin air where every breath was a physical pain. A sudden snow storm made the climb so hazardous that the groups were forced to hole up in the hotel until in the dark of another dawn it was safe for two groups to set out. They had been climbing for more than three hours when a new blizzard struck them but, undeterred, the two groups pressed on. A short rest was made in a lonely mountain hut and then the groups set out, facing the blizzard, a tearing wind which drove ice particles into their faces and poor visibility, which was reduced to less than ten metres. The next two hours were a path of pain and misery as the climbers covered less than 120 metres in their negotiation of a vertical wall of ice, but at last with all the groups combining their strength three assault groups were passed onto the summit.

At 11.00hrs the groups had reached the pinnacle and suddenly as the layers of cloud were torn apart by the icy wind the Gebirgsjäger could see no higher peak in their vicinity. They had conquered the mountain. A sergeant took from his pack the war flag and jammed its staff into a crack in the rock. High on the summit of Mount Elbrus the red, white and black flag of the Third Reich opened up in the icy wind. Then the divisional insignia of both 1st and 4th Alpine divisions were hammered into the rock. One of the highest mountains in the world had been climbed and even though a corps war reporter found that they had not in fact reached the true summit but a peak 67 metres below the real peak, the climb still represented a fine alpinist achievement and was a boost to the morale of the men of the German Alpine divisions.

11

The influence of climate

"The effect of climate in Russia is to make things impassable in the mud of spring and autumn, unbearable in the heat of summer and impossible in the depths of winter. Climate in Russia is a series of natural disasters."

General von Greiffenburg
CHIEF OF STAFF TO 12TH ARMY

"How did we cope with the abnormal climatic conditions experienced during the winter of 1941–42?", asked my visitor. He had, at that time, been a Lieutenant Colonel of the Waffen SS and had lived through three winters of war. "Quite simply, we acclimatised quickly. Those who did not, died."

This answer struck me as so easy, so much the reply of a commander of élite troops recalling, with advantages, the deeds of former days, that I was tempted to reject it. However, from discussions with other survivors of that first winter it seems that the Lieutenant Colonel's reply had been tragically true. Life on the Eastern Front during those months was existence at a basic level, a reversion to a primitive life style and those who could not adapt or hold out went under. Nor was this surprising for, with the exception of front-line comradeship to afford a mutual support, each man fought the cold alone, pitting his moral courage, determination and will to live against the bitterest winter in a century. There had been little preparation made at the highest levels of command to outfit the men in the trenches with the clothing, weapons and food which would enable them to withstand the extreme temperatures. From talks with those who had fought and who had survived a pattern of experience emerged, common to all, and I decided that rather than quote their stories individually they could be collated and related as a single narrative account to give an all-round picture of active service life on the Eastern Front and the effects of Russian climate upon it.

To many field and general officers it had been obvious as early as the autumn of 1941 that OKH was out of touch with the realities of life as it was lived in the battle area. High Command had not anticipated the problems of mud resulting from the drenching rains nor had they plans to combat it and it was clear that the vehicles, equipment and clothing with which the German Army was supplied were defective and inferior to those in service with the Red Army.

The defects, so apparent in autumn, grew more serious as the colder weather developed. Snow fell as early as the first week of October and the severe night frosts made it almost impossible for men who were not clad in warm, protective clothing to remain out in the open. No strong line of field fortifications had been constructed into which the Army might retire during the coming winter, for the intention at OKW was not to halt the advance but to maintain it. The demand was, as always, to attack, particularly to those divisions and corps which were investing Leningrad or pushing onwards toward Moscow.

By the time of the first snows most front-line units had been in action, without relief, since the opening of 'Operation Barbarossa'. The thinness of the German battle line in numbers and the depth of its operational zone made it almost impossible to withdraw whole divisions from the line for resting and refitting. To the physical strain was also added the mental strain of combat without pause and the men were easy victims to respiratory diseases and frost-bite. The type of minor wounds which in summer would have been treated at a regimental field hospital no longer healed quickly and required protracted treatment in base hospitals. Under the double strain of sickness and battle casualties front-line formations were reduced to the level where companies had the strength of a single strong platoon. Nor were sufficient reinforcements being sent forward to replace losses and those which were received were usually recruits without previous front-line experience or else soldiers of the regiments returning from convalescence.

The casualties in dead, wounded and sick widened the gap between the numbers struck off strength and those coming onto strength and this shortage of infantry meant inevitably that fewer and fewer men were available to hold the line.

Sentry duty came round more frequently as a section of perhaps ten men was required to hold a trench line formerly covered by fifteen. Life in the line was an unending grind of guards and patrols. Headquarters staffs demanded information on an almost daily basis and patrols went out to take a prisoner, to identify the Soviet unit opposite them or, sometimes, to subdue the aggressive intentions of the Russian enemy. For the infantry to be able to sleep uninterruptedly for several hours together was a rare luxury; but to be able to sleep until one was rested completely was to yearn for a nirvana denied to the men holding the line. For them there was little rest. Released for a short time from sentry duty or upon returning from patrol, numb with cold they would stumble into the fug of a primitive dug-out whose air was thick with the choking smoke of the little rifle-oil lamps – Hindenburg lights – which were the only source of illumination. Hot food seldom arrived, for dixies of stew sent piping hot from the field kitchens would arrive in the trenches frozen solid after a portered journey of only a kilometre or two. At the beginning of winter most men had little stoves, fuelled with solid

methylated spirit, on which water was heated but the portering
battalions had more important materials to bring forward and fuel
tablets for this simple form of cooking had a low priority.

In the musty, raw earth dug-out the bodies of the newly relieved
sentries would begin to warm a little and then there would be the
slight stirrings and the first irritations as the lice, with which they
were infested, woke from their own torpor and began to feast. It was
out of the question to undress in the cold dug-out or to pick off and kill
the vermin. Nor could there be a change of underclothes for now
every soldier was wearing as much of his clothing, particularly
shirts, pants and vests, as could comfortably fit inside his uniform.
To keep warm it was necessary to wear every piece of clothing, and to
supplement the layers of uniform the dead of both sides were
stripped of overcoats, fur hats and boots, particularly Russian felt
boots, which afforded the best protection in snowy conditions.
German Army standard issue jack-boots were leather and retained
the damp. Constant exposure to the wet caused them to fall apart.
Just as there were no changes of underclothes so there were no socks
and frost-bite began for many men when their socks wore out
completely and left between the chilling snow and the bare feet the
cold leather of jack-boots.

As the winter deepened and as new, lower extremes of
temperature were suffered sentries had to be changed hourly. There
were few men who could hold out even that much and when the time
of the bitterest weather came this period in the open was reduced to
half an hour or even to fifteen minutes. Unprotected, the sentries
stood with the upper part of the body exposed to the full fury of the
elements. The wind was nearly always easterly. When blizzards
came, as they did with irritating frequency, the sentinels would
stand facing into a driving wind which had gathered its bitter cold
from the passage across thousands of kilometres of frozen Siberia,
howling across the treeless steppes and blowing before it a powder
snow that hit the unprotected parts of the body with a bitter touch,
seeming to pierce the face with a thousand frozen needles. The force
of the wind was such that snow did not fall vertically but was
projected, almost horizontally, in vast obliterating white blankets.
The German look-outs wrapped with mufflers, or the fortunate ones
with a captured lamb-skin cap to cover the head and ears, stared out
into the dense white clouds. Goggles to shield the eyes were useless.
All too quickly snow on the eye-pieces froze into a mass of solid ice
and an attempt to remove the shields too quickly from the face tore
skin and flesh from cheek bones and from the forehead, for the low
degrees of frost had the power to weld the goggles to the face in a
matter of minutes.

Suddenly – and it was always sudden figures who would loom out
of the snow – Siberian ski troops appeared, camouflaged in white
and inured to sub-zero temperatures. They would sweep across the
trench line to spray sentries with bullets from machine pistols or to

hurl grenades before vanishing into the concealing snow clouds, usually before fire could be returned. Or there might be borne on the wind the howling battle cry of the Russian infantry, to meet whose attack the grenadiers, survivors of months of battle, would stream out of the crumbling dug-outs to stand ready. With hands cupped over the rifle breeches to keep these from freezing they would man the firing step until they saw, like phantoms, wraiths, dimly as the whirling snow storms first exposed and then hid them again, the lines of Soviet infantry coming towards them. Wading slowly through the snow, these advanced line after line after line. Then would be fought battles of an almost primaeval fury. These frantic struggles for a handful of weapon pits would not be proclaimed in OKW communiqués which nightly were heralded in heroic fanfares sounded in far-off Berlin. They would be recalled, however, with horror decades later by the men who had fought them. The battles were to hold the line; the line of shallow trenches and primitive shelters which they were occupying. Cold, bare and miserable though these dug-outs were they represented a sort of warmth, a protection from the wind, and in a sense were 'home'. To be driven from them would mean that the grenadiers would have to retreat, to God knows where, and then start again to scrape out other shelters. If the present living conditions were frightful, future prospects, if they were to be forced back, were unspeakable. To defend their little kingdom each man aimed and fought with a lunatic desperation, with the knowledge always present in his mind that to be wounded and left behind in a retreat was certain death. This was warfare at its most primitive: kill or be killed – survive or die.

No eyes sighted along rifles more carefully than did those of the grenadiers of the Eastern Front in those winter months. Every man prayed that his rifle or machine gun would function. They had all known cases where intense cold had made metal as brittle as glass and the slender firing pins had snapped, rendering the weapons useless. There had been occasions when the bolt actions of machine guns had seized up in temperatures which reached to thirty and forty degrees below freezing. It was a cold which numbed and deadened from the feet up until the whole body was one aching mass of frozen misery. Yet, in the fury of battling against a Russian attack or when they themselves were launched into the assault, the pains of cold would vanish as more urgent priorities filled the mind.

Soon the grenadiers in their trenches could see the first Russian troops clearly and in their minds' eyes saw the steamy breath ejected from panting and open mouths as, gasping with exertion, the Red Army infantry struggled slowly forward through the deep snow. Then the German machine guns alone opened up. Mortars were as useless as artillery in such extremes of temperature, for even if their fuses detonated the effect of the explosion was nullified in deep snow. From left to right the machine guns traversed the Russian line. Belt after belt of ammunition jerked through the breeches. A sudden jam, soon put right, when over-eager hands tried to force the bullets faster into the feed slit. From the wide spread out rifle pits came rapid and sustained fire into the mass of men moving towards the German line. Red attackers collapsed in the snow, staggered as the bullets hit them. Great gaps appeared in the extended lines where a long, continuous burst of machine gun fire had found its mark and soon the huddled bodies marked the progress, the awful slow progress of the Russian assault.

Hand-grenades burst with small clouds of black smoke among the ranks of the Soviet soldiers now almost into the German trenches. Perhaps the first wave of Red troops would be driven back but before the grenadiers could pause to take breath a second line would be upon them. This was the testing time. Men sobbed with strain, cursed out loud, screamed in frustration and fury and in mortal fear for their very lives. Steadily and inexorably an anger grew within them. Against the snow which cut visibility, against the cold which numbed the brain, against the weapons which did not fire fast enough and against the stubborn, stupid enemy who would not halt his futile attacks. Then as the anger mounted and desperation grew, a lust was born, a lust to destroy the advancing foe. Reeling senses dictated that if one could get rid of them, of enough of them, the war would stop and one could sleep and sleep in a place where it was warm.

Inflamed by this lust the grenadiers would climb out of the trenches and move forward to close with the attackers. Chests rose and fell with the strain, eyes stared with fear and hatred, oaths screamed aloud were torn away by that damnable east wind. Then it was no longer the time for the impersonal rifle or machine pistol but for close combat. Man against man. The knife, the bayonet or the entrenching tool with its sharpened edge that would cut, or pierce or cleave the enemy. Hacking and chopping, gouging, stabbing and killing until suddenly it was all over and the enemy had gone. If that really was the result, then would come a feeling of anti-climax, of being drained completely. Exhaustion would sweep in, covering the body with great waves of tiredness and of lethargy. This was the hour when the body trembled uncontrollably but not with cold. Of men who sat with their heads buried in their cupped hands and who would suddenly become conscious that these were bleeding. Bayonet blades had torn the skin. Knives had slipped through the fingers or else ungloved trigger fingers had frozen to the metal. Pieces of skin and flesh would be left on the trigger when the fingers stopped firing and blood, dark red in that cold, would run slowly at first and then more slowly as it began to freeze only inches from the wound. Quickly a handkerchief would be wrapped round the finger to staunch the bleeding and to protect it from the cold; for cold was a killer. It either weakened a badly wounded man, causing him to slide into sleep, then coma and death, or else it mortified to the extent that a simple wound would require amputation if the life was to be saved.

As the fear died away the consciousness of the cold flooded back and then it was a return to the abnormal normality of the everlasting sentry-go and the unending patrols that made up front-line life.

But the initiative was not always with the Red Army. The German offensive continued, but hopelessly now for the fighting troops who bore the suffering. More confident of victory was the Supreme Command and one further indication of how isolated it was from reality was the objective set by it to follow the fall of Moscow. Even as the frantic assaults of the German Army to reach the Russian capital were freezing into immobility on the open steppes, the new target was given: a town four hundred kilometres east of the city. Supreme Command seemed not to know that the flower of the German Army was dead. The planners seemed to think that the pins on the map corresponded to divisions at full strength and alloted to them, accordingly, divisional tasks to accomplish. The true situation can be seen in the few examples given here. One panzer division leading the advance towards Moscow had a battle strength of just five tanks and in most infantry divisions the company strengths had been reduced to those of weak platoons. The commander of one SS division pleaded, with eyes filled with tears, for socks to issue to his men. They were still keen to fight but needed to protect and to cover their feet. Their own socks had worn out, the number of frostbite cases was increasing and there was no frostbite cream. The SS Grenadiers were freezing to death.

The official solution to the problem of frozen feet was that jack-boots were to be lined with straw or paper, but there was little of those two commodities in Russia's icy wastes. Instructions, tips and practical hints were all that could be given to the men in the frozen boots and uniforms struggling through the snowstorms. Sustained by pride in their army and by a fierce moral discipline the German soldiers pressed home their attacks but the army which had once gone forward in a flood was reduced to a grey-green rivulet crawling towards its goal – Moscow. In day-long blizzards the freezing foot soldiers struggled forward. Their assaults were not like those of the Red Army – massed thousands of infantry – but were handfuls of men making despairing efforts to achieve impossible tasks.

They reached the outskirts of Moscow: the tram terminus of a line which ran near the Kremlin. Their goal was only a handful of kilometres distant. One more push and the objective of Army Group Centre would have been attained. But this was not to be. Across the Red Square were marching fresh regiments of Siberian riflemen, swinging past the saluting bases and tramping westwards out of the city, prepared to drive back the Fascist invaders. Behind the thickening line of riflemen Red guns and tanks were massing. Holding the line were the battalions of workmen, hastily conscripted, scantily armed and put into battle. Their defence had been of short duration but it had been sufficient to slow down the grenadiers until the counter-stroke could be launched. The domes of

Moscow shining in the brief bursts of sunshine in those short December days were all that most German troops were ever to see of their Army Group objective. On 5 December there crashed down upon them a hail of fire behind whose destructive curtain advanced the infantry masses of the Red Army.

For their counter-offensive STAVKA had taken the artillery principles of General Voronov and had enlarged them. He had proposed that divisions of artillery be formed and in pursuit of this objective had actually taken from combat divisions, fighting for their very existence, batteries and even whole regiments of field guns. In the short term the Soviet infantry had paid dearly but the Red Army had a mighty hammer which it now wielded to smash open the German front. For the opening barrage the Soviet artillery was massed not in divisions but in corps and began a bombardment which could only be adequately described as earth shattering. Thousands of guns of every calibre, marshalled under STAVKA direction and well supplied with ammunition, fired simultaneously. It was claimed that for this single bombardment on the central front more guns were brought together than had been assembled in the armies of all the major Powers throughout the First World War.

The storm of steel smashed down upon the grenadiers, and behind it moving into the assault were one and a half million Red infantrymen whose attacks were spearheaded by the Siberians, whole battalions of whom were armed with machine pistols. Opposing this giant wave were the freezing and lousy survivors, six hundred thousand of them, who had once been in the divisions of Army Group Centre forming the cutting edge of the German sword. In guns the Soviet superiority was immeasurable, in armour the imbalance was in places more than twenty to one, and in infantry it was more than three to one. The aim of the Russian Command was not merely to save the capital but to destroy completely Army Group Centre.

Local penetrations of the German line became breaches and these were then expanded as division was separated from division and corps was split from its neighbouring corps. The adjustment of the battle line then became a tactical withdrawal and soon much of the army which had marched eastwards with such high hopes was struggling westwards in the throes of a bitter retreat. In vain were orders given to hold fast; the retreat continued and began to suck into its movement other corps, other armies who moved back westwards to conform with the general manoeuvre. It did not, however, deteriorate into a rout. Indeed in some sectors commanders mastered the situation quickly and moved back by bounds from one sketchy defence position to another. Each of these would be a so-called hedgehog, centred around a village, a cluster of houses, even an individual house: some place in which the men could find a little rest or warmth, some fixed point in which they could hold, turn at bay and resist the assaults of the onstorming Red Army.

During the middle weeks of December there was a partial thaw, a not unusual phenomenon of winter in Russia. The ground unfroze, there was mud again, soaked boots and saturated uniforms before the cold returned to hold the country once again in an iron grip. The few days of mud, immediately preceding Christmas, had been enough to bog down the Russians and strong hedgehogs were established within which the German troops sought to obey Hitler's direct order to stand fast. Behind these hedgehog positions reserves were being assembled for a counter-attack which would not only seal the gaps in the line but would sweep back the advancing Russians.

Thus it was that another feature of military tactics was developed, for the first time, on the Eastern Front – deliberate encirclement. In this troops stayed put and held out, allowing Cossack cavalry, Siberian ski-troops, T 34s and the Red infantry masses to sweep past their positions but inflicting upon them during this passage damage and casualties and all the time denying to the Russians the road and rail junctions, the strategically and tactically important places they needed to nourish and to maintain their advance. In later pages of this book there are described some of the encirclement operations fought on the Russian Front.

By the end of December the line had been partially stabilised. On some sectors there was still a desperate retreat fought by men weakened by privation and exertion, frightened by the hostility of the severe weather, by the fierce assaults of the enemy and obsessed with fear of being wounded and left behind. Those were the days during which the legend was born that officers of SS units would administer the *coup de grâce* to those of their men too badly wounded to be moved, for fear that they should fall alive into the hands of the Red Army. On other sectors of the German line wise commanders had used the mild weather of autumn to prepare or to restore defensive positions against which the Red infantry flung itself in vain assault. In other areas there was little fighting; supplies and post came regularly and there was at Christmas and at New Year the opportunity to take a mental break from the primitive conditions and to remember past Christmases. The following accounts recall the situation of that first Christmas in Russia.

The dying hours of New Year's Eve along those sectors of the German front not immediately under attack were filled with unusual light and activity.

Shortly before midnight our divisional artillery opened up and this bombardment was followed by that of our regimental mortars. The Russian area, one cannot speak of a line under such conditions, was filled with the lights of explosions. Then the sentries in our trenches fired Very lights and our machine gunners fired streams of tracer into the Russian positions. It really was a very pretty sight. The night was clear and the vast expanses of snow reflected the little light there was and seemed to magnify it so that visibility was quite good. Clearly visible were the dancing points of light from shell explosions, green and red beads of tracer arching across the snow and then the Very lights; white, green, violet and red rising and falling along the line. It reminded me, as I watched from the doorway of our house, of pictures I had seen of Flanders during the First World War.

We had had a Christmas of sorts. We even had a Christmas tree. Not a big one but it was at least real and had been brought back from Germany by one of our returning convalescents. The aroma of those few German twigs in this desert was truly a breath of home. There were even a few candles to light when the Colonel came round to wish us a Merry Christmas. We stood around the tree and sang the old familiar German carols. Imagine if you can the scene. Apart from our few miserable huts there was no proper habitation for miles around. We existed in a desert of snow and ice but within this desolation we had brought our German traditions, our songs and our spirit. It was in situations like that that one realised how strong were the bonds of religion and tradition. Like all the married men I felt the loss of the family more keenly at such times, but it had been for their future that we were in Russia.

A deserter told us to expect a heavy attack on Christmas Eve but there was none; nor on Christmas Day. We, however, sent Ivan a New Year's greeting in steel and high explosive and we hoped that he enjoyed it.

The thin and broken German line allowed the Russian troops and partisans to infiltrate and to send back to the Soviet leaders intelligence on the strength and disposition of the German troops. Hidden in woods and concealed in dug-outs those agents watched for smoke rising from chimneys indicating that the houses were occupied. The grenadiers stayed indoors as much as possible, for they were aware of those sharp eyes watching them and waiting for careless movements. In some cases the German commanders forbade the lighting of fires by day so that no wisp of smoke would betray the positions. In the weeks of the deepest freezing temperatures, when it was vital to bring every man under cover at night, there was often too little room for all the men of a unit to lie down or even sit down at the same time. So they stood or lay down in shifts, pressed close to each other for warmth, the strongest men giving up the chance of a lay down in favour of weaker or lightly wounded comrades.

Life was basic. Eat the food, evacuate the food, sleep, guard, fight. The rations, although usually cold, were sufficient to keep the senses alert and the body fit to carry out the combat activities. The more basic requirement to evacuate the food was a tiresome procedure. So much so that many men were glad that they were suffering from constipation, even though this brought with it headaches and stomach cramps. Lavatories in rural houses were usually a small shed on the western side of the house so as to shield it from the prevailing east wind. Inside the shed would be a primitive latrine trench, although in some houses the lavatory was actually a room in which there was a bucket. Within the shed or room there would be an unpeeling of layers of clothing, then a few agonising minutes and then, once again, the cocooning process. Those in hedgehog positions who caught dysentery suffered more than most, for the first traces of blood were often a sentence of a death as long and as agonising as were the black and stinking evidences of frost gangrene in the feet or hands.

The latrine shed, even though bitterly cold, was still better than the open steppe. "The blizzards and the bitter cold seemed to stop most of our natural functions but when it became necessary then a ravine, a dip, even a low snow wall would give that protection from the wind which was essential. Of course, the winter of 1942–43 was neither so severe nor were we unprepared so that there were not the great number of frostbite cases which we had suffered in the first year. We had had, in that first year, also many cases of cystitis and the inability to urinate quickly as well as the intense burning sensation which accompanied the act, which made even this simple toilet procedure a long and painful business. Out of fear of frostbite most men wrapped that part of their body in a thick cloth that was used over and over again. Together with all the odours produced by unwashed bodies, feet and clothing, you can imagine that we did not smell very sweet. The term 'Russian winter of 1941' brings back to me very strongly a compound of smells: stale urine, excrement, suppurating wounds, Russian tobacco and the not unpleasant smell of Kascha, a sort of buckwheat porridge."

As the Russian offensive slowed and began to falter there was a certain return to the pre-winter confidence among many German soldiers. They knew that the winter through which they had passed had been a testing experience and that they had emerged from that test and had survived. Now in the first weeks of January 1942 the worst seemed to be past and spring, with its promise of warmer weather, was only ten or more weeks away. They had survived and they were going to get a medal to prove that they had been there at that time of crisis. There was also the possibility of being granted privilege leave. Orders had come round well before Christmas asking for the names of two men from each company, or its equivalent, but the Russian offensive had destroyed all chances of furlough and, indeed, many of the men told off for leave had been killed during the winter fighting. Now leave was being reintroduced and the lucky men were on the way home.

Anglo-Saxon armies go overseas to fight and it is, therefore, with some surprise that the realisation comes that a German soldier on the Eastern Front could travel almost from his trench to his home town by train. Of course, in reality, it was never quite so easy. At a collecting point behind the line the leave men would be formed into anti-partisan detachments. The slender life-line of the railway was a major terrorist target and passengers on the train had to be able to move out to fight and destroy the partisan groups. One can well imagine the feelings of men going on leave who are confronted with the demand to fight pitched battles against an enemy who were indistinguishable from the peasants among whom they moved.

At Przemysl, Smolensk or some other large collecting point de-lousing stations were set up to cleanse the combat soldier before he re-entered the Fatherland. For some there would be a change of uniform but for most it was the same old combat clothes with the lice baked dead from the infestation cleaners. The appearance of the furlough men in the first trainloads excited comment because they were wearing Russian fur caps and felt boots as well as other miscellaneous items of Red Army uniform. As leave from the Russian Front swung into a regular routine, checks were carried out to see that each man was correctly dressed as well as being properly armed and duly authorised.

The leave trains were not elegant nor were they heated in winter. In this context it should be mentioned that there was also a lack of heating in ambulance trains which had been halted and shunted into sidings to allow supplies to go up to the Front. In 1941–42 and 1944–45 ambulance trains arriving in the rear areas were found to be conveying corpses, for the wounded had frozen to death in their beds. Even though the leave trains lacked comfort they were heading westwards and that was the most important thing. Commanders of certain corps had set up regular, properly-staffed meal halts. Quite often the staff manning these canteens were native Russians whose employment had released another German soldier for the fighting line. The attitude of the military authorities towards these people was seldom constant. At times some units would be encouraged to enlist help so as to make soldiers available for the Front, or else to give the natives employment to keep them out of mischief. At other times these civilians would be looked upon as possible agents for partisan groups, a threat to security, and orders would come down that they be discharged. After one such order was received senior NCOs, wise in army lore, checked and found a loophole in the regulations which allowed a whole family to be employed, and bewildered but happy Russians working in army kitchens suddenly found that, by a stroke of the pen, they had all been given the same family name and that by this simple subterfuge they could stay employed and receive the supplementary rations which kept them alive.

At home the front-line soldier found, as such men have always found, that the gulf between the Homeland and the Front was an unbridgeable one. Whisked from a slit trench onto a leave train was dramatic enough. In the train, rolling past the windows were the empty wastes of steppe land with cow-dung houses and thatched roofs, until as the train moved deeper westwards there was an improvement in architecture, the husbandry of the fields, a simple caring for the goods one had. Then for them was the realisation of how neat and orderly was their own country but once in the cities the full realisation of how different conditions were began to strike home. The Soviet Union was a nation geared for war. Women fought alongside the men, even piloted planes and were dedicated to the task of achieving victory. In the Fatherland it seemed that hair-dressing salons and permanent waving were more important than turning out component parts for panzers. Thousands of foreign workers were employed to do the factory work that the unconscripted German women should have been doing.

In certain cities life was punctuated by air raids and there was rationing, but the ration was ample. Propaganda and Party control were absolute and unceasing and Goebbels' ministry turned out a continual stream of optimistic and inspiring slogans, most of which were hollow. The soldiers found that Germany was an empty shell, a glittering gem that turned out on closer inspection to be a tawdry bauble, a country whose people would not comprehend reality and were only playing at war. The Germany that the fighting men knew was out there in the East where the green glare of a Very light brought the men of an understrength unit to their feet in response to the rocket's alarm call. There where the tired and hungry grenadiers lay was home, was the real Germany. Home was the worn-out panzer or the gun lines. There amid the lice and the smells, that was home, and many, particularly the single men, cut short their leave and returned to those things which were lacking at home: the comrade-ship of their peers and a sense of purpose.

At the Front in that first winter the Russian offensive was once again gathering momentum and the weather was deteriorating, day-long blizzards bringing with them a cold more intense than that experienced in December. The promised winter clothing had still not arrived and without it men could not stay exposed on the open steppes for a night. The medical return for the 4th Army showed that frostbite casualties in the three weeks of bitterest weather were more than twice as many as the battle casualties and that many of the troops affected had been the drivers or the passengers in open trucks, moving up to or out of the line.

The Front was in motion once more and the retreat which the German Army had resumed was again a race from village to village, to occupy it before the Red Army arrived. Winter warfare showed that even in retreat the defenders still held the advantage. In the open their positions were not usually visible and thus when fire was opened upon the attacker the surprise effect was greater. In addition the Red Army's lines of advance were frequently dictated by natural obstacles so that the grenadiers could concentrate their fire power to cover those avenues. Russian attempts to outpace the retreating Germans or to outflank them often failed because their numbers were insufficient to destroy the defence.

It must not be thought that only the Germans suffered during the winter. The abnormally low temperatures affected both sides alike, for it should not be believed that all Red Army soldiers had equal resistance to the cold or that each man was at ease in such conditions. It was training, discipline and upbringing that held the Soviet units together in the most appalling conditions of climate but

German intelligence reports speak of many formations upon whom winter left its mark in a breakdown in military cohesion and a lessening in unit efficiency.

12

The effect of winter upon a Red Army unit at Rzhev

One example of the effects of the sub-zero temperatures upon a Red Army detachment was that reported from the Rzhev salient. Other sections of this book will deal more closely with the importance of Rzhev to the strategic plans of both sides and it is sufficient to say here that STAVKA considered its capture imperative and poured men and materials into repeated assaults to take the town. As a result of one series of attacks a German force, whose strength had shrunk to that of a weak battle group, was surrounded in a small village to the north of Rzhev. The grenadier and artillery group had withdrawn into the protection of the wooden houses of the village and had set up an all-round defence perimeter against which repeated but unsuccessful Soviet assaults were launched.

The length of an overcast and cloudy winter day in midwinter in the Soviet Union is a matter of a few hours during which there is adequate light. For much of the remaining time the only illumination is a pearly opaque luminescence, in which light it is difficult to judge distances or to identify men and vehicles.

The village in which the German garrison was holding out was stormed by Red infantry in attacks which lasted from first light until twilight and each was flung back. The assaults continued as twilight turned to dusk and as the night grew nearer the assaults betrayed a desperate urgency on the part of the Russian soldiers. It was clear to the Germans that the real reason for the Russian fury was the need to secure wind-proof, warm billets. It was less the need to kill Germans than the desire to spend a night out of the freezing temperatures of the open steppe which directed the assaults of the Russian infantry. The winter night closed in and immediately the already low temperatures began to sink even further. The Russian regiment searched about with feverish intensity for shelter but there was none and the men stood in thin ranks or lay in the snow. Even their superb woollen greatcoats, fur caps and felt boots could not prevent the cold from slowly chilling them. Field kitchens with hot food had not come up. These, the leading troops of the Russian offensive, had outrun their supply columns and for the battalions forced to spend the night on that frozen swamp there was neither shelter nor food.

Stand-to for the grenadiers in the village was well before sun-up and then as the light grew stronger they could see the massed ranks of Soviet troops grouped round the village and encircling it. From those solid blocks of brown-coated soldiers there came neither sound nor movement and the first thought of many of the defenders was that this was some sort of new Russian infantry tactic. Minutes passed and still the silent enemy gave neither sign nor sound of life. Meanwhile orders had come through to the grenadier commander to withdraw the battle group through the Soviet ring and to strike southwards towards Rzhev and the main German line.

The German troops were well aware of the dangers which they faced in running a gauntlet of Russian fire. They all knew the simple equation of the Eastern Front: a bad wound equalled death. A battle patrol was sent out to find a way through the Russian investment.

Wading through the deep snow was tiring but at least the action warmed the body and, sweating furiously, the patrol moved laboriously closer to the blocks of Soviet infantry. No shot greeted them and the grenadiers were convinced that the Red Army soldiers were dead, frozen to death in temperatures which had sunk to thirty degrees below freezing point. Slowly, uncertainly, hesitatingly, the grenadiers moved nearer to the silent Soviets and they then saw that there was some sort of trembling motion in the ranks – the Russians were shivering. The Red battalions were not dead but had been numbed by cold into such a comatose state that only the trembling and the misery in their eyes showed them to be still alive. They made no move to intercept the German patrol. It might be, reasoned the patrol leader, that their senses were not functioning clearly and that they had not appreciated the danger of the appearance of the German soldiers. This was a tactical advantage which could be exploited. Here was a chance for the German garrison to escape through the Russian ring.

Quickly the information was taken back to the commander in the village. The artillery pieces were limbered up, the engines of the few remaining serviceable vehicles were started and a small convoy assembled. The snow-covered dirt road out of the village curved to skirt a piece of woodland before straightening up and running straight southwards, parallel to the railway line which lay some kilometres away. Behind the first bend and on either side of the road there was a large body of Russian infantry holding a defensive position. Cautiously the German lorries moved towards the Red Army group and being unchallenged then drove slowly past it. Not a Russian soldier moved to stop the vehicles as they moved along the icy road, their engines roaring with the strain and the artillery pieces swinging from side to side as they skidded on the slippery road surface.

The whole battle group passed out of the encirclement and even though, at times, the nearest Soviet post was within a hundred metres there was no interference. The effects of having been exposed to the cruel cold without shelter or food for an entire night had weakened the Russian soldiers' capacity to act to destroy the Germans.

13

The German Army resolves the problems of winter warfare

THE 1942 HANDBOOK

When the first really low temperatures were recorded during the winter of 1941, the Quartermaster's Department of the Army was inundated with urgent demands for grease, oil and lubricants with cold-resistant properties. Units needed these special supplies to keep vehicles and guns in action, for the lubricants on general issue were found to be ineffective in the cold of the Russian winter.

There were, however, no special cold-resistant materials. None had been developed for the German Army because there had been, up to that time, no need of them. The Red Army, for its part, had faced and overcome the problem of special lubricants many years before and the research work of Russian scientists in those fields had been aided by the simple, natural fact that oil produced from native wells had fewer impurities, and was usable at temperatures lower than that from the sources available to the Germans.

The German Army made recourse to ad hoc methods. It was found that to prevent the action of rifles and machine guns from freezing solid every trace of oil and grease had to be removed. To ensure a smooth bolt action a finely-ground powder was sprinkled on the action. One SS unit on the central sector found that finely-textured flowers of sulphur to be particularly effective. Corps and divisions fighting in the Ukraine and in southern Russia were less severely affected than those on the central or northern fronts and used sunflower seed oil in place of the standard German Army rifle oil.

Cold affected the large metal areas of armoured fighting vehicles and guns. Engines of vehicles parked in the open were usually found to have frozen solid, including the anti-freeze solution with which the radiators were filled, for that was only effective at normal winter temperatures. To prevent the distortion of their plates, batteries had to be removed and then stored in a warm room, or else they were individually wrapped and set inside straw-lined wooden boxes. In some detachments when it became necessary to move vehicles, motors were started using the most primitive means. Small fires were lit under radiators and gear boxes, or else petrol was poured into the gear box to make the movement easier. Other units which did not light fires to warm the radiators kept on standby a number of vehicles whose engines were started at hourly intervals. When orders to move were received the hot water from the radiators of the running engines was pumped into the drained radiators of the other vehicles. This hot water could be passed from machine to machine so quickly that within an hour a regiment could be at battle readiness.

Those formations which could quarter men, weapons and machines under cover were able to avoid most of the acute problems encountered by those whose personnel and equipment had to stay in the open. For the artillery arm there were particular difficulties. Oil and grease froze in the recoil systems of artillery pieces, even those covered with heavy tarpaulins. Breech blocks which had frozen solid had to be heated before they could be opened. Some protection for the sensitive elevating and traversing gear was obtained by building walls of straw bales up to and around them, but delicate optical sighting equipment had to be removed, for the rubber eye pieces crumbled in the extreme cold.

But it was not only that the guns required special attention. The whole concept of handling artillery had to be rethought and new ideas introduced to counter the peculiar effect which temperature had upon the propellant charges, the flight of the projectile and its characteristics. Conventional flash and sound ranging suffered and firing by map co-ordinates was totally unreliable. The deep snow not only reduced the force of the explosions of light shells but also concealed the fall of shot from FOOs or spotters in light aircraft.

Under such circumstances it is not surprising that the infantry, denied artillery support, relied upon machine guns and hand grenades and the failure of the artillery to give covering fire, the inability of panzers to cope with snow, the lack of preparation at the highest levels of command and the strain of the worst winter for a century had its effect upon the German Army on the Eastern Front.

In an attempt to restore that high morale which had been lost as a result of its experiences the Army produced a handbook on winter warfare and issued it in the August of 1942, well before the onset of bad weather. This book assured the German soldiers that they could meet and overcome the strains and difficulties of campaigning in sub-zero temperatures and that, whatever the circumstance, they could defeat the Red Army in winter, whether in attack or in defence. Moral preparation to meet the hard winter was essential. There was training which had to be undergone, acclimatisation and familiarisation with new equipment. All these would produce a confidence in their own ability to meet and to overcome the disadvantages of winter. Much was made of the moral factor, for it was claimed that most frostbite cases might have been avoided had sufficient care and attention been paid. There were dangers in over-tiredness or of going for long periods without sleep. It was precisely at such times that the lack of moral fibre manifested itself and soldiers refused to take those simple precautions which would prevent frostbite.

Much of the book concerned itself with the various ways of overcoming the severity of the cold weather season in Russia. Whole chapters dealt with the construction of shelters; igloos were included in the buildings recommended, but these proved to be unpopular habitats even for soldiers on open and treeless steppes. Pages were devoted to the construction of primitive but effective stoves, the production of charcoal to heat these and instructions on how to avoid carbon-monoxide poisoning. Other chapters dealt with clothing, food, animal care, the maintenance of vehicles and the effect of climate upon the railway systems. Vehicle camouflage was also dealt with and the way in which tank track marks could be concealed.

Much of what the 372-page handbook laid out has been taken into the winter warfare handbooks of the Western Powers and much of what was written is basic common sense. For example, German Army units marked the depth of snow by using on roads lines of black painted poles, cut to a standard length and set up along road verges.

The common belief in the West, and accepted by many Germans, that the Russian winter produces a snow-bound wilderness for more than six months of the year is not one which stands close scrutiny. It was seldom appreciated that the snowfall amounts differed from region to region and that the depth of the amounts impeded operations to a greater or lesser degree. The period of time which snow stayed on the ground also varied. Snowfall was heaviest (100cm) and stayed longest (six to seven months) in the north, while in the south snow and frost endured for only four months and varied in depth between 10 and 40cm. In the winter of 1942–43 along the line of the lower Don and Donets snow did not fall until mid-December and subsequent precipitations in the months which followed were so light that the mobility of the German forces was hardly affected.

When frost hardened the mud which had bogged down whole columns of vehicles and guns, movement was restored to sectors of the front which had been paralysed. Not only did the frost harden the ground but it also froze streams and lakes, enabling these to be used as auxiliary roads by light carts. Heavier or longer periods of deep frost were sufficient to freeze a river so solidly that it could be used by quite heavy vehicles. A chapter within this section of the book describes how, in the winter of 1941–42, German engineers constructed and ran a railway across the frozen surface of one of the major rivers of western Russia.

Although the handbook mentioned that swamps were usually covered by only a very thin layer of ice, this is not borne out by the evidence of a letter written by an officer of a security division. He was stationed in a partisan-infected area along the southern edge of the Pripet Marsh and wrote that in the fairly mild winter of 1942–43, "The bandits make their way across the frozen marsh sliding on a type of low sledge. Some whom we killed the other night were carrying food. I suppose they push themselves (on their sledges) using feet and hands ... Everything in this country seems to be against us ... in summer the swamps are a barrier halting the movement of our men. In winter they make a bridge across which our enemies attack us ..." The ability of the partisan groups to cross the frozen marshes represented yet another drain upon the German rear area troops, for now a far greater number of soldiers was required, more infantry, more cavalry and artillery to patrol the area which cold had made passable to the Soviet forces.

In the handbook strenuous efforts were made to convince the German soldiers that snow could also serve as an ally and not merely as an enemy to be feared. The disadvantages that snow brought did not need to be stressed; they were obvious and familiar, but the advantages were less apparent. Snow, the book said, was wind-resistant so that walls acting as windshields could be erected to protect engines of vehicles parked in the open. Thick and hard packed snow was reasonably bullet-proof. It was particularly easy to work and trenches, particularly communication trenches, could be easily cut out of this soft and plastic material. It also had excellent camouflage properties and trenches could not be easily detected as there was no spoil to betray the position. It was absolutely vital for camouflage to be effective that there was no unusual mark or feature, in or near the trenches, which might betray the positions. To a good observer a single thing out of place or unusual, startled birds, or animals moving in panic flight indicated the presence of man.

In the following extract from a letter written by an NCO of the SS Viking Division he relates how a patrol was saved from ambush by a sharp-eyed observer:

A few days ago we carried out a reconnaissance patrol into the Russian zone. It was a beautiful clear day. On such days the visibility is quite unbelievable. One can see literally for miles and every detail is pronounced and clear. I mention this because it had a bearing on the patrol.

From our form-up position we crossed open ground and then moved into a wide shallow depression. This was the limit of our first bound. We lay down in this and took up defensive positions, recovering our breath, before making the next bound which was a small wood. Our Sturmführer looked through his glasses at a low ridge in front of which we would have to pass. The Sturmführer called to me and pointed at something on the ridge. I looked through the glasses and saw it immediately. Clearly seen in the bright sunlight there were long black streaks across the snow; the marks made by a machine gun which had been firing for a long time. Through the glasses I was then able to pick out a white cloth which covered a hole in the snow wall of a trench and through which the machine gun had been fired.

This was something so surprising as to be completely abnormal. Ivan has the ability to camouflage his positions in such a way as to make him almost invisible and will spend hours removing every trace of his presence. Yet here he had left marks which were distinct, clear and unmistakable. Thanks to the slackness of one Red machine gun group the whole position, a trench system not marked on our maps, had been betrayed ...

There were circumstances in which the extreme low temperatures immobilised completely. It was frequently found, when attempts were made to withdraw heavy guns in the face of a Soviet advance, that they had frozen to the ground, forming solid blocks which defied every effort to move. Some German units acquired Russian-built tractors, simple in construction but with a power out of all proportion to their size. It was not unusual to see a single one of these machines acting as a prime mover to two or more heavy guns. When the task was too great for even the Soviet vehicles to achieve and the guns could not be withdrawn and thus prevented from falling into Soviet hands, they were destroyed by a commando of gunners who had had to be specially trained for this unhappy task. In the early days of the campaign when artillery had not accepted the fact of Soviet infiltration, the sight of a Red Army patrol had often caused artillery pieces and vehicles to be abandoned. Such penetrations of the German line eventually became commonplace and gunners were then trained in infantry combat methods so that they could defend both their guns and themselves.

The maintenance of mobility and the task of maintaining road or rail communications were repeatedly stressed, for the fear of a complete break down in the supply system haunted the German staffs. They had need to be concerned. In 1941 Hitler had been given a choice. He had been told that the amount of Russian-gauge rolling stock in German hands was sufficient to supply the armies in the field with only one of the three most urgent priorities: warm clothing, food or ammunition. Hitler had chosen ammunition and the results of his decision are clear from earlier pages of this work. Even so, although only one main material was being transported, in that first winter the railway life-line had often failed and on the sector of Army Group Centre, to quote just one example, only nine out of the twenty-seven trains which were required daily to sustain the Front had ever completed the journey. One reason lay in the faults in the construction of German locomotives, seventy per cent of which broke down as a result of extreme temperatures. The situation was not resolved until specially designed locomotive types came into service during 1943. In that year, too, the organised employment of battalions of civilians kept the permanent way open and the points free from ice.

By a strange paradox it was found that road travel was sometimes easier in winter than in summer, although this statement needs to be qualified by adding, so long as the surface was kept free of snow. Local civilians were employed to carry out this task with hand shovels or by driving snow-ploughs. The work battalions were not committed until the blizzards or snowstorms had blown themselves out, but once in action the civilian workers achieved rapid results and a single battalion could keep clear a 48-kilometre stretch of highway. To increase the number of passable highways in wintry conditions alternative routes were laid out to pass through forests or along hill crests and ridges where snow did not build up to form drifts.

Cross-country mobility for ration carts, wounded sleds or even light guns could be improved by the addition of skis or sled runners. Skis also gave infantry patrols the speed which conventional foot marches lacked.

It should not be believed that all units had been unprepared for the severe conditions. Quartermasters of some divisions set up excellent liaison networks through the depots of units under their command, and by coded messages were able to send representatives to collect the vehicle spare parts which would keep their tanks or lorries moving. At times of the most severe shortages a form of black market in spares and components was in operation and unit representatives scoured the factories.

Units which had prepared were usually the ones which, in the days of heady advances during the autumn of 1941, had organised supplies of winter clothing. In those few weeks of clear weather, which occur between the end of the autumn rains and the first snows of winter, the quartermasters had brought forward into the combat zone and had organised in well-guarded and weather-proof dumps, the food and fuel supplies, the warm clothing and ammunition with which to equip their men. The number of such quartermasters was few and their men were the fortunate ones during that first winter. Too many quartermasters believed the propaganda stories of the war being over before winter, had organised no supplies and their men had suffered accordingly.

On the subject of clothing suitable for the Russian winter the handbook admitted that the garments collected in Germany from civilians during that first winter had generally not reached the Front until the worst weather had passed, but went on to reassure the reader that for the future adequate supplies of reversible, quilted jackets and trousers had been produced. Sufficient numbers of fur caps were available so that it was no longer necessary for German soldiers to wear Russian pattern caps and to run, thereby, the risk of being wrongly identified and fired at.

The handbook conceded that there were no special tactics to be used in snowy or wintry conditions. Emphasis was laid upon the slowness of infantry movement through snow and it was suggested that to speed the pace of an attack the cover of woods or forests be utilised in which the snow would lie less deeply.

The slow pace of infantrymen through snow required a very close co-operation between the grenadiers and the supporting arms. If artillery was meshed into the attack it was necessary for the forward observation officer up with the infantry to be in close and immediate contact with his batteries, so as to switch targets or to call back the guns which were increasing their range too quickly. It was often found that unless there was this strict control the pace of the grenadier advance allowed Soviet machine gunners to man their weapons in the interval between the barrage marching over them and the appearance of the German infantry.

It was not considered advisable for German troops to follow in tank tracks through the snow, although this was usually done by Red Army infantry. Although admitting that the going was easier for the foot soldiers it was emphasised that a tank drew artillery fire which might cause casualties to the grenadiers.

The German Army handbook on winter warfare was a well-written, simple-to-understand and excellently researched work. Much of its text was obvious to anyone who had lived in a cold climate and much was based upon the results of trial and error. Whole sections of this work have been translated and reprinted in the winter survival handbooks of the British and American Armies and the techniques which were advised have become standard practice in the NATO forces.

14

The construction of an ice railway bridge across the Dnieper

WINTER 1941-1942

The German Army handbook on winter warfare expressed the conviction that the severe conditions which were met in Russia could often be turned so as to become an advantage instead of a disadvantage. An example to prove that statement is that in which a German railway staff overcame the difficulties of an over-extended and tenuous supply line to a front-line army by constructing a railway line across a frozen river along which they passed sufficient materials to build up that army's strength and reserves.

This ice-bridge construction was unique in the German service at that time although the Russians had run an efficient rail link to beat the blockade of Leningrad and had, in the past, often had recourse to such enterprises.

The account of this German Army venture is recorded here because it demonstrates how a unit faced with a difficult problem was able to utilise a natural element transformed by extremes of climate into an unusual platform, and through these means to achieve a desired objective.

During the winter of 1941–42 the problem of maintaining supplies to the 6th Army, which was holding the line from south of Kursk to well below Kharkov, sharpened. As a result of the climatic conditions convoys of lorries proved insufficient to sustain the required levels and the situation quickly became critical. One of the reasons for this supply block was that as the Soviets had withdrawn eastwards they had destroyed all the Dnieper bridges, including the giant railway bridge which linked Kiev, Poltava and Kursk. The first named town was the main supply depot for the 6th Army and the other two towns the southern and northern depot points behind the Army's front.

In the yards at Kiev there was a great number of wide-gauge wagons available to transport the supplies but there was no rail link to bring these across the wide and swift flowing Dnieper and to nourish the 6th Army, which lay east of the river.

German engineers, had, of course, erected light and temporary wooden bridges but these were certain to be swept away by the breaking ice when the spring thaw came. Nor was there time to repair and bring into use the existing railway bridge and even less to erect a new span. The needs of the 6th Army were immediate and they could not hold out until April, the month by which construction of a permanent bridge might be completed. Nor were there suitable heavy road bridges capable of carrying the flow of traffic which would be needed to bring forward the materials of war. There was, in fact, only one usable heavy bridge, a 22-tonner, for the whole area between Kremenchug and the Pripet Marsh. Among the solutions which were suggested to the task of making the traffic flow between the western and eastern banks of the Dnieper was that of building a railway line across the frozen river; in other words to use the surface of the river as an ice bridge.

The construction of this, according to Colonel Willemer, upon whose report this account is based, was fraught with several difficulties, the chief of which was the lack of data on the load-bearing capabilities of ice. The proposal met with opposition, chiefly from senior engineers, both civil and military, who refused to accept the responsibility for its construction. The task was then left to the local headquarters of Railway Transport Command to undertake and to complete.

The first task was to muster a work force and this consisted of between 300 and 800 Ukrainian civilians and 300 German soldiers from 88th Infantry Division.

Three eight-hour shifts were worked and Sunday was considered to be a normal work day. In order that there would be no interruption to the construction and to supply the civilians with hot and nourishing food the army's field kitchens were brought on to site. Extra petrol had to be obtained both for supplying the field kitchens and for bringing forward the building materials. The requisitioning of these extra fuel supplies was not an easy task as at that time there was a critical shortage of petrol throughout the entire army on the Eastern Front. To save on fuel, horses and sledges were obtained and used to porter the building materials from outlying areas to a central point from which they were picked up by motor transport. Sledges were also used to transport the blocks of ice from the downstream cutting areas to the ice bridge site.

A thorough reconnaissance was made and a site which contained several natural advantages selected. Firstly the banks were low enough not to require special gradient treatment; secondly, between the eastern and western banks of the river there was a natural island of some 150 metres in width; and thirdly the eastern and western terminals of the ice railway could be connected to existing railway lines. The ice bridge would, therefore, be in two halves, each supported by the central island and the river banks. To overcome the problem of gradients on the island the soldiers of 88th Division dug a cutting 3.5 metres deep across its width. The western terminal of the ice railway connected to a spur line in a timber yard which then joined a main line. The eastern terminal also connected with a spur line in the grounds of a saw mill and this line also joined a main line.

Weather was a great difficulty and temperatures encountered during the building time sank to twenty-nine degrees below freezing.

There were also severe snow showers which slowed the pace of the work. Snow had to be cleared from the site area as well as from the cut ice blocks, for it was discovered that when melted snow was refrozen it lacked the strength of a compact pure ice mass.

The river surface was a layer of ice some 50cm thick and it was decided to build upon this further layers of ice blocks to a width of about 12 metres. This would be the foundation. The blocks were cut from ice pits set downstream of the site and were brought up by sledge. These blocks between 40 and 80cm long had a width of between 40 and 60cm and a thickness of about 50cm. The blocks were dressed and laid on the river surface. Gaps between the blocks were filled with ice chippings. As the extra weight was added it was noted that the whole ice layer had created a concave bow whose depth varied between 10 and 40cm. Ice had little elasticity and wide cracks appeared at about 15 metres on either side of the bridge. Through these gaps water poured and flooded the bridge section and when this water froze it was discovered that not only had it strengthened the bridge bed but that it had also sealed the cracks. The flood water had acted as a sort of natural weld.

A second layer of ice blocks was laid to a width of 5 metres upon the first layer and once again there was the concave effect which caused the construction to sink by a further 30cm at its maximum and 10cm at its minimum. As there were no breaks in the ice to bring about the desired flooding holes were bored and water hosed over the two layers. These then froze into a compact ice mass and the bridge had been constructed. All that then remained was to lay two double lines of tree trunks longitudinally on each side of the bridge as a reinforcement. These tree trunks were cut from oak and pine, were about 35cm in diameter and between 4 and 6 metres long. Upon these four longitudinal sections were laid the sleepers and the rails. A third ice strip made up of blocks was laid alongside the tree trunks and all the hollow spaces were filled with ice chippings. Hosing of the structure again took place and when the water had frozen there was a solid railway bridge between 130 and 170cm thick.

To test the construction a locomotive was driven on to the ice. The weight of the test piece was 120 tons and its passage caused the construction to bow to a maximum extent of 45cm. Once the weight was released the ice rose again.

Colonel Willemer's report concluded with facts and figures which show that 15,640 ice blocks were cut, brought to the site, dressed and put into position. The length of track required to connect both sides of the ice bridge to existing spurs was 1,600 metres, 6,200 metres of timber were cut and 2,465 sleepers were laid. To keep the ice surface clear 13,500 cubic metres of snow were removed at the start of the operation and this work had to be continued during the many snowfalls which occurred throughout the construction period.

Construction time had been twelve days and it proved possible to use the ice line for about a month. The first service began at the beginning of February and continued to the beginning of the thaw, that is during the first week of March. If a similar project could have been begun and completed by the end of December the constructors may have been faced with the problem of a thinner ice surface on the Dnieper but this could have been built up by the addition of a third layer of blocks. A bridge built in early December would have eased the supply difficulties of the 6th Army enormously. No dismantling of the site was necessary. When the thaw came the steel railway lines were removed and the remaining sections of the bridge were allowed to break up and float downstream.

During the time of its service more than 4,500 wagon loads of supplies and materials were brought across the ice bridge and this figure could have been doubled but for the fact that there was a limit to the number of wagons which could be carried at any one time by the spur lines. An unsuccessful attempt was made to build a direct line.

Jams, therefore, built up and these halted the flow of traffic from west to east and the return of empty wagons from the 6th Army, across the ice bridge and back to the Kiev depot. Nevertheless, the aims had been fulfilled; the transport of wide-gauge stock across the Dnieper had been accomplished and the 6th Army had been supplied with sufficient reserves of war materials.

It would have been neat to be able to record that those who had been responsible for the planning and executing of this project had been promoted or rewarded but Colonel Willemer makes no mention of this. One can only hope that the soldiers of the 6th Army strung out along the lines of the Donets river were aware of this unusual feat of military engineering and were grateful.

15

The frustrating mud and the scouring dust

From the previous chapter it can be appreciated how the cold weather affected the nature of the campaign. But there was another product of the Russian climate which the German Army met as early as the opening weeks of the new war and whose grip, if not as iron as that of winter, was as tenacious. This condition was Russia's oldest ally - mud.

The cold of winter killed quickly but mud broke men spiritually and emotionally. It destroyed mobility and the effect of mud produced by the rains of autumn and spring upon military operations on the Eastern Front cannot be too strongly emphasised. In the first months of the new war men of the German motorised columns became frighteningly aware that a few hours' downpour of rain upon what was technically a main highway, reduced this to a slough of mire. The mud produced by a half day of rain was sufficient to immobilise whole columns of wheeled transport and even tanks were bogged down in the apparently bottomless slime. During the Kiev encirclement, which is dealt with in later pages, a thrust by one of the panzer battalions of the 3rd Panzer Division, was halted by mud and the machines were bogged down. Held immobile they were sitting targets for the Russian armour whose broader tracks coped more easily with the poor going and gave freedom of manoeuvre. It was only superior gunnery, better wireless communication and the small force of grenadiers which accompanied them that saved the German column from complete destruction, but so many vehicles were held fast at that place and at other places during the subsequent advance that Model's panzer spearhead was reduced, at one time, to only three machines.

Although rain was liable to come at any time the wet season usually began during October and lasted for a month. This was then followed by a short windy period which dried out the ground surface and restored mobility until the onset of winter. Except for periods of thaw the ground then froze solid until the warmer weather of spring melted the snow blanket. The soil which remained deep frozen was unable to absorb the sudden and large amounts of water produced by the melting snow and as this could not drain rapidly away there was vast and severe flooding and a consequent increase in mud.

These weather conditions were not, of course, constant along the whole battle line. There was a lighter covering of snow and an earlier thaw in the temperate zone of southern Russia and as the ground was also not frozen to so great a depth there was less flooding than on the northern sectors with their harder frosts and deeper snow layer. In the central and northern regions of western Russia the already vast areas of swamp were extended by flood waters produced as a result of the thaw and even high summer did not always dry the ground sufficiently for it to be used by wheeled transport. In some of the vast wooded areas of those regions, even the hottest summers did not bring about this result.

The Russian commanders, aware of the restricting effect of mud, were prepared to submit to its dictates and frequently brought their largest military operations to a quick close when the thaw arrived. Their tanks were robustly constructed and were fitted with extra wide tracks to cope with the bad going, but even these were not always sufficient and many offensives using armour, and which had been ordered to take place despite the mud, were halted as a consequence of the staggering fall-out losses suffered by the Soviet tank units. Generally, however, the Russian field commanders reasoned that if their tanks could not manoeuvre in the mud then neither could the wheeled transport and that there was little point in wasting petrol and in wearing out engines seeking to overcome the bad ground conditions.

This acceptance of the power of mud is demonstrated by the fact that the Russian winter offensive was halted when, on 18 April 1942, the weather on the central front changed and produced a warm and sunny day. The thaw had set in. The strategic intent behind the Soviet winter offensive, the smashing of the German salient in front of Moscow, lay within the Red Army's grasp, but STAVKA halted its armies in sight of a major strategic goal, because it was aware of the effect of mud.

For the Germans with their lesser experience of such conditions the situation at first was frightening. They had observed, with alarm, how road surfaces vanished completely under a few hours' rain and soon realised that they were totally dependent upon the very few all-weather roads which had been built in western Russia. Fighting was then to gain those few highways and for the possession of the equally few railway tracks. But the main all-weather roads had not been constructed to carry the amount and the weight of the traffic which now used them and the surfaces began to break up under the strain. On the Orel sector, for example, the surface of the Roslavl highway broke up and soon the road was a mud track more than a metre deep. Wheeled transport was either pushed to one side or else towed through the worst stretches by tracked vehicles. In these and similar conditions only the horse could be used and German animals died in hundreds from heart strain brought on by their efforts to haul artillery pieces through the mud. The ubiquitous civilian *panje* cart came into its own and was taken on the establishment of many units, often for the first time. The light wagon and its seemingly inexhaustible horses still retained mobility in conditions which were difficult even for foot soldiers.

Conscious of their absolute dependence upon the Russian roads, the German commanders drew up plans to regulate the flow of traffic along them, as well as the types of vehicle which could use them, and also brought in engineering experts to advise on how the existing surfaces could be improved.

The magnitude of the task varied from sector to sector but certain actions were general on every front. Some very efficient corps produced maps showing road states and regulated the daily movement of traffic along the roads within its area. In such areas the columns were well regulated, the speeds were fast and supplies were frequent. As a general rule, in muddy conditions, minor roads which could not be used for wheeled traffic were blocked off completely even though diversions to reach a major road added considerably to the length of a journey and a higher petrol consumption. Main roads were restricted, generally, to priority class vehicles, such as ammunition columns, petrol lorry convoys and the reinforcements needed to nourish the advance. Of course, no civil traffic was allowed to use the main roads, chiefly because this would have slowed down the pace of the military traffic, but also because there was always the fear of partisan attack upsetting the flow of supplies and reinforcements to the Front.

In extremely muddy conditions all wheeled traffic was halted and removed from the road, leaving it clear for tracked and half-tracked vehicles. Single lorries were allowed to use a track parallel to the main road, but only under a strictly controlled 'block' system. Where the road was of sufficient width four lanes of traffic could be accommodated. One lane was for slow, single, wheeled vehicles going up the line. Then there was a main stream up, a main stream down and a slow down lane.

Maintenance of the road surface was all important and in the early days the Reichs Arbeitsdienst or the Organisation Todt had been used to carry out this task, but then locally-recruited labour groups were formed into construction battalions and made responsible for carrying out repair over a given distance of the road. One simple but effective measure to drain the road was to dig ditches and, where time allowed, the whole surface of the road was often removed and then laid afresh to prepare it for the next crisis of climate. German engineers improved many of the main highways and, using civilian labour, often built up the roads to a standard of all-weather capability that they had never had. These improvements and the rigid application of road discipline reduced the influence of mud so that, in later years, its onset was disliked but it no longer held the awful terror that it once had.

The story of Russian mud is not confined to its influence on road traffic alone. It affected cross-country movement particularly in regions in which the fiercest battles were fought. The nearer one approached to the battle zone the worse did the mud become, for the action of the vehicles upon the ground was to churn it up and to turn this into a swamp. In an attack using armoured fighting vehicles there was often little cohesion, for each driver was more concerned to find good firm going and to maintain the forward movement than with keeping formation in a concerted assault.

An army as flexible as the German reacted quickly to counter the limitations placed upon it by the effect of mud. They seized every initiative which would aid their operations. In March 1944, to take one example of this flexibility, one of the corps belonging to the 1st Panzer Army, which was threatened with encirclement, realised that a sudden rise in temperature had dried out a road which had been, until then, impassable. The German vehicle columns were quickly assembled and passed along this road at fast speeds. The suddenness of the German action surprised the Russians who were unable to bring their own units into a counter move at such short notice and the German corps escaped from the ring which STAVKA had planned to cast around it.

German armoured fighting vehicles, constructed for the terrain conditions met with in western Europe and therefore less sturdily built, broke down more frequently than the less sophisticated but more robust Russian machines. The losses from fall-out in German units were so high that forty per cent of a unit's establishment in workshops at any one time was acceptable. Losses in the 2nd Panzer Group rose, on one occasion, to as high as sixty per cent and this at a time when German industry was still producing fewer than one hundred tanks each month. The gap between losses and replacements inevitably widened and unit strengths already reduced by long months of campaigning fell to a dramatically low level. There were some formations which lost most of their effective strength not to Russian armour but to mud. A full chronicle of the misery produced by the mud of Russia has never been told and the cost in suffering has never been computed.

Artillery units made local and limited attempts to overcome the problem of ammunition supply by building corduroy roads* from an access point to the battery positions. Even though the roads betrayed the gun positions, this was acceptable. The most important thing was that the guns should be fed and this could only be accomplished by the construction of corduroy roads.

The need to bring forward supplies in good time and well before the onset of the two great periods of muddy weather, was stressed in divisional and corps orders. Some units were able to build up sufficient reserves but the majority were accorded very low priorities on the road despatcher's list. "There were many times in that first autumn when we had no bread at all for days at a time and there was little that could be requisitioned or even bought from the civil

*Logs placed side by side

population." Attempts to overcome the supply problem by using aircraft were initiated but proved to be so costly both in terms of petrol consumption and aircraft lost that this was discontinued. This same inability to maintain a regular flow of supplies and reinforcements led to the premature evacuation of bridgeheads, for often the sense of isolation was increased by the raging flood waters which cut off the lonely outposts from the main body.

The whole story of the German Army's experiences in Russia is dominated by stories concerning mud. It was a phenomenon unparalleled in the experience of those who fought there and stories of jack-boots being sucked off the wearer's feet are commonplace. However serious the problem may have been, not once, in any diary, letter or interview did I hear or read the equivalent of stories current in Britain following the battle of Passchendaele in 1917, where Flanders' mud simply swallowed up many of the wounded.

In addition to the difficulties of supply and transport the rainy season also brought with it medical problems different from those met with in the cold and hot months. Some regions of the Soviet Union were malarial and to this mosquito-carried illness there were other insect-borne sicknesses as well as fevers brought about by the damp conditions. Despite the wet conditions there were few sufferers from 'trench foot' and, indeed, those who contracted this were considered to have a self-inflicted wound. There were many types of stomach illness brought on by the swampy conditions, wet clothing and the damp, warm air. Mild dysentery, colic and inflammation of the bowels were common and lice were, as always, a problem.

To conclude this description of the effects of mud on military operations is an account of the effort made by the 6th Panzer Division in the opening weeks of 'Operation Barbarossa'.

The first offensives of the new war in the sector of Army Group North had been very successful but as 1st Panzer Division pushed westwards and closer towards Leningrad the resistance put up by Soviet units of the 8th Red Army became stiffer and soon the forward movement of Hoepner's Panzer Group was threatened. To add weight to 1st Panzer's faltering advance the 6th Panzer Division was brought forward and diverted northwards. To spearhead the divisional thrust a battle group was formed and was sent out to establish a bridgehead across the Plyussa river.

The distance from the start line was not a great one and from the maps which had been issued it seemed as if much of the journey would be made on good roads, although it was also clear that these ran through swamps. The battle group set off along one of the roads marked on the map and soon found that this ended in a marsh. No road past that point had existed since the Russo-Japanese war of 1905. The route now became a struggle as the column diverted from one piece of firm ground to the other. Bridges, wooden and half-rotten with age, collapsed under the weight of the heavy armoured vehicles and had to be rebuilt before the advance could continue.

Where the going was not marsh then it was loose sand and drivers had to avoid the tracks of the lorries in front of them, for to follow in these was to become bogged down. From sand patch to firm going, from swamp to hard ground and across small streams the column wound its weary way. There were on that first day twelve rivers which had to be crossed and at each of them the bridge collapsed and had to be rebuilt.

Attempts to move off the path and to follow an independent route met with total disaster as the half tracks and lorries 'bellied' in the swamps. Inviting green patches which seemed to be meadows turned out to be vegetation covering the surface of a pond or patch or marshland. In those places where the going was almost impassable and almost every vehicle was bogged down it frequently happened that the vehicles employed to tow out the stranded machine were themselves stuck fast. Then there were long waiting periods while the recovery vehicles dragged themselves along the narrow paths and the bad going and then sought firm ground from which to drag out the lorries or tanks now deeply enmired.

The column spread in length as the lead vehicles were separated from those still trapped in the mud and halts became more frequent in an effort to keep the column closed up. Shortly before last light the final stop was made and a bivouac sought. The first vehicles laagered for the night at 20.00hrs and the last ones reached the concentration area at 04.00hrs the next morning. The rate of march had been a little under two kilometres per hour. The mud, the swamps, burning heat and insects had all combined to make the day a miserably memorable one for the spearhead detachment of the 6th Panzer Division.

A patrol sent out at first light the following morning found that there was a strong defensive position guarding the road but that the sentries did not seem to be too alert. A battle group was formed and rushed the position, sweeping opposition aside in a swift determined assault. The Soviet garrison had, however, had time to destroy the bridge across the river and once the German engineers had come forward a new erection was completed and the column was moving forward again by 10.00hrs. Ahead of the point group there was another Red Army road block and an assault from the flank rolled up the Soviet line in the area and left the way clear for the main of the division coming up. Orders were then received that the pursuit battle would be taken up by the 1st Panzer Division and that the battle group could stand down but before the crews could begin to carry out the overdue maintenance on their vehicles the group was ordered to seize the river bridges at Lyady.

Once again the terrain was wide with deep swamps and the tribulations of the previous days were repeated. Only light opposition was met during the advance and this was brushed aside with little difficulty. Late in the evening the advance guard rushed the objective and, having seized the bridges, set up a defensive perimeter on the far bank. They had accomplished their task after a strenuous march of fifty kilometres which had taken nine hours to complete.

Once again the battle group was ordered to stand down. Once again the drivers and fitters began work overhauling the half tracks, the tanks and the lorries and for the second time within two days the stand-down order was cancelled and a new set of objectives given. The task was now to capture two bridges across the Luga river near Porechye. The situation facing the German forces on that sector was that frontal attacks from the west had been held by determined resistance and that the forward movement of a whole German Army and a complete panzer group was held. The intention was that the 6th Panzer Division's battle group should strike the defenders on the Luga river from their southern flank and in the ensuing confusion the Soviet line could be overrun by the panzer group.

The column set out again towards the objectives, some 100 kilometres distant. Progress was fast along a good road but south of Lake Samros the going deteriorated and soon the road had vanished into the worst swamp conditions which had been met. The whole column was stuck fast. Vehicles which tried to bypass those already bogged down ran off the path and vanished almost completely in the swamps. Other machines held in the mud tried to force their way through the mire using all possible power from their motors but only succeeded in building a small wall of mud which soon proved too thick for the vehicle to move. In an attempt to make some sort of foundation upon which the column could advance every piece of timber that was carried on the Engineer trucks was laid down in the mud. Trees were cut down, the branches laid across the road, the few houses in the area were destroyed and the materials from them flung into the mud to form a platform upon which the tanks and lorries could obtain a firm purchase. Hours of back-breaking labour in searing heat amid a cloud of stinging marsh insects finally brought the column across this veritable slough of despond and once again there was a good surface and speed increased.

Inevitably conditions deteriorated and now there was an added problem. The scorched earth tactics introduced by the Soviets resulted in the route forward being marked by a series of burning villages and in every case the whole column had to halt until the houses had burnt themselves out. The pace of the march slowed almost to a halt as the evening drew on but then orders were received from Corps. There would be no halt, the advance must be maintained throughout the night. It may well be imagined what strain had already been borne by the drivers of the vehicles in their struggle through the mud, and to those difficulties were added those of night driving. There was no light to guide the leading vehicles of the column and there were also the bridges which had to be rebuilt in the inky blackness of the Russian night. In many cases tree-trunks were flung across the piers of the bridge in an effort to keep the advance flowing, for orders from Corps became more and more insistent.

By first light the head of the column was near the village of Zaruchye and a stretch of good road surface which enabled the vehicles to roar forward and on to the bridges which the Soviets had ignited before they withdrew. The lead tanks rumbled through the flames, reached the northern bank of the river and took up defensive positions. Behind the advance guard engineers had fought down the fire and strengthened the weakened timbers. Hurtling forward in support came half tracks and lorries and strengthened the bridgehead perimeter allowing the panzer to move forward and to attack the local aerodrome. The mission had been accomplished.

From start line to objective the distance had been nearly 250 kilometres and it had taken three days to cover this. Not so much was this slow rate due to the resistance of the Red Army but rather the effect of mud, marsh and terrain.

The capture of the two bridges had brought the battle group to a point only 120 kilometres from Leningrad and it had traversed an area which the Russians had believed to be impassable to motorised traffic and which they had, correspondingly held with only weak forces.

There is a sequel to the successful capture of the two bridges. The very success of the mission had been its undoing, for in its passage it had torn up the roads and the ground to such an extent that the follow-up troops could hardly use them. New roads had had to be constructed and paths for light traffic laid alongside the main track. The main column made only slow, painfully slow progress towards the battle group now under constant and severe attack by hastily assembled proletarian divisions supported by armour and by every aircraft in the Leningrad garrison. Isolated, besieged and running short of essential supplies there was no logical solution other than to abandon the bridgehead. The columns were brought back across the bridges so recently taken and soon the entire advanced guard was withdrawing towards the main of the panzer division. Mud and swamp had defeated the *élan* and the best efforts of the men of this crack unit. General Mud had proved, indeed, to be the best commander on the Russian staff.

Of the other season, summer, there is little to say. There were no special tactics and the only noteworthy things from the campaigning point of view were the shortage of water experienced particularly in the Ukraine and in the Caucasus and in the absence of dust filters on German tanks. No provision had been made to fit these simple but essential pieces of equipment to panzer engines and the scouring dust of the provinces of southern Russia wore out the pistons within weeks. Not until fine dust filters were issued did German tank engines have so long a life as those in Russian vehicles.

The absence of good roads had less effect in summer but

conversely it was harder for the columns to conceal themselves, for the slightest movement threw up clouds of dust which betrayed the position of the panzers and brought the Soviet fighter-bombers roaring down upon them. They could hardly miss. A panzer division's vehicles on the move covered an area of 11 square miles and in the early days there was no anti-aircraft protection.

16

To Moscow by horse

It is not only human beings who suffer during times of war. Animals, too, particularly horses, have always been exploited and used in battle. One benefit, perhaps, of the invention of the internal combustion engine is in the replacement of animals by machines so that never again will men on battle fields hear the screams of wounded and dying horses.

At the outbreak of the Second World War the British Army was the only completely mechanised force in the world. Except for the mounted troops of the then Household Brigade horses had been replaced in cavalry units by armoured cars or tanks and quads had taken over from horses the task of towing artillery pieces. In every other army there was a great dependence upon the horse. The German leaders, anxious to impress the world with the degree of mechanisation that their own force had achieved, displayed their handful of steel grey, half-tracked vehicles on every possible occasion and thus convinced the world that all their regiments were equipped with armoured carriers and prime movers. The truth was completely the opposite; there was an absolute dependence upon the horse for over eighty per cent of the motive power. The mass of the army which followed in the wake of the driving armoured divisions moved on foot at the pace of the infantryman or of the plodding horse.

It is quite likely that Hitler may have had every intention of making his army an all-mechanised armoured force, and it was perhaps in pursuit of that plan that he scaled down its horsed establishment to a single Cavalry Brigade made up of two mounted regiments. In actual strength the Cavalry Brigade was about that of an infantry regiment but it had a greater artillery establishment than was usual in an infantry regiment of comparable size. Its role was reconnaissance, for it was classified as a highly mobile unit. The Brigade saw service in the campaign in the West and for 'Operation Barbarossa' formed part of Guderian's Panzer Group. It had crossed the river Bug on 22 June and then took part in the battles along the Beresina; had carried out patrols in the Pripet Marsh and covered the left flank of the panzer group as this carried out the great encirclement battle around Kiev.

Surprisingly, the successes which had been achieved and the dependence upon horsed units in the roadless expanses of the Soviet Union were not appreciated and on 3 November 1941 the formation, now the 1st Cavalry Division, was dismounted and converted into the 24th Panzer Division. In order to indicate its horsed antecedents the arm of service colour remained yellow and did not change to pink, the colour of panzer troops. Units within the 24th Panzer Division were organised as if they were still cavalry and titles and ranks formerly used were retained.

At the time of the Cavalry Division's disbandment a number of squadrons were serving on detached duty as divisional cavalry with infantry divisions and, for some reason, were excluded from the conversion. Around the now parentless units there grew up a light cavalry organisation, for events had demonstrated how essential were horses to operations on the Eastern Front. By the middle of 1942 there were strong German cavalry units operational with divisions in such crisis sectors as Rzhev. At a higher military level, some Army commanders formed horsed units of up to battalion strength to carry out patrols and other duties for which infantry would have been too slow and in conditions under which vehicles would have become bogged down. The expansion of these, at first quite unofficial, detachments was then regularised and by the summer of 1943 there was a complete regiment, Prinz Karl zu Salm-Hordomar, serving on the northern front, and another, Prinz zu Sayn-Wittgenstein, serving in the south. Expansions of those regiments in mid-1944 and then amalgamations with the 1st Hungarian Cavalry Division produced the Harteneck Cavalry Corps with its constituent divisions numbered 3 and 4.

Cavalry influences in the German Army must have been unusually strong, for once again special distinctions were permitted. The 3rd Cavalry Division, for example, carried the Schwedter eagle and the 5th Regiment wore a distinction formerly associated with the Imperial Life Guard Hussar Regiment.

How great was the reliance of the German war machine upon horses can best be appreciated by the fact that two and a half million beasts served on the Eastern Front and that more than three quarters of a million were used in the opening battles of 'Barbarossa'. The losses were enormous: an average of one thousand horses died each day of the war with Russia and to obtain replacement animals a vast remount organisation was established in German-occupied Europe and there were great cattle drives of horses from the occupied parts of the Soviet Union to the German Army's remount depots.

Research has shown that the greatest number of beasts which were lost on the Eastern Front were killed by shell-fire or else fell victim to aerial machine-gunning, and that seventeen per cent died of heart failure brought about by the exertion of towing guns or vehicles through the clinging mud. Disease killed the remaining eight per cent: diseases brought about by the mange, lice infestation, or respiratory complaints brought on by the low temperatures. Horses had less resistance to cold than humans. Men could remain alive on the open steppe for a whole night and at temperatures as low as minus ten degrees. German horses died if subjected to the same length of exposure and at temperatures of only minus four degrees. Research also found that one certain strain suffered particularly from lameness while others were prone to ulcers or exhaustion. It is understandable, therefore, that German units tried to bring onto their establishment as many of the native *Panje* horses as they could, for these were immune to most diseases, could resist lower temperatures of cold and were almost tireless.

The beasts used by the Cossack and Kalmuck soldiers who volunteered for service with the German Army were, of course, riding horses but they, too, were smaller than German cavalry mounts although they retained the qualities of stamina and endurance found in the *Panje* horses.

It may seem strange that it is in a chapter on animals that I shall include a short account of those men of the peoples of Russia who fought for Germany. The reason is that it was the mounted units which actually saw active service with the German forces. Most Russian infantry detachments who volunteered to serve did not actually go into battle. This statement requires perhaps a certain qualification. There were small groups of Russians who did serve in German combat units, including certain national groups such as those from Aberdijan. But major units of divisional strength were not fielded by the Germans under the command of Vlassov until so late in the war that their first battle was actually against the Germans – in Prague during May 1945.

At about the time when unofficial horsed units were being formed at divisional, corps and army level, that is as early as autumn 1942, men of the Cossack peoples had approached the leaders of the German forces driving into the Caucasus and had volunteered the services of the men of their nation against the Communist government in Moscow. In common with many national groups in the USSR the Cossacks resented the restrictions placed upon them by the central authority and longed for the free and independent life that they had once lived under the Tsars. To achieve this liberty they were prepared to ally themselves with the Germans. The first squadrons had proved to be of such value, particularly on anti-partisan patrols, that by December regular recruiting had begun and on 1 August 1943 the 1st Cossack Cavalry Division was formally established. In common with most foreign volunteer detachments at that time, there were German officers, administrators and instructors with the regiments, usually in a proportion of 160 Germans to 2,000 Russians.

The constitution of the 1st Division was two brigades, each of three sabre squadrons and an artillery battalion. As an indication of the wide variety of men in the Cossack nation there were regiments from the Don, Siberia, Kuban and Cherkassia in the mounted detachments while men from the Caucasus manned the artillery units. Expansions of the constituent regiments produced a 2nd and a 3rd Division and these then combined to form a Cossack Corps whose language of command was Russian and not German. The Corps eventually passed under SS control in December 1944 and was then posted to Croatia, but before it passes out of this account, some details of the uniform may be of interest.

The fur cap associated with the Cossack peoples was worn by most units and even in action the Cossacks preferred not to wear a steel helmet. On the Kubanka or the Papascha fur cap was worn the German eagle badge and some former officers of the Tsarist army wore the Imperial cockade and carried the Cossack sword, the Shashka. A standard-pattern German Army tunic was worn, in the case of the 2nd Division complete with German badges and with the shoulder straps piped in cavalry yellow. Other units wore the traditional loose trousers of the Cossacks: blue piped in red. The high-shouldered black wool cloak and hood scarf completed the uniform.

Such was the respect that grew up between the Cossacks and their German officers that the commanding general was elected by the Cossack council to be the Hetman, an honour bestowed previously only on the Tsar. To reward these traditionally brave soldiers the Germans instituted and distributed, as early as 1942, a special Eastern Peoples medal.

Another nation, fiercely independent and associated traditionally with the Russian cavalry, was the Kalmuck. Like the Cossacks these volunteered for service, were accepted and then formed into cavalry units by the 1st Panzer Army about July 1942. By August the original detachments had grown to a two-brigade establishment, each of which contained two regiments. German writers, both during the war and those writing more recently, are almost unanimous in their statements that the Kalmucks were the most loyal and the most efficient of all the Russian peoples who volunteered to serve with the Germans. Such was the pride and the independence of the men of that nation that they did not see themselves as fighting for the Germans but rather as fighting with the Germans as allies in a common cause. The Germans serving with the Kalmucks could not give battle orders to the native warriors but had to restrict themselves to instructions on administrative or medical matters. There were, in fact, no German personnel at squadron or battalion level and advisers were to be found only at regiment or division level. The native officers were most proficient for many were graduates of Soviet military academies.

In addition to the army cavalry units and those of the foreign volunteers there were also SS cavalry divisions of which 'Florian Geyer', the 8th SS Division, was the most important. This unit had its antecedents in the horsed troops which were formed before the Second World War and which, by 1940, had been amalgamated into a Totenkopf squadron. Further squadrons were formed during 1941 and by April 1942 there were sufficient to form a regiment. Other expansions during that year raised the strength to that of a brigade and then to that of a division. Some of its regiments were seconded to form the nucleus of other SS cavalry units, particularly that of the 22nd or the 'Maria Theresa' Cavalry Division. This was formed late in 1944 and had hardly reached its establishment when it was put into battle to defend Budapest. In that city it, together with 'Florian Geyer', fought and was destroyed.

From the remnants of men and units which had been in depots or at training schools a new SS cavalry division was formed and this, named 'Lützow', was in action in Poland and in Germany for the whole of its very short life.

On the Russian side there had been cavalry units on the Red Army's establishment from the time of the revolution and Marshal Budyenny, himself a cavalryman, was responsible for the eminent position which mounted units had in the Russian force. In his belief that the horse still had a prominent role to play in war he was supported by Voroshilov who, at the Party Congress of 1934, called for an end to those who demanded the replacing of the horse in the military sphere.

It was not until 1936 that the five cavalry divisions in the Red Army received once again the title of Cossack, for the Soviet authorities had made the most strenuous efforts to break the nationalistic feelings of the Cossack nation. With the restoration of the name the principles of the mounted arm were laid out afresh. The 1938 Cavalry Field Service Regulations laid great stress on the light and mobile role of cavalry but stressed also that mounted units were capable not only of tactical operations but that they could make independent, strategical moves. To achieve these they could be totally self-reliant or could be combined with other arms of service to give increased impetus to their actions. The role which was given to the cavalry unit determined the fire-power which it controlled and this could be increased to any required degree.

The standard cavalry division had three mounted regiments and an armoured component which varied in size from battalion to regiment, depending, as stated above, on the role which was given to the division. The standard artillery regiment was of five batteries but this, too, could be increased for added support. Each cavalry regiment, although smaller in size than an infantry regiment, had the same fire-power and this amount of support indicates the importance which the Red Army Command placed upon their mounted arm.

By the opening of 'Operation Barbarossa' the total number of cavalry divisions serving with the Red Army in western Russia was twenty-eight and these covered the withdrawal of the Soviet Army in the first months of the war. The vital part played by Cossack units is reflected in the fact that four corps of cavalry were promoted to the status of Guards Cavalry Corps. It was cavalry which led the counter-offensive in the winter of 1941–42, just as it had been attacks by Cossacks which had surprised German units who had believed themselves to be safe in rear-line areas. The Soviet cavalry proved that no part of the hinterland was safe from their infiltration, that no river was a barrier and no terrain condition an obstacle. Just as they had formed the rearguards, as they had brought in their spoiling attacks against the German assaults, so did the Red cavalry spearhead the advances of the Red Army and were the first troops into the outskirts of Berlin.

The use of dogs in war has generally been restricted to their carrying messages or mess tins of food to isolated trenches in dangerously exposed sectors of the line. The Soviets during the Second World War, however, employed them in a new and more sinister role. On some sectors of the Front in the early months of the campaign the animals were used as anti-tank mines.

This phenomenon was first encountered on the central Front and, initially, the connection between packs of dogs on the battlefield and the destruction of tanks was not apparent. Then the body of a dog killed before it had had the chance to carry out its destructive mission betrayed the Russian secret and more details were gained through interrogation of prisoners. The principle of training was simple. Meat was thrown under the body of Russian tanks and thus the dogs grew to accept the link between the vehicle and the food. In action the dogs had explosive strapped round their body. A detonator was fitted so that it stood up like an antenna and the head of the detonator was fitted with a graze fuse.

In action the dogs would be kept hungry for a day or two and then would be fitted with their exploding devices. When released the animals would race to find the expected food under the oncoming German tanks. The graze fuse would be activated and the panzer would be destroyed. The alarm caused by the presence of the animals racing across the battlefields led to a wholesale destruction by the German Army of all dogs which were found. Suddenly the use of dogs ceased and the reason was a simple one. The tactic had recoiled upon the Russians. The dogs, of course, were not selective and could not distinguish between German and Russian vehicles. There were sufficient cases where the Soviet machines were blown up by mine-carrying dogs for the Red Army to order their withdrawal and thus the exploitation of dogs in this fashion ceased.

The German tank men would well be forgiven if they thought that every living creature in Russia was against them, particularly in view of the telex message from Army Operations Section of OKH and sent to all Army Groups. This read: "A panzer division on the Eastern Front which had placed its vehicles under cover and in a warm place, in accordance to standing orders, found that when an alarm call was received only 30 per cent of its vehicles were ready for action. Mice had gnawed through the electric leads on the engines of the tanks."

A Staff Officer with a sense of humour had annotated the document with the words "Soviet mice!!!!"

Ruki verch (hands up). A line of Soviet soldiers, captured in the summer offensive of 1942, file past a German infantryman with a raised MP 40.

In the summer of 1942 armour and infantry collaborate closely in clearing a village in the Ukraine.

Grenadiers of Army Group South on an anti-partisan sweep in the autumn of 1941.

A panzer division begins to deploy for attack during the first weeks of the war with Russia.

The face of the German soldier. A young lieutenant and his men fighting in the battles along the Don during the summer of 1942.

Right: The German front line along the Donets river during the summer offensive of 1942.

Forward Observation Officers of the artillery, wearing camouflage nets; Rzhev front, 1942.

Above: This rutted track along which the motor cycle combination is travelling is the road through the vast fields of sunflowers to be found in the Ukraine.

Right: By the winter of 1942/43 suitable winter clothing had been issued to the German Army. Men of a panzer grenadier unit from Army Group North keep warm round a fire.

Below: A panzer division moving up the road towards Stalingrad, during the summer offensive of 1942.

Above: A blizzard on a road in the central front sector during the winter of 1942/43.

Below left: A German staff car driving through the slush on a main road in Russia during the winter of 1942/43.

Below: A grenadier patrol in protective clothing, moving out. On the central front during the winter of 1942/43.

The German winter warfare handbook of 1942. These drawings from the handbook indicate the thoroughness of German research into the problems of winter warfare.

Drawing 63 shows how trenches could be covered with brushwood and snow so as to provide both cover and camouflage. Drawing 67 shows how a tree dragged behind a vehicle will cover the marks of tyres or tracks.

Bild 63.

Bild 67.

Bild 79.

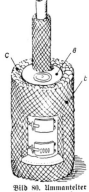

Bild 80. Ummantelter Schützengrabenofen.

Figures 79 and 80 indicate how heating methods were tried. In fig. 80 stones placed around the central stove become hot and can be carried by sentries as a sort of hot water bottle while in the open.

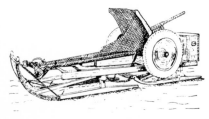

Bild 18. 3,7-cm-Pak, verlastet auf Schlitten 500 kg (Hs. 3).

Bild 20. Kleine Feldküche auf Schlitten 500 kg (Hs. 3).
10 Winterkrieg

Bild 19. Pak 38, verlastet auf Schlitten 1000 kg (Hs. 5) (mit verladenen Schlittenkufen zum Instellungbringen).

Wheels were useless in snow and sledges were used to transport weapons or vehicles which would otherwise have been immobile. The three drawings 18, 19 and 20, show how the German Army attempted to overcome the problem of moving heavy pieces of equipment through snow.

Drawings 54 and 55 show face camouflage and the correct way in which a man dressed in winter-camouflage overalls should move forward so that he is not silhouetted against the dark trees.

Bild 54.

richtig   falsch

Bild 55.

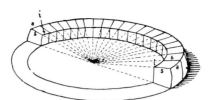

Bild 5. Der erste Ring des Iglu, halbfertig.

Bild 6. Iglu mit 4 Widerlagern im 4. Ring.

The construction of igloos would have been effective in the more extreme cold temperatures of the northern front, but this type of shelter was unpopular with German troops. Figures 5 and 6 show stages in the construction of this ice shelter.

warme Sohle

Stroh-Einlage

Bild 70.

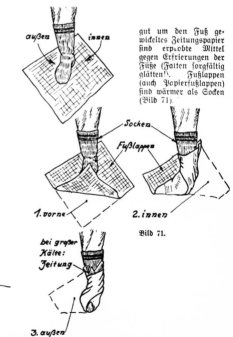

gut um den Fuß gewickeltes Zeitungspapier sind erprobte Mittel gegen Erfrierungen der Füße (Falten sorgfältig glätten!). Fußlappen (auch Papierfußlappen) sind wärmer als Socken (Bild 71).

außen   innen

Socken

Fußlappen

1. vorne   2. innen

Bild 71.

bei großer Kälte: Zeitung

3. außen

richtig   falsch

Mit Stroh oder Papier ausstopfen

seits vom Ofen aufhängen oder aufstellen.

Bild 75.

Personal protection against extreme cold included the insertion of straw into jack boots and the wrapping of feet in foot-cloths or even newspaper. Drawing 75 shows the wrong and the right way in which wet boots should be dried out.

A sentry in a communication trench on the northern front in the winter of 1942/43. He is properly equipped with the camouflage mantle and draw string hood.

Below left: German ski-troops after having stormed a Soviet-held position during the winter of 1942/43.

Below: Part of a German armoured column advancing into the recaptured city of Kharkov in March 1943.

17

The weapons of the Eastern Front

"Bring up the assault artillery ..."

*"The life of a soldier of the assault
artillery is short but eventful"*

Although it cannot be claimed that the concept of self-propelled
assault artillery was a German one, nor that such vehicles were first
used in the war between Germany and Russia, it cannot be denied
that they set their mark upon the fighting on the Eastern Front, that
it was in that war that their potential was first fully realised and that
it was there that they achieved the importance which kept them for
decades as a main weapon in military armouries.

Since the invention of cannon one fact has been obvious, a fact
which the battles of the First World War had served to underline:
namely that when infantry broke into enemy defences it was then
that they stood in the greatest need of massive and well-directed
artillery support. The communications systems of former days had
lacked the flexibility required to switch the guns with speed on to
fresh targets and to bring down concentrations of fire immediately
these were required. German attempts during the First World War to
resolve the problem of an 'artillery fire gap' included the use of horse-
drawn or man-towed infantry assault guns, whose volunteer teams
brought their pieces forward with the infantry wave and thus gave
the required close support to the attack. These were assault guns in
the truest sense of that term and their daring occasioned the crews'
heavy losses which rose even higher when, after the introduction of
tanks, they formed the first anti-tank gun teams.

In 1935, von Manstein, at that time serving in OKH, reconsidered
the idea of assault artillery in the light of modern developments and
suggested that a tracked chassis, powered by an internal combustion engine, should form the gun platform. There is not space
here to record the arguments which took place in the German Army
for and against this new concept.

The main opposition came from the 'panzer idea' officers who
feared that the production of SP guns on tank chassis would reduce
the flow of tanks to them, reduce the numbers in service and,
consequently, weaken their particular arm of service. Although a
need for assault artillery was eventually conceded neither the
panzer nor the artillery high commands were willing to devote effort
to organise the new arm. Neither would accept it as part of their area
of responsibility although it did eventually come under the aegis of
the Gunners. As a direct result of this procrastination SP battalions,

and later brigades, did not form part of the establishment of every infantry division as it had been intended they should but were held as a sort of strategic reserve and designated as army troops.

With the principle of assault artillery accepted the time had come for practical planning. A variety of tracked chassis were tried but it is, perhaps, with those of the Pz Kw III and Pz Kw IV that the German assault artillery of the Second World War is most closely identified. To accommodate the 7.5cm L/24 gun, which was mounted upon the chassis, the entire turret had to be removed. This reduced the vehicle's total weight and lowered both its centre of gravity and its silhouette: two considerable advantages.

To protect the crew against shell-splinters and small arms fire an unroofed box of 2cm-thick armoured shields was fitted round the outside of the machine. Later in the war more sophisticated designs, totally enclosing the gun platforms came into service. Nevertheless, some guns continued for the whole of the war to be mounted within an open box shield.

Since the gun was considered simply as a forward firing artillery piece on a mobile platform the traverse was limited to twelve degrees on either side of a central line and elevation to plus thirty degrees. Certain improvements in both traverse and elevation were later found to be essential but it can be seen that, as opposed to the rotating turret of a tank which could swing the gun to bear on its target, the whole SP vehicle had to be pointed directly at its objective.

Preliminary trials carried out in 1937 demonstrated that SP crews could hit a target faster and more accurately than tank gunners. SP men, bracketing their mark like conventional gunners, could effect a killing shot within three rounds. Panzer gunners, on the other hand, shot themselves towards their objectives, required more ammunition and thus more time to achieve the same result. Despite these satisfactory tests and the fact that SPs were cheaper to manufacture, their production was still delayed and of the six batteries which had been raised by the time that the campaign against France opened during May 1940, only four saw active service. The successes which those few guns achieved convinced even the most sceptical officers that here was a weapon of unusual versatility. Full-scale production was ordered, but to make good the years of neglect was not an easy task and by the opening of 'Operation Barbarossa', there were still only eleven battalions on establishment. An immediate and dramatic expansion was ordered when SPs demonstrated their great value and flexibility during the opening months of the campaign in the East.

Although there were many changes and improvements in the gun carriage the standard weapon remained the 7.5cm gun. In 1943 the L/48, a longer barrelled version of the original L/24, was introduced and the increased range of which it was capable allowed it to 'kill' Russian tanks at great distances. A further upgunning was carried out between the end of 1944 and the beginning of 1945, when the L/70 version of the 7.5cm was fitted.

For as long as the SP was considered solely as a piece of assault artillery to accompany the infantry, it was clear that, in addition to the flat trajectory field gun, a high-angle weapon for indirect fire was also needed. Retention of the 10.5cm howitzer after the circumstances on the Eastern Front had changed completely did not find total approval. This reluctance on the part of SP crews was justified when the role of the SP vehicle changed to that of a tank destroyer, a task for which the howitzer was completely unsuited. In the context of that change in the war situation which came about during 1943, it must be mentioned that, in addition to the standard SP gun, there were others in service which were in effect purely anti-tank guns on SP chassis. In the latter stages of the war it was not possible to distinguish between the SP and A/T roles, for both types of artillery were then used for the same purpose. Thus it was possible to find in early 1944 units named as assault artillery brigades, SP anti-tank battalions and tank hunting battalions all carrying out the same tasks in the same fashion.

There was a range of vehicles as varied as the names they bore and some types of chassis lent themselves to their new role more readily than others. Among the most successful can be considered the 'Hetzer' a 16-ton Czech Pz 38(t) chassis carrying the L/48. The Jagdpanzer IV, a tank destroyer on a Pz Kw IV chassis, was fitted with the L/48 when it first entered service during 1943 and was then upgunned with the L/70. In the same year the 'Ferdinand', later to become the 'Elefant', was introduced. This was a piece of SP anti-tank artillery, armed with an 8.8cm gun, L/71, carried on the chassis of a Porsche Tiger, the Pz Kw VI.

During 1944, the Jagdpanther, an 8.8cm L/71 anti-tank gun on a Pz Kw V chassis was introduced and towards the end of the war a 12.8cm gun, L/55, was fitted into the chassis of a Tiger II, the Henschel Tiger. Only a few of these vehicles ever saw action.

Keeping pace with the development of the SP guns was the parallel development of close quarter anti-tank weapons capable of being used by a team of two or, sometimes, by a single man. These constituted such a danger to SP guns that a permanent escort of infantry had to be assigned to each gun. Thus, to sum up this introductory section, the concept of assault artillery within the German Army changed from the initial idea of a mobile gun whose task it would be to blast a way forward for the infantry, to become a mobile anti-tank gun, so vulnerable to assaults by enemy close range weapons that a permanent guard was needed to protect it.

That SP guns were successful cannot be doubted and their achievement in the German service can be assessed in the number of 'kills' which were claimed. By the end of May 1944, more than 20,000 had been logged and this figure rose to 30,000 by the end of the war. The greatest number of victories were achieved on the Eastern Front against the T 34 and other Soviet tanks with their 7.5cm and 8.5cm guns. So successful were the German SP gunners that it was a standing order to Russian tanks crews to avoid a duel with an SP if at all possible.

The startling numbers of 'kills' claimed by SP crews were met with scepticism until certain senior officers carried out personal inspections of battlefields and were convinced that the tallies had, indeed, been accurate. To quote the example of only one brigade: this, during a fifteen month period in Russia, destroyed more than 1,000 Soviet machines. When it is considered that the average daily strength of the brigade was twenty 'runners' and that the unit must also have spent some time out of the line refitting and resting, then the full measure of the fighting ability of the gun grews can be gauged. According to Alfred Müller and Hugo Primozic, two of Germany's most able SP commanders, the secret of the German victories lay in the fact that they were better gunners than the Russians and in battle usually scored the first shot. A comparison between the assault artillery and the panzer arms also shows that, gun for gun, the SPs gained more 'kills' than did the tanks.

Until 1943 each man in the SP gun arm of service had been a volunteer, maintaining, thereby, a tradition born during the First World War. If the same proud claim could not be made in 1944–45 on behalf of each and every man of the assault artillery, then it was certainly true of the great majority, for no fewer that seventy per cent of the gunners were still volunteers, men whose pride it was to answer the call "Bring up the assault guns".

Tactics developed for new weapons are often rules of thumb, elementary and sensible practices put into writing, then refined, codified and set out as guidelines for the successors of those who pioneered them. Before going on to describe the actions of a few assault gun units and personalities, let us consider the instructions as these were laid down in 1945 in 'Leadership and Employment of Assault Artillery', a document brought out by the OKH.

From the 10,000 word text the following points have been taken and must be considered as the way in which, theoretically, it was intended that assault artillery was to be used.

> Assault guns are armoured artillery whose task it is to serve in the front line and to give close support to the infantry attack by beating down the enemy's weapons or fire. The platform is mounted on tracks, capable of cross country performance and armed either with a gun or a howitzer. Through a combination of fire-power, mobility, armoured protection and instant combat readiness, whether leading an advance guard or forming the point unit during a pursuit battle, assault guns are the decisive means by which a commander can control the changing circumstances of an engagement; enabling a point of maximum effort to be formed quickly, to support a weak flank or to add power to a counter attack.

The basic organisation is along the lines of field artillery and when used as front line artillery, SPs close the gap formerly existing by providing maximum support during those times of crisis which occur during an attack. In cases where field artillery is unable to support front line troops SP guns can be called upon, as a temporary measure, to carry out that role. Assault guns have a decisive effect when formed into a compact group and put in at the point of main thrust. This effect is reduced or lost completely if the unit is split up.

The handbook stated that the assault gun brigades were usually allocated to infantry or to panzer-grenadier divisions and less frequently to panzer divisions. Although the brigade was administered by the senior artillery commander the regulations laid down that an assault gun unit would come under the command and orders of the formation which it was to support – one generally not lower than a regiment. In fact, commanders of assault gun units had had more experience in SP/infantry collaboration than the infantry to which they were subordinate. It was not uncommon, therefore, for a junior officer of the assault artillery to advise an infantry commander of higher rank on the tactics which should be used, on the lines of approach which he wished to follow and, in some cases, on the conduct of the battle. This situation was particularly apposite in those circumstances where it was essential not to waste the element of surprise by the premature employment of the SP guns, and it says much for the flexibility of the German military system that such advice was not merely accepted but was often sought by the infantry commanders.

Continual emphasis was laid on the employment of the whole brigade as a single unit in a single mission although it was appreciated that terrain conditions or the tactical situation would not always allow this. Under such circumstances it was allowable to employ a battery but finer sub-division into troops was to be avoided wherever possible. Once again it was appreciated that, for example, in street fighting or in forests a whole battery could not be deployed and single troops might be employed. It was absolutely forbidden, however, to commit a single gun to offensive operations, for experience showed how important it was to have a second vehicle to hand to overcome the difficulties of ground or of mechanical failure. This last instruction could not always be adhered to in the latter stages of the war, for all too often there were only single guns to cover vast stretches of the front line. The initial establishment of independent batteries in 1940 led eventually to amalgamation into battalions, each of three batteries. There then followed an increase in the number of guns per battery from six to nine and, subsequently, to ten. These thirty-one gun battalions were eventually renamed brigades at the end of 1943, without, however, receiving any increase in strength. The brigade was the major tactical unit and plans were made to raise the establishment of guns from thirty-one to forty-five but the deteriorating situation in the latter years of the war prevented this proposal being completely carried out.

The composition of a brigade was an HQ with a troop of guns, varying in number between one and three, under direct control. The HQ battery also contained a supply squadron, a light workshops platoon and a recovery troop. The fighting component of each brigade was three batteries. Within each of these there was a battle squadron, an ammunition squadron, a workshops group and the train.

Each battle squadron retained one gun for the CO and disposed the others in two troops each of three guns and another troop of three howitzers. The war establishment of an Assault Artillery Brigade was:

HQ staff and headquarters
    battery: 143   All Ranks including 8 officers
Each fighting battery: 101   All Ranks including 3 officers
The grenadier escort: 198   All Ranks including 2 officers
Motor cycles or tracked vehicles: 9
Light trucks and cars: 23
Heavy trucks: 62
Half-track vehicles: 8
Trailers: 18

Each gun had a crew of four men: commander, driver, loader and gun-aimer. The loader also operated the wireless set. The standard uniform worn by assault gun crews was a double-breasted tunic, similar in cut to that of the tank crew but was in field grey and not in 'panzer' black. Red piping, indicating the Artillery arm of service, was worn round the shoulder straps.

According to the section in the manual which dealt with tactical employment the gun was used while the machine was halted. This usually happened while the infantry was moving from one bound to another, according to the principles of fire and movement. Using direct fire good results could be achieved at distances up to 2,000 metres but the most effective distances were up to 1,000 metres. The 7.5cm gun with a high muzzle velocity, flat trajectory, accuracy and good powers of penetration fired several types of shell, the selection of which depended upon the target to be engaged. High explosive was recommended for use against field fortifications, heavy weapons and observation posts. Tanks, of course, were fought with armour-piercing shot and the same type of ammunition was used to destroy pill-boxes. The 10.5cm howitzer, firing high explosive ammunition, was particularly effective against infantry targets, soft skin vehicles and marching columns.

Where the enemy made an attack combining both armour and infantry, SP guns engaged the tanks while the howitzers bombarded the follow up infantry in order to separate these from the armour and to leave this unsupported.

Although another of the most important tasks in any operation was to fight down enemy armour, the early regulations stressed that assault guns were not to be used in a purely anti-tank role and emphasised indeed that, unlike tanks, they were not suitable for independent operations but could only achieve their successes when collaborating closely with infantry or tanks. Events were to show the reverse to be true and that it was SPs upon whom the infantry relied, convinced that as long as the assault artillery was in the line the situation was in hand. By the end of the war it was the panzer which had had to become the SP gun.

The greatest advantage possessed by SP units was the element of surprise. Shock is, possibly, the better word. To preserve this advantage movement forward was made if possible by night. The noise of the SP approach during this march into the front line positions was concealed by the use of loud speakers, by driving tractors around on other sectors of the front or even the firing of an artillery barrage. Assault artillery usually took no part in pre-battle reconnaissance and was not intended for use in roles which could be carried out by the field artillery or by the heavy weapons sections of an infantry unit.

Experience soon showed that not only could SP artillery undertake approach marches to battle by night but could also move long distances during the hours of darkness; always accepting that adequate reconnaissance had shown the ground to be passable, with neither swamps, heavily cratered areas, trenches or steep slopes to negotiate. Night marches did, however, require an even closer co-operation with the infantry and also imposed a severe strain on the vehicle driver.

This was especially true of driving in wintry conditions and where possible night marches at that season of the year were avoided. More than fifty centimetres of snow reduced the vehicle's performance and increased the petrol consumption. Thus, except when fighting a battle, the assault artillery was tied to roads free of ice and snow. It was even more important in winter that vehicles travelled in pairs for, in bad going, it was only towing by the second machine which enabled another machine ditched or trapped in snow-drifts to be still a 'runner'.

Across country the radius of action of assault artillery was up to eighty kilometres but this distance was reduced by terrain conditions, climate factors and the strain to which the worn-out vehicle motors had been subjected. The amount of time which could be spent in a battle depended, of course, upon the amount of ammunition carried and the speed with which this was shot off.

The gun platform was fitted with internal racks to hold the forty-four rounds of ammunition which made up the standard load, but battle experience soon showed that this number was far too few and most vehicles were then fitted with unofficial, external racks. By this means the gun could stay longer in action without having to return for fresh ammunition, but experienced crews who were aware that the imminent battle might be a long one or that there might be difficulties with supplies of ammunition would layer the gun platform floor with shells. In this fashion it was possible to on-load up to 120 rounds but it does not need to be stressed that this extra weight strained the SP's engine, reduced its performance and shortened its life as well bringing about a dramatic increase in fuel consumption.

In addition to these difficulties when the L/48 gun was brought into service the extra weight of the gun raised the machine's centre of gravity and made the SP top-heavy. There was also a reduction in the number of rounds of L/48 ammunition which could be carried and even with layering the gun platform the maximum was ninety-six.

In the earliest days the infantry group being supported by the gun moved on foot, but the practice was then introduced of carrying them on the vehicle and of towing the heavy weapons behind the SP. Eventually, this portering developed to the point where the infantry were 'lifted' for long distances and thus brought very quickly into action. The portered infantry had certain duties and had to indicate to the SP commander areas of bad going, minefields, the presence of enemy anti-tank guns or enemy aircraft.

The regulations stressed the importance of the SP commander advising the infantry that at certain times during the battle his vehicles would have to withdraw for refuelling. To maintain infantry morale and to reassure them that they were not being abandoned, the SP commander had to ensure that not all his vehicles were withdrawn at one time and that, if possible, there were always more guns in the battle line than were being refuelled or re-ammunitioned. Another factor to maintain morale was that where possible a permanent infantry detachment was allocated to a particular SP. Where this was not practicable it was stressed that the same SPs should support the same infantry unit.

In those chapters of the regulations covering collaboration with other arms of service emphasis was placed upon the absolute need for the closest possible liaison. It has already been explained that under usual circumstances an assault gun stayed with or slightly behind the infantry line and bombarded the enemy positions. Then, when the infantry moved into the final assault the gun would pass through the foot troops to engage the enemy more closely. This stage of the assault was made in open formation and the infantry were warned of the dangers of gathering behind the SP or of walking in its tracks; heavy losses could be caused to men clustering close to the machine, for enemy artillery fire was always directed against the SP guns.

During an advance the gun could move ahead of the infantry, in effect blasting them on to the enemy position, but in close country, or when driving through such crops as maize or sunflowers, the infantry moved ahead of the vehicle to protect it against enemy close-quarter attacks.

Later, when the development and use of short range anti-tank weapons threatened the safety of the assault artillery each brigade had seconded to it a permanent escort of Panzergrenadiers. This escort divided on a platoon basis: one to each battery. A further sub-division allocated sections of grenadiers to troops which then apportioned these to the individual vehicles. The main task of the grenadier escort was to ensure the security of the vehicle while it was in the line, to protect it when it had fallen out through mechanical defect and to guard it when out of the line. The regulations warned infantry commanders against considering the grenadier escort as storm troops and stressed that they were not intended to carry out operations independent of the machines which it was their duty to guard. When the SP unit was withdrawn from the line the grenadier escort went with it.

Subordinate detachments of SPs with the infantry reverted back to battery control at the end of a mission and a battery returned to brigade until the next operation. During the longer intervals maintenance tasks were carried out and the mechanical perform-ance of the vehicle was checked. At the end of four or five days of combat it was essential that assault artillery detachments were withdrawn from the line for a long period to enable vital maintenance to be undertaken. Where the withdrawal of the entire unit could not be undertaken due to the intensity of the fighting, then the local infantry commander had to accept that these would be a lower degree of support, as some part of the SP unit would always be in workshops, and that this situation would continue for consider-able periods of time.

These workshops were located, whenever possible, in large buildings so that repairs could be carried out under cover and in well lit surroundings. Warm conditions, it was stressed, were particularly important during the winter when maintenance and repairs both took longer to carry out and to complete.

To maintain the close collaboration which was required in SP brigades, an extensive and very sophisticated communications network existed, both within the brigade and from it to those whom it supported or who supported it. The means of communication were wireless, telephone or runner. Messages passed by wireless were subject to interception by the Red Army and the Germans, being aware of this, ordered that radio was only to be used out of the line for messages which could not be relayed by other means, during action or at such times when an order could be immediately obeyed. Morse messages were usually sent in code but on those occasions when they were sent *en clair*, no unit names were given, nor positions stated. Ranks, titles, dates, times and figures were omitted.

Each SP in the battle squadrons had a 10-watt short-wave set (Fu5) and there was a 30-watt Command network which went out on a 'brigade wavelength' and whose subscribers were the brigadier, the three battle squadrons and the several liaison officers. Telephone hand-sets were used to communicate with the grenadier platoons, where tracer, pistol flares, arm movements and verbal messages were also used to pass orders or to indicate direction.

Liaison with the Luftwaffe was maintained by an Air Force officer at Brigade HQ equipped with a Fu7 wireless set and who received reports from aircraft and directed the SPs on to centres of enemy resistance. In like fashion the Luftwaffe liaison officer could bring down his aircraft to support a forward movement by the assault artillery. By day orange smoke or markers indicated the position of friendly troops to the aircraft and the direction or location of enemy targets was indicated by firing tracer ammunition.

The regulations detailed very exactly the duties and tasks of the components of an assault artillery brigade. The document was intended to be the handbook on assault artillery and tactics but by the time that it appeared circumstances on the Eastern Front had changed. Assault artillery was, in the final years of the war, no longer able to be used in the sense of artillery closely supporting the attacking infantry. Rather had the role changed to that of a tank hunter and as Germany's military situation deteriorated the task of the SP and the tank became interchangeable. Neither arm of service could initiate extensive operations but was put in, seldom in brigade or battalion strength and more usually as a troop or even as a single vehicle, to carry out tasks beyond their capabilities.

Assault artillery brigades were army troops and were usually committed to battle in small numbers. There are left to us, therefore, only the actions of sub-units: miniature dramas played out by a handful of machines in some isolated sector of the vast battle line. Thus the accounts which follow are short and deal with a single mission of limited duration. Often only the barest details are given in the unit war diary and it is the reader who must imagine for himself the drama, and the feeling of the gunners as they fought from the first intoxicating weeks of the new war through bitter winters, scorching summers, grinding dust and clinging mud against what became an ever increasing flood of Soviet armoured fighting vehicles and who continued the fight for nearly four years.

Theirs was the courage of desperation and many, particularly in the final days of the war in East Prussia, went out as the last vehicle in a unit, riding out to certain death but determined to show by their action that the spirit which had animated the first assault gun teams was still alive.

From the stories of the hundred or more battalions, brigades of assault artillery and the fifteen independent batteries which served during the Second World War it is difficult to select just a few. The accounts given on the following pages are only examples of the type of action in which the SPs took part and must serve to illustrate the record of all who fought that arm of service.

18

Assault artillery in action on the central front in the early days of the war with the Soviet Union

During the second day of the war with the Soviet Union, men of an infantry corps in Army Group Centre broke through the Soviet field defences which lined the frontier but were unable to exploit the situation because of the determined resistance which was being maintained in a small village east of the river Bug. The situation was not clear and no idea of the type and weight of the Russian resistance could be gained from the garbled accounts which were reaching divisional headquarters. One thing was certain: the infantry attack could not continue until the resistance had been broken. This was a perfect opportunity for the SPs to prove their ability and a battery was ordered forward to break the tenacious Soviet defence whose main resistance was located in the houses and gardens at the eastern end of the village.

The guns came up to the western outskirts and a plan of attack was agreed with the infantry CO, whose battalion had been separated from the reconnaissance detachment which it had been his task to support. Soviet resistance had to be broken as quickly as possible so as to gain touch with that isolated detachment of the advance guard.

The lead troop rolled into the village halting and firing as they located points of resistance and had soon broken the infantry resistance. Then as the lead vehicle turned a corner to enter the main square it saw and identified a heavy Soviet tank; it halted, swung round, opened fire and with three shots had destroyed this. The three guns of the troop then passed out of the village, deployed into line abreast as a vedette on either side of the dirt road and waited for the infantry to come up so as to lead them forward. As they were moving into position three Soviet T 60s roared towards them in line ahead. The SPs now at the halt opened fire. One shot hit the third tank of the Soviet line and the 7.5cm shell tore apart the five-ton machine. Meanwhile the other T 60s, relying upon speed to outflank the German gun line, had deployed and had closed to within 100 metres, firing their 2cm cannon as they advanced. The commander of the nearest SP swung round his vehicle in a tight arc to meet the threat from the flank and even as the manoeuvre was completed his gunner reported 'on target' and opened fire. The lead tank was hit and burst into flames. The surviving Soviet machine tried to turn away to break off the engagement but was hit and destroyed before he could escape.

Then ahead of the SPs and on both left and right flank violet flares rose into the summer sky. The reconnaissance detachments were reporting the advance of a heavy concentration of Russian armour and it was clear that a major attack was developing. The divisional commander sent anti-tank and 8.8cm flak guns to reinforce the SP troop and all was made ready to receive the enemy. But he was still hidden by the lie of the land and could not be seen. The first indications of his presence were the sudden explosions which crashed around the SPs. A heavy Russian tank, probably a KV I, concealed in some woods, had moved out of cover and opened fire. The German 3.7cm anti-tank guns returned fire and although they lacked the velocity to penetrate the thick armour, hits which were scored forced the KV I to withdraw into the cover of the trees from which he had emerged. His action had, however, served to distract the attention of the gun line from the Red tanks which now swept down like a cavalry charge.

A mass of Soviet armour in line abreast roared across the open ground and the three SPs deployed into open order to receive them. The flak and pak line remained silent, ready to engage any break-through which the Soviet wave might achieve. The SP tactic was constant and rhythmic: advance, halt, fire, advance, halt, fire. The SPs had the advantage of firing from a halted, and therefore stable, platform; their crews had greater experience and their guns had better sighting equipment. Quickly they began to pick off the Soviet machines with precision. The muzzle velocity of a 7.5cm gun firing solid shot was 580 metres per second, and this force tore the Red machines apart like over-ripe fruit. They were stopped or caught fire and then blew up as the flames reached the ammunition lockers.

The open heathland was now dotted with the wrecked and burning hulks of the first wave but then charging through the black and greasy smoke came another advancing and firing as it charged. Meanwhile in front of the SP line an infantry battle was being fought out. A German battle patrol had been given the task of capturing the Soviet soft-skin vehicles which had accompanied the first tank wave but it was fought back with great determination by the lorry drivers, by baled-out tank crews and by the Soviet infantry who had been escorting the lorries. Even as this miniature battle was taking place the SPs had opened fire upon, and had destroyed, the second wave of Red armour. Following close behind this and charging between the broken hulks of the first two ruined waves came a third, charging at the German line.

The pace and fury of the battle had by now produced a crisis for the SP guns; they were running short of shells and fuel. Instead of withdrawing the vehicles to 'A' Echelon, the battery commander brought the lorries up to the guns and set chains of soldiers to carry ammunition to the waiting vehicles. The men worked like demons, all the time under the fire of the Russian guns and completely exposed to the open terrain. The machines were refuelled and rearmed in time to engage the third line of Soviet tanks as they approached to within killing range. This wave, too, was tumbled into ruin and with its destruction the heart went out of the Soviet troops, for no further attempt was made by the Red armour to impede the German advance. With the destruction of the third wave the way forward seemed to be clear; the SPs could withdraw.

As the guns moved westwards through the village and towards their concentration area, there to carry out repairs and maintenance, a column of T 60s, which had probably broken through on the right flank, emerged from a small wood about a kilometre's distance from the village. Quickly the troop commander disposed his guns in the gardens of the houses and under the trees in the village. The Red tank line came on, seemingly not having seen the SPs, and these waited, holding their fire, until the T 60s were at point blank range. The three 7.5cm guns spoke; three T 60s began to burn and before the Soviet machines could deploy the guns had fired again and again until the whole Soviet group had been destroyed.

When the battery took tally of its 'kills' at the end of the day, only those Soviet machines totally wrecked or destroyed by fire were allowed to be included as 'confirmed'. Even with these limitations it was found that the SP guns had destroyed forty Soviet machines. Within twenty-four hours of the opening of the campaign these weapons had proved their worth and had gained the confidence of the infantry of Army Group Centre.

19

An SP detachment in the closing stages of the encirclement battles around the Kiev pocket

AUTUMN 1941

Other chapters of this book will describe the encirclement which took place around six Red armies in a pocket near Kiev during the autumn of 1941. From that account of the movement of armies and corps, let us pass to warfare on the Eastern Front as it was lived by one assault gun group which battled long after the actual investment had ended, to compel the trapped Soviet forces to surrender. The following account records the passage of about a week in the time during which the Red forces were dissipated or destroyed.

The assault gun unit had been resting after a long day's march, the men wrapped in a single blanket and trying to sleep in the oppressive heat. The fierceness of summer had already passed but this was an Indian summer of abnormally high temperatures and a terrible humidity. There was no other sound than the sentries moving among the parked vehicles. But from the west came the distant thunder of gunfire and on the far distant horizon Very lights rose and fell in the hot and sticky night. Theoretically, the group was a long way behind the German front and in what should have been a safe area. This belief was soon shattered when sudden bursts of machine-gun fire were heard close at hand, the bullets whistling through the dark and ricocheting off the steel sides of the assault guns.

The crews, who had been lying huddled on the ground around their guns, responded immediately and took post waiting for orders. To the rattle of machine-gun fire was now added the dry coughing sound of Soviet mortar bomb explosions and fragments of casing went whining through the night air. The detonations followed each other in close succession so that it was difficult to determine the sector from which the mortars were being fired but it was alarming to realise that the machine-gun fire was coming from a hillside which neighbouring troops had declared to be free of the enemy.

From the first burst of Russian machine-gun fire to readiness for action had taken no more than two minutes but these 120 seconds seemed to last an eternity. There was a sudden break in the noise of machine-gun and mortar fire and in the heavy, sudden silence there came from the upper slopes of the hill from which the machine-gun fire had come the long drawn out 'Ooray' of the Russian battle cry coming nearer as the Soviet infantry charged downhill towards the SP battery.

Magnesium flares fired from the SPs lit up the dark night and the battery crews began firing their MG 34s and firing HE into where they thought the enemy should be. 'Cease-fire' and then it was quiet again with no noise save that of a single mortar bomb or an odd burst of machine-gun fire where an anxious gunner thought he could detect movement. The flares sank and died, seeming to make the darkness of the night more intense. The German gunners stood straining their eyes and ears trying to pierce the silence and frantically guessing at the identity of every unusual noise. Now there was an absolute quiet which lasted and lasted. The gunners began to show signs of restlessness. They could not believe that they had crushed the Soviet infantry attack so quickly, but on the other hand, why had they not persisted in the assault. When the minutes grew and stretched into half an hour the battery commander ordered a partial stand-down but with a double sentry on each gun.

Shortly after midnight the Russian attack pattern was repeated. Machine-gun fire, a barrage of mortar bombs and then the battle cry. The alarming feature of this new attack was that the 'Ooray' came from much nearer, indicating that the Soviet soldiers had been crawling forward undetected through the dark night. At the first burst of Russian machine-gun fire the SP gun crews had begun to sweep the area with machine-gun and with machine-pistol fire but from the almost continuous 'Oorays' it was clear that the distance between the Soviets and the guns had been reduced. Soon Soviet hand grenades began to fall in the German perimeter.

Near the SPs a battalion of infantry had been alerted at the first bursts of firing and had begun to organise a counter attack. One of the SPs was sent to liaise with the infantry and at battalion HQ a short O group decided on a plan of action. The SP together with a 2cm flak went forward until it had reached the leading company of the infantry battalion which was already engaged in a fire fight with Red Army infantry. The SP loaded with high explosive and moved to a better tactical position and opened fire. For twenty minutes the gunners loaded and fired while the other crew members fired machine guns, their tracer bullets indicating to the 7.5cm gunners the direction of the enemy groups. Belts of ammunition rattled through the breeches; gun barrels glowed red from the rounds which were being fired through them, but fire was not halted for long. A quick flip to open the casing – out with the hot barrel and in with a new one. Carry on firing.

Slowly the Soviet troops, illuminated clearly in the light of the white flares, began to give ground and, the assault artillery leading, the German infantry drove back the retreating enemy across the ground out of which they had poured.

Slowly the fighting died away and the front began to quieten. The SP gun returned to its battery area to refuel and to stock up with fresh ammunition. The main stage of the battle which had begun shortly after midnight had lasted nearly two hours and already the stars in the eastern sky were beginning to pale.

Dawn was misty, indicating another hot and humid day, and the battery moved forward on a general north-westerly line, passed through the infantry battalion's positions and began to climb a small rise from which the commander expected to gain an idea of the terrain before him. The guns had been in almost continuous action since July and with lack of maintenance it was no surprise that during the day's drive several of them developed faults and had dropped out. Only two 7.5s, a 10.5 howitzer and a 4.7cm continued the drive. The latter was mounted on a Panzer I chassis and was unsuitable to engage any target save small tanks and infantry groupings.

During the greater part of the morning drive there had been no sign of the enemy and no sound of battle. The Ukraine lay silent and shimmering under the hot sun. Clouds of dust which the vehicle tracks threw up showed the route which had been taken. At the top of a slight rise the small group halted for a rest, a cigarette and the chance to eat. In front of the SPs the ground dropped gently for two to three kilometres before rising again to a ridge some four kilometres distant. The advance continued towards the far ridge and when the group reached the foot of the rise it halted again, resting the engines before they pulled the SP carriages up the ridge to the high ground.

The CO who had been observing the countryside through his glasses suddenly halted his traverse and concentrated upon a small mound, one of a dozen or so which dotted the ground. The more he looked the more he was convinced that the mounds were artificial and his suspicions were confirmed when a group of Soviet soldiers sprang out of cover, ran to a mound and began to tear at the foliage. The leaves and branches fell away, exposing the barrel of a gun which began to bombard the SP group. Even as the first Soviet shots were still whistling through the air the other mounds began to move and soon it was clear that these were the vehicles of a Red tank battalion which had been carefully dug in and camouflaged.

The Russian tank engines roared as the vehicles backed out of the hollows in which they had been hidden and with a squealing of tracks the machines stood on the upper ground forming a rough semi-circle around the four German guns. The Soviets had already begun to open fire but their guns did not have the range and as they did not move it was obvious that they were under orders not to advance.

On the German side the battery commander had already radioed for assistance and had been told to stand fast until the other vehicles of the battery could reach him together with other reinforcements. Both sides lay there in the hot afternoon sunshine, each waiting for the other to move. Inside the metal boxes which formed the protection for the crews of the SP guns the heat was oppressive, for there was little shade and none could be sought, as constant vigilance was needed. As the afternoon wore on the heat became more intense and by 14.00hrs it was almost unbearable.

A Soviet T 34 made the first move. In an obvious attempt to test the alertness of the German gunners it was driven downhill and disappeared into a *balka*, one of the gulleys which are a feature of the Ukrainian landscape. The intention was perhaps to attack from a flank and the crews of the SP guns could hear the roar of the T 34 engine as the vehicle traversed the group's front. Through binoculars the battery commander saw where the T 34 would emerge from the *balka* and ordered one of the 7.5s to cover the gap. The roar of the Russian tank engine echoed from the walls of the shallow ravine and then increased to a deafening scream as the driver revved up. The T 34 shot out of the *balka* and the first shot from the 7.5 exploded behind him for the gunner had not allowed for such a turn of speed. The second shot was a direct hit and even though the Russian tank maintained its course for a few seconds and even fired off a shot, there was a sudden burst of flame, an explosion and a cloud of thick and heavy black smoke.

There was again a short period of silence as both sides waited and then a KV I charged downhill firing its machine gun. The great tank then halted and opened fire with its main armament, advanced, halted and fired again. A third advance brought it to within 1,500 metres of the German group and then as it drew nearer but still remained on the upper ground an SP opened up. Simultaneously the KV fired and although the Russian gun had the higher rate of fire the gun laying was poor. The second shot from the German 7.5 was a direct hit. Only two of the Russian crew were seen to escape. A third Soviet machine, another T 34, then made the downhill descent but instead of pressing home its attack concentrated on trying to drag the KV back into the Russian positions.

The 7.5 gun opened up and its fire was supplemented by the howitzer which bombarded the area around the two Russian machines with high explosive shells, driving into cover the crews attempting to fasten the tow ropes. With both machines now immobile the German SP had sitting targets and with one shot the T 34's turret was blown off and the machine began to burn.

Another long pause followed and then a T 34 came down to try a second rescue attempt. This machine, too, was shot to pieces and brewed up. Pillars of smoke rose into the still September air. A fourth T 34 made its move to rescue the KV, and to cover the charge it made the remaining Russian machines opened fire. Their shot fell short but the 7.5 scored another hit. There was another hiatus in the fighting and although the Russian tanks milled about the area none of them dared to come down to engage the Germans who were still surprised that the Soviets had not made a mass move or at least attempted to enfilade the German guns.

The hot and humid weather was followed by a thunderstorm which now broke and drenching rain fell, turning the churned up surface into thick clinging mud. It was fortunate that the supply lorries had by this time reached the battery position for soon they were held immobile.

Under cover of the pelting rain the Soviets mounted an attack, a combined infantry and armour assault whose approach was first hidden in sheets of rain, and not until they were as near as 800 metres did the infantry wave supported by three T 34s come into view. The SPs deployed ready to destroy them. The first two Soviet tanks were destroyed, each with a single shot, and seeing this the third turned away but was hit just below the turret. The force of the impact knocked this off and it flew through the air for a considerable distance. The fire from the SPs and machine guns crushed the infantry assault and the Red Army men retreated into dead ground. The howitzer then began to 'search' the area and from the shouts and screams which were heard it was clear that the gunners had hit a strong concentration of enemy soldiers. Action finished then and the rain slackened off to a drizzle. By last light even that had stopped and the battery leaguered for the night, secure in the knowledge that other troops had come up and that another SP battery was on its right flank.

Just after 'stand-to' next morning a Fieseler Storch dropped a message to the battery that two groups of Soviet tanks were approaching: one from the north-west and one from the south-east. This was obviously a major attempt to escape the Kiev encirclement and all units in the area were put on full alert. A defensive line extended for about five kilometres in length and was manned by the SP batteries. Behind this mobile gun line was a battery of 8.8cm flak guns and echeloned in depth a company of panzers.

There was no action during the whole of that day and the two enemy tank groupings seemed to have gone to ground. The gun lines were stood down at last light. In the early hours of the following morning, just before first light, the German force was brought to instant readiness when tank track noises and engines were heard. Once again the morning mist reduced visibility and the outlines of the Soviet vehicles did not become visible until the group was under two kilometres away. The tactic which the Red armour adopted was one of desperation. The tanks advanced in a single block, making no attempt to deploy but charged with all guns firing. The German gun line held its fire as the Russian machines entered a killing ground. The flexibility of the German Command had changed the battle plan even as the Soviet tanks advanced and these were now being lured into a three-sided trap. Each flank was an SP battery and the base of the trap was the 8.8cm flak gun line. The panzer company made ready to close the neck of the trap once the Soviet machines had entered it. Still the Soviet machines raced on; still there was no sound from the German guns.

When all the Soviet tanks were inside the trap the order to fire was given and in the growing light each tank was clearly visible. As a single volley the German guns fired and within five minutes fourteen Soviet vehicles had been destroyed or were burning. A few turned to escape but others pressed home their attack, charging forward right up to the muzzles of the 8.8s.

There was firing on the right flank of one SP battery and a fresh group of Soviet tanks, determined to escape the encirclement, attacked the German gun line. The SPs swung to meet the new challenge, opened up and shot the Russian charge to pieces. Other attacks came in, every fifteen minutes, precise and unfailing. This punctuality allowed the German guns to be replenished with ammunition and for the gunners to prepare to meet the next charge.

There was silence again and through the radio the battery commander received the news that the two Soviet tank groups had been destroyed or dispersed. The fighting was over. On the next day there would be a move westwards to invest more closely the Soviet pockets still holding out or seeking to escape through the German panzer ring, but for that evening there would be a chance to rest.

A tally before darkness fell showed that during the morning of the Soviet escape attempt forty-nine Russian machines had been destroyed. The SP 'score' was twenty-nine. September 1941 had been a good month for the assault artillery battalions.

A Winter Drive

Although it has been stated in former pages that night drives during the winter were to be avoided there were circumstances and crises which required SP battalions to undertake such moves.

The following pages recount one drive undertaken during the Soviet winter offensive of 1941–42 when the German line was broken through on a massive scale. Only the prompt intervention and determined resistance of assault gun battalions were able to halt the Russian advance and, to stiffen the crumbling German front, SP units were gathered from sectors of the front hundreds of kilometres distant from the scene of the bitter fighting. This account speaks of the strain of a drive in winter along bad roads and in pitch blackness.

We used the bell in the village church tower as a signal and one night it began to ring. Our unit was supposed to be out of the line but this was an alarm call and an O Group was summoned. Fitters had to report to the Transport Officer on the state of their vehicles while the gun commanders went to battery headquarters. The information which we received was that we were to bolster up the defensive front at Volkov about 300 kilometres away. Army and divisional reports spoke of the appalling road conditions. In addition to the poor surfaces was added the fact that the weather was terribly bad, with constant snowstorms and freezing temperatures.

Quickly we stowed our kit and then came the hardest part of the operation – we had to start the engine. You can imagine the difficulties if I tell you that it was twenty-eight degrees below zero and that our vehicles were in the open although covered with tarpaulins. The method we used to thaw out the engine was to partly fill empty ration tins with earth and to pour on to these either methylated spirit or petrol which we set fire to and put one under the engine and another under the differential. Of course we had to do this under cover of the tarpaulin firstly because the heavy material acted as a windshield and, secondly, because we had to hide the light from the little Russian Rata aircraft which flew over us all night long dropping anti-personnel bombs.

The driver and his mate made the last minute adjustments; we had to cover 300 kilometres in winter conditions and we had to make the distance in the shortest possible time.

By the time that the engines were running smoothly we had had a hasty breakfast and within an hour of the alarm bell sounding we were on our way through the pitch dark night. Can you imagine what it was like for the driver? The roads were rutted and icy and we skidded from one side of the highway to the other. Of course, we were driving without any lights, not even the blacked-out headlights were allowed for fear of Soviet air attacks and it was a most difficult task to keep in touch with the vehicle in front without crashing into him. Quite frequently one or the other of the heavy machines went into a ditch or ran off the road and had to be brought back again. It was no easy task to reverse on the road; slowly, very slowly, while the crew wrestled to fix the towing cables on to the stranded machine. Then both motors would roar as the one tried to tow the other out.

For us on the gun platform the journey was a nightmare of freezing cold. The platform was open at the top, the wind howled through the many apertures and slits in the armour plating, the snow was pouring down and all through the night one man of us had to be standing up helping the driver to keep in contact with the rest of the column. The maximum period of time that any of us could stand up facing into the wind was a quarter of an hour. Quite literally we turned blue in the face from the freezing cold. The whole body then became an aching mass of pain and when one was relieved, to sit with one's back against the bulkhead but out of the wind and to have the first puff of a cigarette was absolute luxury. We thought the night would never end.

Although we passed through a large number of villages and towns we made no stop until well after first light when we halted for a meal. We had been driving for ten hours. Some of us tied tins of food around the exhausts and heated them that way. It was quick but if they were left in position too long the tins would nearly explode when they were opened, pouring scalding liquid over hands that were freezing with cold. As the light grew stronger we could see that there had been heavy fighting around the town in which we were halted. Trees had been smashed by shell-fire, snow covered tanks and guns lay wrecked and broken all around us.

We turned off the main road and bumped our way across corduroy roads built by our sappers during the summer across a swamp. It took us a couple of hours driving along those poor roads and through the dark, silent woods until eventually we came on to the main highway. The pace of the column increased and we covered fifty kilometres quite quickly and then pulled off the road again to halt under the cover of some trees. This was another meal halt and the hot coffee helped to start the circulation going and enabled us to thaw out a little before we moved off again into the gathering darkness. To give the drivers a rest we halted for the night in a village and were billeted in individual houses.

There was no large barn into which the SPs could be parked and thus be under cover and our drivers tried to keep the engines warm by packing them in straw and by covering the engine area with bales of hay. Others had the sentries start the engines every couple of hours. When we set off again the area through which we were passing was said to be full of partisans and we kept our rifles and machine pistols ready for action. Most of us held our weapons inside our buttoned overcoats but one of us had to have his at constant readiness and that man covered the bolt action with his gloved hands. Of course, the man on the MG 34 was also in a state of instant readiness and our turn to stand up in the freezing cold came round as usual every fifteen minutes.

About midday we had a longer break and during this the machines which had fallen out rejoined the column. The workshops detachment had worked wonders repairing the causes of the breakdowns, often with the mechanics lying on their backs in the deep snow tinkering with something underneath the vehicle or struggling with frozen hands to repair the tracks. With the whole group once more assembled we set off across country, up hills and down dales. In the valleys the snow was so thick that we had to shovel a way through it even though the blizzard which was raging filled in the gaps almost as quickly as we shovelled them clear.

Another night halt in another village and then we spent a day, or the greatest part of it, carrying out maintenance on the vehicles and weapons. We were very near our objective now about eighty kilometres separated us from Volkov and could expect to go into action within a day or two. We had to be in tip-top condition; all our strength was needed, every machine had to be put in.

In the morning the orders were given: "advance to contact" and we carried out the final parts of our journey in tactical formation and across country moving towards the sound of the guns whose fire was brought to us on the incessantly blowing east wind. Our halts were fewer now with just time to eat our haversack rations which we carried inside our coats so that they would not freeze solid.

On one sector through which we passed the casualties were so recent – a Cossack cavalry group – that the dead horses and men had not been completely covered with snow. This must have been a reconnaissance group which had penetrated our forward zone. By midday we had reached the frozen river on whose far side lay our objective. Slowly the drivers negotiated the steep and icy banks, skidding and sliding down on to the ice which was thick enough to bear the weight of our vehicles. We moved across one at a time so as not to strain the icy surface. Then we climbed the eastern bank of the river, crawling up in a slalom fashion, towing other vehicles where this was necessary. The gun crews broke off branches of trees and put these under the tracks so that they could get a purchase on the slippery ice. The engines of our SPs howled like demons with the strain and it was not until after midnight that our battery had grouped in the square of the little village which was our final objective. We were told off for billets and had just settled in when O Group was called. We were under orders to attack the next day. We were back in the line again.

A platoon of SP guns in action against the Soviet thrust to capture Rzhev

AUTUMN 1942

Among the names of the towns and localities on the Eastern Front which appeared frequently in the communiqués of both protagonists there was one, Rzhev, which gained a well-merited reputation for the bitterness of the fighting which raged around it. A glance at the map shows that Rzhev formed a spring-board for any German advance towards Moscow and for any Russian offensive aimed at the capture of Smolensk. The strategic importance of the town cannot be too strongly emphasised and the desire of the Soviet High Command to gain possession is reflected in the masses of men and machines which they poured into the fighting around it. Of all those battles around Rzhev the following two-day account of an SP unit describes at the lowest military level the fighting as it was seen and experienced by the men of that battery during the autumn of 1942.

Only two of the four SP guns which made up the battery were available for the actions which are described here. The other two vehicles were with another infantry regiment. Ground conditions in the area were poor with great areas of swamp preventing the rapid movement of the guns from point to point.

It was the task of the two remaining SP guns to support the German infantry and to break up the Soviet tank assaults. The tactical situation was poor, for along the infantry front ran a deep ravine and on the left flank there was a wood which the Russians could use to concentrate their armour before launching it against the thinly-held German grenadier line. Additional cover to a Red advance was provided by the tall fields of maize. All this natural cover meant that the Soviet attacks could be concealed until at some points their troops were almost within hand grenade distance of the German line. An open slope which ran down to the ravine had been the scene of several Soviet armour thrusts and the hulks of smashed machines dotted the ground. Reports of fire from some of the wrecked vehicles had been unable to determine which machines still had their main armament intact and which would, therefore, act as artillery to cover any future attacks.

Towards mid-morning a sudden puff of smoke from the edge of the wood heralded a barrage of shells which crept towards and then over the German trenches and headquarters. The slight coughing sound of the Soviet field artillery was soon hidden in the bellow of the heavier guns and curtains of black dust from the explosions hung in the still summer air. As soon as the barrage had passed over the grenadier positions these latter quickly emerged from the slit trenches and dugouts fully aware that close behind the drum fire and almost within range of the flying splinters of shell casing there would be the first waves of Red infantry, accepting casualties from their own shell fire in order to cross the German line before a strong defence could be mounted.

The Red infantry had not, on this occasion, kept pace with the barrage and the time which elapsed allowed the grenadiers to make ready for action. To their front they saw advancing some way away down the slope line after line of brown uniformed men, the sunlight reflecting from their fixed bayonets. Much nearer were those Red Army groups which had emerged from the ravine and which were now advancing in long unbroken waves across the open ground.

Even though German machine-gun fire had begun to cut great gaps in the Russian lines the SP platoon commander, observing the pace of the Soviet advance from an observation post on the crest of the hill, saw that the enemy had begun to gain ground on the left and had already begun to outflank the grenadier positions. The Soviet barrage was brought back again to bombard the German defence, Russian heavy machine-guns swept the area and the air was alive with the whistling noise of bullets and of shell splinters. Away on the left flank the fury of the Russian artillery bombardment rose to a climax in an attempt to crush all resistance and to create a gap through which the Red assault might pass. The SP platoon commander knew his time had come and waved – "Bring up the SPs". Once inside his vehicle he gave orders to advance and instructed the second machine to guard his back and flank and to fire independently.

The two guns set off in echelon driving below the hill crest and toward the threatened left flank, the gunners preparing the HE shells as the vehicles bucketed across the ground pock-marked with craters. "Target – Red infantry, 800 metres", "On target", "Fire" – and the shells smashed into the Red infantry marching stolidly forward. The force of the explosion tore bodies apart; limbs and torsoes were flung about and the steel shell fragments cut down all the men within range of the lethal fragments. Still the Red infantry pressed forward. The gunners loaded, aimed and fired with frantic speed until there were only three HE shells left in the locker and then, rolling out of the cover of the woods, through the honey-coloured maize towards the gap which the Red infantry had forced, came wedges of T 34s, each of them covered with sixty soldiers riding into battle. The gun was loaded with AP and the third shot at 800 metres struck the lead tank of one wedge. It caught fire and blew up, flinging the infantry into the air. The other machines tried to make their way into the ravine but a second was hit before he could gain safety.

Not until then did the platoon commander find that his gun had been in action unsupported by the second vehicle. This was nowhere

to be seen and there was not time to use the radio for Soviet infantry
had made fresh gaps in the German line. Quickly the commander
warned battalion and asked for the ammunition truck to be sent up.

With only three HE and eight AP shells left the SP rolled forward
to attack once again the oncoming Soviet enemy. The high explosive
shells smashed back one Red infantry group and the armour-
piercing shells forced back another unit of Soviet tanks which had
begun to emerge from the ravine. By now the SP was almost
surrounded by Russian soldiers firing their rifles at the machine and
at the platoon commander who stood resting a machine pistol upon
and firing over the shield into the thick mass of brown uniforms
which swarmed around his gun. Slowly the SP withdrew through
the Soviet troops, its crew using hand guns to keep the Soviets at
bay. At the refuelling point there was the second machine immobile
with steering trouble. Quickly a human chain was formed to transfer
shells to the platoon commander's vehicle. Russian artillery
observers, up with the forward troops, and who had radioed the
position of the SP gun brought down an accurate and heavy fire all
round it. Fountains of earth rose up around the infantry and
gunners, as they sweated to transfer the ammunition. At last it was
finished, in time to move forward again to support a grenadier
counter-attack. Keeping pace with the infantry line the SP advanced
slowly, every crew member alert for the enemy. Suddenly a small
group of T 34s, six to eight in number, were made out milling about
in the dust and smoke which overhung the battlefield while the
Soviet infantry which had begun to pull back in face of the counter-
attack were moving down into the ravine. Leaving the grenadiers to
deal with the withdrawing infantry, the SP opened fire upon the
armour. Within minutes three of the T 34s were in flames and,
covered by the confusion, the others escaped into the safety of the
ravine.

It then became clear that the Soviet artillery observers had found
the SP again for another heavy barrage fell around the machine. It
was time to pull back to refuel and to load up with fresh ammunition.

It was now late afternoon and the fighting had lasted for the
better part of the day without the Russians having forced a
breakthrough or the Germans having been able to force back the
Soviets from the gains which they had made. Over the radio came
the news that Stukas were coming in to dive-bomb the enemy in the
ravine and there was a bustle of activity in the German line as men
laid out markers to show the front line and draped swastika flags
across the front and rear deck of the SP guns. At 17.05hrs the Stukas
flying high peeled off and screamed down in almost vertical dives,
laying their bomb line only a hundred metres or so ahead of the
grenadiers' trenches. With incendiary and high explosive bombs the
Ju 87s crushed the Russians and as the aircraft flew away T 34s
began to come out of the burning fury of the ravine. They emerged to
be engaged by the SP whose 7.5cm gun firing AP shot destroyed

three of the Soviet machines with only five shots.

At last light the gun withdrew to laager and a tally showed that it had 'killed' nine Soviet machines, of which seven had been T 34s.

On the following day the roar of tank engines from behind the Soviet line well before dawn heralded an attack out of the rising sun. Sixteen machines moved forward towards the SP, unaware that during the night the single gun had been reinforced by a further three pieces. Covered by the darkness in which they were still hidden, the German vehicles moved forward in line abreast, opened the distance between each other and, moving up the reverse slope of the ridge, took position 'hull down' behind the crest. The light of a late summer dawn shone on one T 34, then behind this a second, a third and then others, all maintaining a distance between vehicles and their infantry loads. The platoon commander selected the first tank of the line as victim and with two shots had halted it. The fifth round caused it to burst into flames. Meanwhile the other guns had opened independent fire and had begun to score hits. Those situated on the flanks of the Russian advance could fire into the thinner side armour. Soon a second T 34 was in flames, the bright flames lighting up the dawning day. The other tanks of the Soviet squadron then swung towards the ravine, seeking for safety, but four more were hit and began to burn before they could pass out of sight. Once again the Russian artillery barrage began to crash around the SPs which then withdrew for refuelling.

The next barrage by Russian artillery then showed that there was a lack of communication between guns and armour, for a heavy bombardment suddenly crashed down upon that sector of the line through which the T 34s should have smashed. It was clear that there were no observation officers in the forward zone, otherwise they would have noticed that the armoured assault group had been destroyed. Without orders to cease firing the guns continued to lay a creeping barrage intended to accompany the tanks which had been destroyed and which were burning on the steppe.

A crisis point had been reached in the battle and to force its way through to Rzhev STAVKA brought up masses of men and tanks, regrouped its forces and flung them into the attack. This all-out assault was intended to capture the town. Behind the almost continuous barrages came fresh masses of tanks moving forward in solid blocks and wedges, while further back from the battlefield their advance was in line or column formation.

The SPs had by now been reduced to only three 'runners' – the fourth had dropped out with mechanical trouble. Far away on the left flank a group of Russian tanks moved out of dead ground and headed for the woods in which it was obvious they would group before charging down upon the German grenadiers. As part of the T 34 squadron passed across the front where the SPs lay in hull-down positions the platoon commander opened fire upon the lead tank and gained another victim. With a second shot he hit the last

vehicle in the column and this burst into flames. Immediately in
front of the German machine a small group of Soviet tanks had
swung away from the main body and had begun to drive towards the
ravine but the commander, recognising the danger, swung the
vehicle, laid on to these new targets and opened fire as they came
into range. The second shot claimed another victim – the fourth that
morning.

All across the open land masses of Soviet men and machines were
moving and it was clear that the German SP group could not long
survive. There was a sudden double blow on the chassis of the
commander's vehicle as shells from two Russian artillery pieces
scored hits and slowly the SP moved backwards and across the crest.
But before it could reach the safety of the reverse slope there was a
third hit which caused so much smoke and produced such a burst of
flame that the gun layer thought that the machine was on fire and
baled out.

A quick inspection showed that the damage was only superficial.
The most serious losses had been to the range-finder and the
antenna, both of which had been torn away, and to the recoil
mechanism on the gun, which was damaged. Some plates of the
front armour had also been torn away and the rivets sheared off. The
intensity and accuracy of the Soviet artillery fire was now so great
that two other SPs were hit and damaged so badly that they had to
leave the battle. The platoon commander took over the last
remaining gun, having first had it loaded with as much ammunition
as it could carry, and moved forward again to support the hard-
pressed grenadiers.

The front line zone was now a mêlée of Russian infantry and
armour as the Soviet High Command put more and more squadrons
of tanks and more and more battalions of infantry into the fight.
During the next hour the single German SP destroyed a further four
Soviet tanks, holding back the Red Army men from achieving a
complete breakthrough. Up and down the weakening grenadier line
the SP cruised, bringing moral support to the infantry and at the
same time avoiding being pinpointed and therefore a target for the
enemy gun batteries.

During the afternoon the Stukas came back and a combined force
of all arms – guns, foot and one SP supported by the dive bombers –
crushed the Russian movement and destroyed its will. The STAVKA
plan for a breakthrough had been thwarted and in the counter-
attack which the German troops then launched the single SP went in
against conventional, as well as unconventional, targets. One of
these, a dug-in T 34, was destroyed with two shots, and a second T 34
which came up to support the dug-in machine was shot to pieces.

The evening mist then reduced visibility and made identification
difficult but the commander detected movement as two T 34s
emerged from the ravine in front of the German line and he
destroyed them both. His total of 'kills' for that day had been eleven.

21

The 249th Assault Artillery Brigade in action during the battle for Berlin, 1945

In the first weeks of the new year of 1945, the Red Army opened a major offensive along the whole length of the battle line and the shattered units of Army Group North were driven back under the heavy blows of the Soviets striking for the Baltic in the area of East Prussia.

Among the mass of units fighting desperately to hold back the Russian drive was the 249th Assault Artillery Brigade and this paraphrased account of its final battles and eventual destruction have been taken, with permission, from Franz Kurowski's book *Sturm Artillerie*.

Although regulations stressed the effectiveness of a brigade being used as a single unit, such was the shortage of SP batteries, so thin the infantry line and so great the length of front to be covered that the 249th was divided and sub-divided in order that it could carry out the multitude of tasks which were demanded of it. Inevitably, the assault gun detachments were driven apart from each other as the group which they were supporting separated as they moved back under the Soviet pressure. Thus one battery was forced westwards with the main of the Army Group, while the second was driven back northwards until it was isolated and surrounded in a pocket at Heiligenbeil. There on 14 March the battery's last vehicle was destroyed in action and the unit's survivors were posted en masse to 277th SP Brigade. Constricted by the Soviet pressure the surrounded group, supported by one tank and three lorries, nevertheless fought its way through to Danzig and to the German lines from which port it was shipped to Altengraben.

Towards the end of March 249th Brigade, now reinforced by the men from Altengraben, was concentrated in Krampnitz; the depleted ranks were filled out with new recruits and the brigade, with a headquarters battery and three fighting batteries, together with a grenadier escort battalion, was once again ready for action.

The army vehicle parks had no machines available and the drivers of the 249th went to the Alkett factory at Spandau to collect the SPs. Within a few days these were up to battle standard and in the last week of April the whole brigade went out again on active service and took position in the woods surrounding Spandau. Before it had a chance of going into action it was ordered to move with top speed back to Krampnitz where it was intended that it should be put in against the American Forces nearing the Elbe river. At Krampnitz fresh orders were received: the brigade was to move to Berlin to reinforce the garrison which had begun to battle against the Soviet units which had penetrated into the outskirts of the capital. The SPs of 249th Brigade rolled through the Brandenburger Tor on 27 April and set up a TAC HQ at Freidrichshain, from which sector No. 1 battery went out to stiffen the defence in the Weissensee area.

This first posting away of No. 1 battery was a prelude to further reductions in brigade strength, for in the days which followed the guns were distributed, seldom by troop and more frequently as single pieces, to fight at various points along the perimeter where they destroyed Russian tanks which were advancing towards the heart of the city. An idea of the bitterness of the fighting can be gained from the fact that during one three-day period the Soviets lost 180 armoured fighting vehicles.

On 28 April the Award of the Knight's Cross to one of the brigade's senior officers was recognition of the part which 249th was playing in the defence of Berlin but this accolade could not overcome the sense of outrage which the unit felt at the murder of one of its members. Lieutenant Rupprecht, a young officer who had won the German Cross in Gold and had been mentioned in dispatches for bravery, was arrested by SS men while with his supply company and after a drumhead court-martial was condemned to death. His body was found that evening hanging from a lamp post near the Alexander Platz.

On 29 April the remnants of the brigade were ordered to concentrate in a suburban villa sector of Berlin and in the early afternoon the vehicles, which were strung out along the road, came under attack by Russian bombers. More serious than the heavy casualties was the loss of one of the few guns. The strength of the brigade had now been reduced to only nine SPs which were formed into a battle group and put into action along the Landsberg Strasse and on the Alexander Platz. Within a day the greater part of the battle group had been destroyed and on 30 April the last guns went into action near the Technical High School, within whose cellars the brigade had set up its headquarters. Gunners who had no vehicles were grouped as infantry armed with Panzerfaust rocket launchers and set out on tank-busting missions. Fighting round the Technical High School rose to a climax and the last two SPs, starting from a position in the Berliner Strasse, went out against Soviet armour concentrations. Within minutes the first gun was knocked out. Then the second received a hit which jammed the escape hatch but the crew carried on the struggle and went on to destroy another five Soviet tanks. During this unequal battle the tank-busting teams dodged from one heap of rubble to the other and attacked the remainder of the Soviet vehicles as they forced their way past the High School building.

On 2 May, following the announcement of Hitler's death, the CO informed his men of the situation and of the decision to break out of Berlin and to make for the Elbe. Shortly after midnight on 3 May the remnants of 249th Brigade, mounted in a few personnel carriers and lorries, set out for and reached the area of Potsdam. But the river bridge was in Soviet hands and the grenadiers had to go in to attack at close quarters in order to fight a way through. The slow retreat continued with the 249th, now joined by other fragments of other German units, seeking to break out of the encirclement, making their way through a gauntlet of Russian fire. Soon it was clear that it was no longer possible for large formations to escape and that this would be a matter of small detachments filtering through the Russian ring. The 249th had, in any case, broken into two parts, each of which formed a small battle group.

One of these quickly reached the Elbe but the attempt by the second ended in tragedy. Three SPs which had been abandoned by another unit were repaired and taken over. These, together with three armoured half tracks and about 300 soldiers, were concentrated, with the grenadiers grouped round the guns, until the break out began. The SP covering the right flank of the movement surprised eleven Russian tanks and destroyed them one after the other but at Tetzin the whole group was intercepted by a Soviet heavy anti-aircraft battery. One of its guns scored a direct hit on an SP and destroyed it completely. A second SP broke down at that time and when the third came up to tow it to safety the Russian anti-aircraft artillery fire smashed one vehicle and so badly damaged the other that it had to be blown up.

With the destruction of this last assault gun the life of the 249th came to an end. The great mass of men gathered at Tetzin soon passed into Soviet captivity.

22

Hugo Primozic

Germany's most successful SP fighter in Russia

*"Fighting in an SP is the nearest thing that
contemporary ground warfare can offer to the
soldier's concept of a knight in armour."*

AN SS LIEUTENANT

That "a weapon is only as good as the soldier who uses it" is an
axiom which, if true, would show that the men of the German SP gun
units of the Second World War were very good soldiers indeed, for the
quality of that army's assault artillery was frequently commented
upon by allied intelligence appreciation in the most glowing terms.

That most men were volunteers for that arm of service and for the
dangerous tasks which it undertook is just part of the reason for the
successes which were achieved. Added to that was the shock effect
which was produced by SPs on every battlefield and which helped
them to achieve domination over their Soviet enemy. Even when the
Russians produced their own versions of SP guns and turned these
out in thousands, the skilled training given to the German crews
gave them a superiority which brought them victories, even though
heavily outnumbered, over the armadas of Soviet armoured fighting
vehicles.

Knowledge of the deeds of the assault artillery was spread by the
German Propaganda Ministry to a public which wanted to know
about its heroes. The men of the U-boats and the Luftwaffe aces were
familiar to all readers of German newspapers and now there was a
group in the Army whose best soldiers were aces no less than those
men of the Navy and the Air Force. Their names became familiar
through the incredible deeds which they carried out. Among the men
of the SP arm of service who became known and respected for their
soldierly qualities can be included Alfred Müller of the 191st Brigade
who argued with a general on how a battle should be conducted;
Major Peter Frantz, CO of the SP battalion of Panzergrenadier
Division *Grossdeutschland*; Max Wünsche, the CO of the battalion
in the Leibstandarte SS; and Corporal Bernd Naumann of 184th
Battalion. Above them all, however, stands the person and the
record of Hugo Primozic, an NCO, who in a five-month period of
active service was awarded the second and first grades of the Iron
Cross, the Knight's Cross and then the Oak Leaves to the Knight's
Cross. It is Primozic whom I have selected to be the representative of
all that company of men who fought in the self-propelled assault

artillery and it is the account of his greatest achievement that is recounted here.

Hugo Primozic, born in Backnang in 1914, was trained as a locksmith but decided to serve in the élite 100,000-man army of the Weimar republic. The entrance examination and medical to join that army of potential officers was so severe that Primozic was one of only a handful of men accepted on the day of his enlistment.

He was trained as a gunner in the field artillery and fought in the campaign in the west in 1940, but, becoming dissatisfied with the horsed element which formed the bulk of the German artillery at that time, volunteered for, and was accepted by the motorised assault gun arm.

He showed a natural flair for this new type of artillery and so marked was his ability that he soon became an instructor at the training school. His first attempts to obtain a posting to a combat unit in Russia were unsuccessful but finally, in 1942, he was sent to 667th Assault Gun Battalion which was en route to the Eastern Front. From that time the military career of the professional soldier Hugo Primozic can be said to have blossomed.

His first victim was destroyed at a distance of one and a half kilometres but gradually he began improving his tactical knowledge and training his crews until their most successful day of action came when his platoon of three guns halted a Soviet breakthrough attempt at Rzhev. His principles were simple: it was not always necessary to charge at the enemy, rather the Soviet tanks should be allowed to advance. The lead tank or the nearest was not necessarily the one that should be destroyed first, rather it was the most dangerous or the one with the heaviest armament. To achieve a 'killing' shot with one round Promozic would often wait, coolly patient and under bombardment, until the Soviet machine was only metres or so away before he opened fire. His coolness became a byword in the units to which his platoon was seconded and the intensive pre-war training as a gunner stood him in good stead, for he was aware that the first hit usually decided the issue and that an over-excited gun aimer might miss the target and thus lose the contest.

In the early days of his service in Russia he demonstrated this coolness under fire when one morning one of the guns of his platoon suffered a mechanical defect while in action and faced a combined infantry and armour charge. Primozic left his own machine and, seizing the steel wire tow rope, fixed it to the stranded machine. In the hurricane of fire which was poured down upon the vehicles he calmly directed the rescue, and once both machines were under way Primozic seized an MG 34 and drove back the Red infantry which had by now surrounded both SP guns. For this act he was awarded the Iron Cross First Class.

Towards the end of August 1942, the 667th Battalion was moved to the area around Rzhev and during the succeeding weeks fought

against an overwhelming mass of Soviet armour which had been put
in to smash the salient around that town. One of the crises which
arose during the weeks of bitter battle was reached on 15 September,
when the Stalin Tank Brigade was put in to spearhead the drive
which would break the salient walls and cause its collapse. The
phalanx of Soviet tanks bucketed and rumbled its way across the
cratered fields between the railway embankment and the river, past
the shattered hulks of Soviet tanks destroyed in the earlier fighting
and made for the thin line of German infantry.

Sergeant Primozic's platoon was in the line, his three guns
concealed in bushes which grew abundantly, and, hidden by their
foliage, they moved slowly forward undetected by the Soviet
artillery observers until they reached the edge of cover. There they
halted while Promozic went forward to the infantry slit trenches,
carried out a quick observation, decided upon his plan of attack and
returned to his small command.

His plan was simple. Heavily outnumbered though he was, he
would attack the massive wedges of armour and by fire and
movement smash them. Skilful manoeuvre and accurate, fast firing
would win the day.

At 800 metres Primozic's gun opened up and a T 34 exploded in a
cloud of black smoke, yellow and red flames. Load, aim, fire and a
second vehicle, whose gun had begun to swing menacingly towards
the SP, was hit and halted. No member of the Russian crew was seen
to leave the vehicle. The other guns of the platoon were now also
scoring hits and then the platoon commander noticed that Soviet
infantry were accompanying the attack. He switched his gun on to
these new targets as wave after wave of brown-clad soldiers rose out
of the ground as the tanks passed across their shallow trenches and
began to swing forward at a jog trot. High explosive shells from the
SPs tore great gaps in the lines and the Red infantry advance began
to slow, to waver and then to fall back. Then it was time to load with
armour-piercing shells again and one after the other Russian tanks
were shot to destruction or 'caught fire.

During this engagement the three SPs had been moving from one
firing position to another, avoiding the artillery bombardment, the
anti-tank shells which whistled past and the whispering machine
gun bullets. At the end of one charge Primozic saw before him a
Soviet armoured group led by a heavy tank, a 52-ton Klimenti
Voroshilov, which opened fire and scored a glancing hit on the
sergeant's machine. As the Russian solid shot struck and then
ricocheted it rocked the SP so that the shot which Primozic fired from
his L/48 gun struck but failed to penetrate the giant tank. His second
shot, however, hit the Russian machine fair and square, penetrated
it and probably ignited the fuel, for the tank withdrew with clouds of
smoke pouring from it.

While this duel was being fought three T 34s had moved round to
take the SP in flank but with the engine roaring at the effort

Panzer and panzer grenadier troops fighting through a Russian village during the defensive battles of 1943/44.

Left: The infantry battle. Exhausted grenadiers sleep at the bottom of a hastily dug trench after beating off a succession of Soviet attacks. An NCO with a satchel charge keeps watch as his men rest.

An assault gun platoon of StuG IIIs during the Kursk battle of July 1943.

Mountain troops on the central front sheltering from the fury of a blizzard during the winter of 1944/45.

Left: An SS man taking prisoner the crew of a Soviet tank destroyed during the fighting around Kursk.

Panzer grenadiers forming up ready to move forward into an attack during the fighting which took place during the spring of 1944.

Reconnaissance vehicles of a panzer division preparing to take panzer grenadiers into action during the 1944/45 winter battles on the central front.

Vehicles of an SS panzer division grouped ready to move into a counter-attack in Hungary during the winter of 1944/45.

King Tiger tanks in Budapest during its siege in the late autumn of 1944.

Russian rifles with their muzzles pushed into the earth were the signs that the Red Army men

The Russians who fought for Germany. Men of a volunteer Cossack cavalry detachment and the standard of their new allegiance; southern front, 1943.

had given up the fight and had surrendered; autumn 1941, southern front.

An Italian infantry gun in action with Army Group South in the Ukraine in 1942.

A soldier from a Far Eastern regiment of the Red Army captured during the Kiev encirclement battles in the autumn of 1941.

The capture of a Red Army sniper who had been hiding in a dug-out in a corn field; summer 1943.

Grenadiers, having combed a Ukrainian village for the enemy, move in pursuit through standing crops in which Soviet soldiers might be sheltering.

A Russian main road in winter. The two inner lanes were kept free for fast moving traffic leaving the outside lanes for horsedrawn and marching columns. Halfway up the road on the left side is a tractor to give extra power, if this was needed, to bring the vehicles up the hill.

In the first hard winter often the only means by which frozen vehicles could be brought into running order was to light fires under the engine and the gear box.

War on the Eastern Front meant heavy losses. The dead of one Soviet assault on German positions in the central sector of the front during the winter offensive of 1942/43.

Left: In the wintry conditions of the second winter in Russia, a German soldier heats himself a drink over a methylated tablet stove.

Hugo Primozic an SP gun commander. Here seen with Oak Leaves to the Knight's Cross.

Primozic spun the gun on its left track, the sights came on target and two of the Red machines were destroyed. The third escaped.

The stationary SP was now a target for a number of Russian guns and tanks, one of which scored a hit on the bow of Primozic's machine. Driving through the smoke of the explosion his gun opened fire upon this dangerous opponent and flames rising out of the maize field in which the T 34 was hidden showed that Primozic had scored another victory. The Soviet Command then sent in groups of their tanks against the German SP platoon, with more machines of the KV type leading the charges, but assaults were uncoordinated and so few machines were used in each attack that Primozic's platoon could take time to select and pick off the Russian tanks as they roared forward. Within an hour Primozic had 'killed' seventeen Soviet machines.

By the end of the gruelling day the sergeant's total was twenty-four Soviet tanks destroyed. His other guns had scored well and for his part in halting the assault of the crack Russian tank brigade Primozic was awarded the Knight's Cross of the Iron Cross and promoted to senior sergeant. According to the general officer commanding one infantry division, "The SPs of 667 Battalion saved the infantry and solved the armoured problem around Rzhev". Others were more fulsome in their praise and considered that this action had decided the outcome of the battle of the Rzhev salient.

This is not the end of Primozic's story. Three months later, on 11 December, his SP achieved seven more victories and thereby his sixtieth victim. For his continued bravery and devotion to duty he was awarded the Oak Leaves to the Knight's Cross, the first Non-commissioned Officer to receive this decoration. On 31 January 1943 he was promoted to the rank of lieutenant.

23

Hyazinth von Strachwitz

The German Army's most successful tank man

During the war with Russia there were many tank men who rose to prominence as commanders of panzer armies or as general officers in charge of corps and divisions, but below these men – Guderian, Kleist, Model, von Vietinghoff and the others who directed operations – there were hundreds, if not thousands, whose actions at intermediate and low command level were equally as important to the outcome of the clashes of armour. At that level, that of the lowest command, the names of Wittmann and Peiper are well known, but less famous is Hyazinth von Strachwitz, whose exploits with small panzer battle groups gained him a reputation throughout the German Army for cool-headed courage. His country's recognition was a succession of awards of all the grades of the Iron Cross up to and including the Diamonds to the Swords and Oak Leaves of the Knight's Cross.

This is an outline of some of the exploits of probably the most famous of the German Army's tank men at tactical level during the campaigns with Russia.

The von Strachwitzs were Silesian landed gentry with military backgrounds and Hyazinth, after service in both the First World War and the Freikorps, entered the army of the Third Reich. He transferred from the Cavalry to the 2nd Panzer regiment and with that unit fought both in the Polish and the French campaigns. It was, however, during the war with Russia that his ability first came to the fore. His exploits were legendary and his ability undoubted. He himself claimed to have a sixth sense which made easier his task of fighting Russian armour. But it was not only inside his machine that he could fight. On more than one occasion, but first during the fighting around Ivka, his tank was cut off from the main body and surrounded by Red Army infantry keen on capturing a German panzer commander and his machine. Von Strachwitz dismounted from his tank and fought the Russian soldiers in hand-to-hand combat until the fault which had caused the tank to stop had been repaired. Despite a wound – he was wounded in all a total of fourteen times – he climbed back into his Pz Kw IV and led his battalion into fresh assaults.

In one of the speedy thrusts for which he eventually became famous his group of tanks broke through the rigid Russian defence line, then reached and destroyed the Soviet supply echelons before the Red Army. He was, in effect, advancing faster than the retreating Soviets. His battalion knew no rest for he drove it on, as he drove himself on, in a series of day and night drives to confuse and outflank the Soviet Army.

He seemed to be leading every advance. His tank was the first across the river bridge at Pervomaisk and once on the far bank he attacked and destroyed a column of more than 300 Soviet soft-skin vehicles as well as their protective screen of anti-tank and field artillery pieces. His machine led the 6th Army into Stalingrad and, during the months of battle which his battalion endured in and around that tragic city, hundreds of T 34s and other Soviet machines were destroyed.

Upon return from convalescence, for he had been wounded in the fighting around Stalingrad, he found himself promoted to command the panzer regiment of the German Army's crack division *Grossdeutschland*. It was with this new command that his exploits rose from the unusual to the legendary. The military situation facing the Germans at that time was that the army had fewer men and had to hold back a Red Army flushed with success, well-equipped and armed with all the weapons of victory. For the Germans the days of panzer armies achieving strategic victories were long past. Now a handful of machines, capably handled and brilliantly led, had to wrest tactical successes from the numerically superior Red Army. It was precisely this sort of task in which Count Hyazinth von Strachwitz excelled.

On one occasion his group of four panzers penetrated deep into the area behind the Soviet line and lay concealed, waiting for the tanks which he knew must pass that way. Soon an armada of armoured fighting vehicles approached him, not expecting to meet German tanks so deep in their own army's rear areas. With the advantage of complete surprise to aid him his group opened up and within an hour had shot to ruin 105 Soviet tanks; and all this without the loss of a single German tank.

At Kharkov the fire discipline of his crews brought them success against another mass of Soviet machines. By their deliberately avoiding movement or retaliatory fire the Soviet armour was lured into a trap. A column of eighty machines moved during the night upon what they thought was a weakly-held village. At a distance of less than thirty-five metres von Strachwitz's Tiger (he had helped to form the first Tiger battalions) opened fire and blew the turret off the leading T 34. His other Tigers fired their huge 8.8cm guns and within minutes thirty-six Soviet machines had been destroyed, were blown apart or were burning furiously.

From command of a regiment he went on to lead 1st Panzer Division and was then sent as Commander (Armour) to Army Group North. The war, by now, was entering its final stages and Soviet pressure against the Army Group was forcing back its units towards the Baltic Sea. In one attack, which Strachwitz was assured was essential to the plans of OKH, he captured and held the town of

Tuccum, thereby closing a gap in the line between two German Army corps which were holding the crumbling front. In the course of this successful local operation he destroyed a further fifty T 34s or KVs. Some little time later, having been injured in a car accident, he spent much of his convalescent time organising tank destruction teams before returning prematurely to the Front. Here, there was little armour to carry out destructive raids in the rear of the Red Army, the remaining units and machines were too busily engaged in trying to stave off defeat, and soon the last of the panzer force had been destroyed. The war was closing and von Strachwitz dismissed his remaining men so that they could find their way to surrender to the Western allies. He himself struck southwards through Czechoslovakia and the Bohemian forest until he reached Bavaria. There he surrendered to the Americans and passed into captivity.

24

Anti-tank weapons and tactics

It is a surprising but true fact that the German Army, which had made great strides in the design of its armoured fighting vehicles and the way in which these would be deployed and employed in war, had made no comparable advances in the development of anti-tank artillery. As a result those in service lacked the power to penetrate the armour of contemporary vehicles and, thus, the German infantry was forced to depend upon anti-tank weapons which left them almost defenceless against their enemies.

A total of thirty-six guns formed the establishment for a standard infantry division and these weapons were of 37mm calibre and so weak in penetrative power that they were nick-named 'door knockers'. The 37mm could penetrate vertically mounted armour plate of 20mm thickness at the distance of a kilometre, but when the Germans entered upon the campaign in Russia they soon encountered the T 34, whose sloping hull armour was 45mm thick. The German gunners were forced to wait until the Soviet vehicle was at point blank range before they could fire with the certainty of destroying it.

In addition to the ineffectual 37mm guns there were other anti-tank weapons with infantry battalions: anti-tank rifles which lacked the power even of the 37mm. Of course, during the war there were improvements in anti-tank artillery with the introduction into service of weapons with larger calibres, of tapered bores to give greater muzzle velocity and of recoilless cannon, but for purely anti-tank artillery most German units preferred to rely upon captured Russian weapons. The 76mm was a particularly well-favoured piece.

There were weapons in the divisional artillery component which were capable of destroying enemy armour, but these pieces were field guns which lacked the necessary mobility. Then there was found a gun, part of the standard artillery establishment, which proved almost by accident to have the qualities of both penetrative power and mobility. This was probably the most famous of all German artillery pieces – the '88'.

It had been designed, originally, for anti-aircraft purposes but once used in an anti-tank role – in France in 1940 – went on to prove itself in almost every battle on the Eastern Front. It was capable of destroying Russian armour at very long ranges and was so successful and flexible in operation that it formed, in addition to its anti-tank abilities, the field gun role as the backbone in infantry assaults and that of a rock in defence. It was also the main armament in the Tiger tank and its variants.

An increase in the middle years of the war in the number of Russian armoured fighting vehicles and a sharp decrease in the number of German anti-tank guns led inevitably to the situation where the destruction of armour was no longer a matter of infantry relying upon artillery to carry out the task of destroying the enemy vehicles. Now the grenadiers had to close with the enemy machines and destroy them.

There had always been ways in which an agile and resolute infantryman had been able to meet and destroy his armoured enemy. There were soldiers who actually mounted on to their victims. Men who climbed on to the engine casing, poured petrol from a bottle over the engine and ignited it. Others who trotted alongside the tank and wedged between the vehicle's hull and turret a Teller mine which would explode as soon as the turret was swung. Some grenadiers had the courage to push hand grenades down the gun barrels of Russian tanks, while others were able to drop bombs into the open turret and thus kill the crew.

Among the methods of tank busting had been the hefting of explosive satchels or bundles of hand grenades connected to a common detonator and, the simplest weapon of all, the Molotov cocktail. All of these were flung at the machine.

Each of the methods described above had the disadvantage that the grenadier had to leave the security of his slit trench and move into the open where he would be exposed to the fire of other tanks or of the Red infantry which accompanied them. Once in the open the attacking grenadier fought the Red tanks at the closest possible range and then had to escape, closely followed by Soviet rifle, machine-gun and tank gun fire. The successes achieved were unbelievable in their number and most of their victims were 'killed' by the grenadiers in conditions which favoured the defence: in woods or in built-up areas. Training schools were set up in which the newest methods of tank destruction were taught. Part of a translation of an SS training instruction gives an idea of what was being undertaken in the field of close-quarter, anti-tank combat to cover the serious shortage of more formal anti-tank weapons.

SS Headquarters

Berlin

29.1.1943

Subject: Action to be taken during enemy tank attacks and training to fight tanks at close quarters.

In all major enemy offensives strong tank forces are certain to be employed and the ability of a unit to withstand tank attack is crucial if a successful defence is to be maintained.

Success of a deep enemy thrust is not guaranteed because tanks have broken through our positions, so long as the defending troops use their weapons to cut off the tanks of the armoured spearhead from the follow-up infantry. If this can be achieved then even the heaviest armoured attack will fail since a tank unit by itself cannot hold ground for any length of time and is obliged to turn back to refuel and to rearm. Infantry must allow the tanks to 'sweep' over them.

Training, instruction and drill must aim at strengthening the moral fibre, in helping the men to overcome fear of mass tank attacks and in acquainting them with the defensive measures that can be used to fight tanks.

The following facts must be hammered into all troops, but particularly into new recruits:

(1) The danger which an enemy tank presents should not be exaggerated. Inside a shut-down tank it is very difficult to observe or to maintain direction and the armament of a tank is limited. Commanders standing up in tank turrets make excellent targets for snipers.

(2) For a man to leave his position or slit trench exposes him to a tank's weapons. A deeply-dug slit trench protects against being crushed by a tank and against its fire. To abandon a slit trench results in the speedy and unopposed capture of ground by the enemy infantry and the spread of panic in neighbouring units.

(3) The Russian infantry are poor soldiers and can be beaten by a lesser number of Germans. It is important that the infantry notes: As soon as the enemy tanks have rolled over the positions the follow-up infantry must be engaged so as to separate these from the armour.

(4) In future officers must be able to feel confident that where a division of the Waffen SS holds a post that there the front will be firm.

Fighting tanks at close quarters

It is possible to put tanks out of action using means which are not usually considered to have tank-destroying capabilities. To fight a tank at close quarters is not solely the task of the Pioneers but also that of the infantry. It is also important that as many men as possible, from other arms of service, should be trained to fight tanks at close quarters.

The primary aim in training is to overcome any inherent feelings of inferiority when faced with enemy armour ... No attempt should be made to turn training into a drill manoeuvre. This is pointless for there is neither a standard group of men nor a single tactic for fighting tanks at close quarters. Skill and imagination used to the full are the only answers. ...

Undoubtedly the best of all the close range, anti-tank weapons which the grenadiers received was the hollow-charge grenade, issued during the autumn of 1942. The principle behind the hollow charge had been known as early as 1935 and the weapon had been developed for use against the armoured fortresses and cupolas of the Maginot Line. One far-seeing expert, however, did propose in 1938 that these grenades could be used for anti-tank purposes, but his idea was not taken up at that time.

The bell-shaped charge had on its base a number of small but powerful magnets which held it in position on metal surfaces until a short fuse had detonated. In effect the explosion burnt through the armour plate and projected a force through so small a hole that the concentrated power was enormously destructive. The answer to the magnetic grip was to coat surfaces with an anti-magnetic compound, such as concrete, and to corrugate this so that the magnets could obtain no purchase. A weapon is only effective until its counter is produced.

Late in the war one of the products of German research, rocket propulsion, was applied to infantry weapons and the projectors which were designed fired newer types of hollow-charge grenades. The two weapons which came into service were used to combat armour and both had the advantage that the infantryman could fire them from his trench and thus did not need to expose himself to enemy fire. The first of these rocket launchers was the Panzerfaust, designed and introduced during 1942. This was a single shot projector which fired a grenade capable of striking through 140mm of armour plate. One disadvantage of this weapon was that a 1.50 metre-long flame was ejected and this pinpointed the position of the firer. It was also essential that the Panzerfaust be fired from a position which allowed the flame sufficient area in which to escape. In the early days there were hundreds of cases of burning, many of them fatal, brought about by men unaware of this requirement and who had fired the rocket launcher in a confined space.

Improvements increased the weight, range and penetrative power of the Panzerfaust and by the end of the war the bomb could be projected a distance of 150 metres, five times the original range. So effective was this weapon and so feared was it that a determined grenadier group armed with the launchers could halt a major tank attack. Crews of allied tanks took protective measures and some Russian tank men fitted mattresses as an emergency measure until armoured skirts could be welded on to the outside of their vehicles to protect wheels, tracks and transmission.

The simple, robust and very effective Panzerfaust was lavishly distributed on every front and to every type of unit, including the Volkssturm and the Hitler Youth tank-busting teams which fought the advancing Red Army in the eastern provinces of Germany. There were even reports of uniformed women, perhaps telegraphists in Wehrmacht service, using the launchers against Soviet armoured vehicles during the fighting in Breslau.

Another rocket-propelled weapon was the Panzerschreck, a variant of the American Army's bazooka. The German launcher came into general service during 1944 and was a two-man weapon, for it was not a single-shot launcher but a piece of anti-tank ordnance capable of firing a grenade over great distances. Some reports speak of it hitting and destroying a target at distances of up to 400 metres. It was soon realised that the Panzerschreck was capable of use other than in a purely anti-tank role. Its bombs were able to destroy pill-boxes, houses or field fortifications as well as being fired into the air as a short-range but powerful rocket capable of breaking up Soviet infantry assaults: a sort of poor man's Nebelwerfer.

This section is completed by part of a letter written by a young grenadier describing the fighting of the late autumn of 1944 during which he had destroyed his first Soviet tank at close quarters by using a hollow-charge grenade.

The regiment lay with its back to a great forest which covered much of the sector on which we were holding back Ivan's offensive. My company was in position in a small thicket as an outpost line forward of the main body. We were in slit trenches, well positioned in echelon formation and very well camouflaged. We had learnt the tricks of this from Ivan and changed the wilting leaves every few hours. The trees in our copse were not old and sturdy like those of the great woods but were thicker than saplings. We were hidden under the trees because of the Russian aircraft which attacked without mercy anything which moved on our side of the line. Even individual soldiers were shot at with machine gun and cannon fire. If we had been detected the whole sky would have been full of aircraft seeking to destroy us. Prudently we hid ourselves in the slight but adequate shelter of the trees.

One Sunday morning a rolling barrage walked up the rising ground, smashed through our copse and marched on behind us towards the forest. Almost before we had time to regain breath the tanks were upon us and some distance behind them came the Red infantry labouring up the slope.

The first group of T 34s crashed through the undergrowth. My trench was almost in the first line. A tank passed some distance to my left while a second was on my right and in front of me about twenty metres distant. I heard my officer shout to me to take the right hand machine and I watched it rumble along. All that I had learned in the training school suddenly came flooding back and gave me confidence, but I must admit that I was frightened. We, who were in the front line of trenches, had the hollow-charge grenades and those farther back had the stovepipes [Panzerschreck: translator's note]. It had been planned that we should allow the first group of T 34s to roll over us and for them then to be engaged by the stovepipe men. In the confusion of their attacks we grenadiers with the hollow-charges could strike hard at the halted or slowed down vehicles. Things did not work out that way and we were ordered to attack just as the tanks entered the thicket.

My T 34 was now so close that I was in a dead corner and not in any immediate danger. The crew could not see me but even if they had been able to see me they could not have fired at me. The grenade had a safety cap which had to be unscrewed to reach the rip-cord. My fingers were trembling as I unscrewed the cap, felt the loop of the cord tighten in the crook of my first finger and holding the grenade in my right hand, climbed out of the trench using my left hand to help me. The T 34 was now only a few metres away on my right and I prepared to attack it. Crouching low I started towards the monster, pulled the detonating cord and prepared to fix the charge. I had now nine seconds before the grenade exploded and then I noticed, to my horror, that the outside of the tank was covered in concrete like our Zimmerit paste. My bomb could not stick on such a surface. It had to be flat and metal. Worse was yet to come. The tank suddenly spun on its right track, turned so that it pointed straight at me and moved forward as if to run over me.

I flung myself backwards and fell straight into a partly dug slit trench and so shallow that I was only just below the surface of the ground. Luckily I had fallen face upwards and was still holding tight in my hand the sizzling hand grenade. As the tank rolled over me there was a sudden and total blackness. Luckily the tracks passed on either side of me but so close that the shallow earth walls of the trench began to collapse. As the belly of the monster passed over me I reached up instinctively as if to push it away and, certainly without any conscious thought, stuck the charge on the smooth, unpasted metal. The three magnets held the bomb in position and barely had the tank passed over me than there was a loud explosion. Smoke poured out, then with a tremendous roar the vehicle burst into flames and blew up. I was alive and the Russians were dead. I was trembling in every limb but felt elated. My comrades afterwards told me that they thought that I had been knocked over and crushed by the tracks of my T 34. The company broke the cohesion of the first tank attack and our artillery caught their infantry in the open. In the resulting confusion we fell back to our main line in the woods. I now have a black and silver badge on my right sleeve. [This was the tank destruction award for the single-handed destruction of an enemy tank by the use of infantry weapons only: translator's note.]

The situation facing the grenadiers in the slit trenches was a desperate one when the heavy tanks came in and rolled over their positions. The man with a Panzerfaust or Panzerschreck who, through excitement or fear, did not achieve a killing shot was usually doomed. The lumbering heavy vehicle would move down upon his slit trench and there would place a track across it. Full lock would be applied and the machine would spin slowly on its track, its engine roaring with the effort and the strain. But often above that noise could be heard the high-pitched screaming of the grenadiers as they were crushed to death under the flat, broad tracks of the Soviet vehicle. It was a fearful end to an heroic gesture.

25

Rocket propulsion

A new form of artillery, first used on the Eastern Front

"For decades to come the powder-propelled rocket will maintain its importance as a weapon ..."

Dr. Dornberger
DESIGNER OF THE NEBELWERFER

Two German weapons which, more than any others in the first years of the Second World War, served to destroy the morale of allied soldiers were the dive bomber and the Nebelwerfer (smoke projector). In both, nerve-racking, screaming, whistling or moaning sounds were followed by violent explosions of bomb or shells. It was the noise which frightened many troops into abandoning their positions and it was the explosions which killed them as they ran.

Of those two weapons it is the Nebelwerfer which is written about here. The Stuka had already demonstrated its potential during the campaign in the West during 1940, but the Nebelwerfer was a weapon used for the first time in Russia, can be said to have shaped the artillery tactics of that war and was the forerunner of many of the rocket weapons in service with contemporary major armies.

Basically, the Nebelwerfer were mortars but mortars with the differences that they were multi-barrelled and fired rocket bombs. The term Nebelwerfer was given to projectors which were originally intended to discharge smoke and the name was retained even when it was quite evident that it was not smoke screens which the new types of projectors were designed to lay but curtains of poison gas. Mortars had proved during the First World War to be the most efficient means of saturating the enemy with gas: the weight ratio of noxious filling to casing and propellant were better than those of artillery shells. From projecting a bomb filled with chemical substances to becoming a multi-barrelled 'Walking Stuka' firing patterns of heavy, high explosive bombs, proved to be but a short step, and soon the Nebelwerfer were in action along the entire Eastern Front and then in every theatre of war.

Their close association with the infantry led to their suffering bitter losses, particularly in the last weeks of the fighting when some regiments and battalions battled to the last, firing often literally over open sights, to cover the evacuation of infantry units from Baltic harbours – infantry whom they had served for so long. In this self-sacrifice the Nebelwerfer troops were following the lead given by one unit which served as a rearguard in the Crimea. This regiment had concealed the withdrawal of the main German body by firing a continuous barrage of smoke shells, and had then gone under with all the crews being either killed or taken prisoner when the final Soviet infantry assault went in.

As has already been explained in the section on armoured assault artillery, there is a difficulty in writing about sub-units who support the battle actions fought by the two major arms of service – infantry and armour. Each Nebelwerfer engagement was like all the others, except in the minor details of place, time and target engaged. From the months and years of battle two accounts have been selected to represent the German rocket-propelled artillery. The first of these is a description by a former Red Army man of his first experience under a Nebelwerfer bombardment, and the second is a record of a Nebelwerfer unit during some days of battle in the German summer offensive of 1942.

But first it is necessary to describe the genesis and development of the Nebelwerfer, to give an account of their destructive capabilities and to detail the various types of projector and the ammunition which they fired.

One of the earliest discoveries connected with gunpowder was that the gases given off by the burning powder could be channelled and exhausted to propel rockets and these fireworks were first used as a means of entertainment, then later as signalling devices and, finally, in a warlike role as artillery pieces to bombard the enemy.

It was flight instability and short range, vis-à-vis conventional artillery, which had caused the rocket to be removed from the armouries of most major armies well before the end of the 19th century and the First World War was fought without recourse to rocket-propelled missiles. The situation might have remained thus that all armies had excluded them from their weapons systems but the Germans introduced, or rather re-introduced, them during the Second World War under the general term Nebelwerfer. There is no doubt that the Germans pioneered and then developed this type of weapon in its modern form and the reason for their interest in this type of propulsion went back to the Treaty of Versailles. Under its terms Germany was forbidden to have, among other things, tanks, aircraft, heavy artillery and the means to wage chemical warfare, but there were no clauses which specifically forbade the use of artificial smoke or the development of rockets. Consequently, in 1929, the High Command and the Reichswehr's Weapons Department used this loophole to seek an alternative to the heavy artillery which was forbidden them and also to cast about for means with which to smother an enemy's positions with a dense chemical smoke.

As stated above one of the principal drawbacks to the successful application of the rocket as a military weapon had been its erratic flight path due to the uneven burning of the gunpowder charge and the resultant fluctuations in the propellant power of the gases produced. It was not unknown for rockets to be deflected or to be turned completely round by head winds. This problem had to be overcome. A team of scientists under the direction of Captain Dornberger (as he then was) considered the issues of how to direct the energy flow and by 1931 had brought their development to a point where a completely new principle designed to maintain the projectile on a straight course had been successfully tested. This was achieved by discarding any type of stabilising fins and producing stable flight by spinning the rocket like a rifle bullet. The problem had been how to achieve this twist which is given to a bullet or shell as a result of being fired from a long and rifled barrel, on behalf of a bomb fired from a smooth-bored and very short barrel.

To bring about this result Dornberger first altered the centre of gravity and placed the rocket motor at the head of the missile and mounted the explosive section behind this so that the rocket could be said to be towing rather than propelling the payload. Then he surrounded the rocket body with a ring of twenty-six venturi tubes, each of which was set at an angle of fourteen degrees to the axis of the motor. The propellant gases exhausted through these tubes and the thrust which was produced took the rocket through the air and at the same time spun it.

The new projectile was troop-tested by No. 2 Squadron of 4th Motorised Battalion, stationed at that time in Dresden, and to enable them to carry out their test firing satisfactorily the unit was brought up to fully motorised establishment. At that time the projector was still seen as a smoke bomb discharger whose task it was to blanket the enemy very quickly and effectively with chemical smoke but the scope, the scale and the pace of the experiments developed so rapidly that in the summer of 1933 the squadron had expanded to become a battalion. It was at this time that the role of the 'smoke' battalion changed to that of a chemical warfare detachment, able not only to clear areas contaminated by poison gas but also to retaliate and to discharge gas at the enemy using rocket-propelled canisters.

By 1937 Dornberger had designed and produced the 15cm Nebelwerfer 41, which was also known as the 'Dornberger' or 'DO' projector. Although still relying upon black powder as a propellant the venturi tubes proved satisfactory and held the rocket on a true course. An added advantage was that no violent explosion was necessary to launch the rocket and, therefore, there was no recoil. There was no need, in any case, to re-aim the piece since it could not achieve high accuracy and thus instead of a one-barrel projector it was, theoretically, possible to erect multiple projectors on a single frame. This, in fact, is what the 15cm Nebelwerfer 41 was – a six-barrelled launcher mounted on a wheeled, split-trail carriage. Into the smooth barrels the rockets fitted, each with its jets level with the rear end of the tube. Wire leads from an electric igniter set inside one of the venturis clipped to terminals which were fitted alongside each tube. A remote lead was plugged into the control box on the launcher and at the other end was a selector box containing the firing unit. The handle of a magneto was spun by a gunner taking cover in a hole some fifteen metres distant from the weapons; current flowed to the selector and from that box to the rocket igniters. The choice of alternatives in the selector determined whether the six rockets were discharged singly, or at intervals, or in a single volley with a two-second interval between each launch. Two seconds was considered sufficient time for the flight of one rocket not to be disturbed by the launch of the next.

The maximum range of missiles fired from the standard or 15cm Nebelwerfer 41 was 7,000 metres and the bomb was fitted with a highly sensitive contact type of fuse. When the missile struck home the fuse detonated the explosive which, it will be remembered, was located behind the rocket. When the explosion came it occurred some fifty to sixty centimetres above the ground, and as no deep crater was made the shell casing fragments were widespread so that each detonation was more destructive than the shell from a conventional artillery piece. Then, too, the rate of fire of a Nebelwerfer was high and a battery of six projectors, manned by experienced crews, could let lose a salvo of thirty-six rounds in ten seconds and follow this with a second salvo within sixty seconds.

Because of its excellent fragmenting qualities the 15cm bomb was used against human or other ground targets, whereas the bomb of the heavy mortar, the 21cm 42, a five-barrelled weapon, was used primarily against field fortifications. The rate of fire of this weapon was the same as that for the 15cm weapon, but reloading took longer, usually between two and three minutes. This 21cm projectile was a reversion to conventional rocket principles, for the propellant was located behind the war-head. For greater destructive effect the detonating mechanism could be retarded so that the missile would have time to bury itself deep into the earth before it exploded with a force equivalent to that of a land mine.

The Nebelwerfer as a weapon had certain positive advantages and disadvantages. In comparison with conventional artillery pieces it was light and more manoeuvrable across country. The men needed to serve the projectors were few: the standard crew consisted of only five men and they could man-tow the piece if it was necessary. The mortar's simple but robust design made it cheap and easy to produce. The chief disadvantages were that it was imprecise and that it could not bombard a small target with accuracy.

The short range was another disadvantage, for the weapons had to be brought closer to the battle line than was usual for artillery pieces. Heavy losses to the crews were the inevitable result and the casualty rate was frequently as high as that in the infantry.

Finally, there was the disadvantage that when the rockets were discharged the sheets of flame and clouds of smoke which were produced betrayed the position of the mortars both by day and by night. Late in 1942 a new propellant increased the range and also considerably reduced the betraying smoke trails, but these could never be totally eliminated.

Organisation was originally by battery, each with an establishment of six projectors, and during 1940 battalions were created out of the amalgamation of the batteries. With the introduction into service of heavy mortars, details of which will be given below, battalions were designated either as 'Projector' or as 'Heavy Projector', depending upon the weapon with which they were equipped. Then as the war progressed regiments were formed from the battalions and brigades from the regiments.

The changes in organisation and the increase in establishments can also be seen in the manpower growth of the new arm of service. At the beginning of the Second World War the effective strength of the 'Smoke Troops' was 100 Officers, 332 NCOs and 1,612 men. By 1945 the numbers serving with the Nebelwerfer had increased to a strength of 5,257 Officers, 18,150 NCOs and 112,321 men. During the years of war twenty brigades of thirty-one standard regiments were raised, together with fifteen heavy projector regiments, three regiments in permanently fixed positions, four training and replacement regiments and twenty-five independent battalions. If these numbers seem small, given the length of the eastern battle line and the duration of the conflict, then it must be understood that regiments which had been wiped out in battle were often reformed under their old number. One of the very first Nebelwerfer regiments to be raised, the 51st, was destroyed three times in little more than a year.

As an indication of the confidence which eventually was reposed in the ability of the Nebelwerfer units the 51st Regiment during one five-month period, between July and December 1943, fired 68,344 high explosive missiles of 15cm calibre and 8,325 of 21cm calibre. During the course of those months the regiment attacked forty-three tank groupings, 342 forming up areas, helped to beat back 145 Soviet infantry assaults and bombarded forty-two enemy gun positions.

What the power of the Nebelwerfer represented can be shown by the density of shot with which they were able to saturate an area. A brigade made up of a standard and a heavy regiment controlled the fire power of 384 barrels of 15cm calibre and 325 of 21cm calibre. German reports speak of such a regiment being able to bombard a target area with six tons of explosive or incendiary war-heads in five seconds and to produce this barrage every minute. Conventional artillery could only achieve the same saturation with the equivalent tonnage by deploying eighty-one batteries of guns. A battalion could smother an area 2,000 metres long by 100 metres deep with 108 rockets in ten seconds.

The Germany Army did appreciate, however, that the Nebelwerfer was unable to replace conventional artillery for it had neither the range nor the accuracy to do this. But more and more the Army began to appreciate that rocket detachments and particularly those grouped in regiments or brigades could bring together, and with only minimal delay, the fire power of a corps grouping of field artillery, that they would require less manpower to produce this effect and could bring this about with weapons that were more mobile than artillery, easier to maintain and cheaper to build.

A surprising fact concerning the use of the Nebelwerfer is that it was kept secret from the Soviet High Command for so many years. Indeed it was not until some of the weapons were captured during the Soviet winter offensive of 1943 that the Red Army knew for certain the design and potential of the weapon which their soldiers had been reporting since the earliest days of the campaign. The Russians had, by this time, developed their own rocket launchers, the best known of which was the *Katyusha*, known to the German soldiers of the Russian front as the Stalin Organ.

That the Germans had rocket units may have been known to STAVKA but it was not at first disclosed to the Soviet units and the shock that bombardment by rocket had upon troops can only be imagined. It may not be too much of an exaggeration to claim that during the German advances of 1941, as well as in the Soviet winter offensive of that year, it was Nebelwerfer which played a major part in destroying Soviet morale, in bringing the German armies forward during the opening offensives and in destroying Russian assaults during their attacks to break the German winter line. Time after time German infantry war diaries speak of Red Army attacks halted and flung back whenever the advancing waves of soldiers came under the fire of the Nebelwerfer. When it is remembered that in those early days the projector units were often still in battery organisation and that it was not unusual for a single piece to be sent forward to support the front then the full impact of the weapon's effect on morale can be appreciated. In fact the frightfulness of the new weapon was so great and the loss of morale within the Red Army units so high that the Soviet government threatened to use chemical warfare if the Nebelwerfer continued to be employed.

Two examples of the projectors in action are given – one by a former Russian soldier who endured a bombardment and, the second, an account of a detachment in action during the German summer offensive of 1942.

From the earliest beginnings with the primitive 10cm muzzle-loading, smoke-projecting Nebelwerfer 40, which had been used in Poland and again in France, more efficient projectors were produced and were in service. These are described below and, in addition to them, there were several interesting but still-born projects, one of which was a 50cm calibre projector with a 210 kilometre range. This, it was intended, was to have been mounted on a Tiger tank chassis. Another project was to be a huge projector with an 85cm calibre. Neither idea was developed.

Of the principal Nebelwerfer types the 15cm projector fired six rockets of 35kg weight to a maximum range of 7,000 metres. This weapon came into service during May 1941, a month before the opening of 'Operation Barbarossa' but not until early 1942 did it receive the designation 15cm Nebelwerfer 41. The second multiple-barrelled weapon to enter service was the 21cm 42, authorised for issue on 30 June 1943. This was a five-tube projector mounted on the 15cm carriage and firing 200kg rockets of which total weight just under 10kg was a war-head. The range of this weapon, which continued to use the same propellant as the 15cm projector, was only slightly greater than the 41 pattern: a little over 800 metres.

The 15cm 42 projector was next introduced, mounted on half-track vehicles, the Sdkfz 4/1 or Maultier. The weapon which was fired was a ten-tube projector served by a three-man crew and the vehicle driver. A battery of these weapons consisted of eight projectors and not the standard six pieces.

During 1943 the 28/32cm Nebelwerfer 41 was introduced and this had the capability of firing either a 28cm HE or a 32cm incendiary bomb. The design of the projector was different in that it consisted of six cage-type racks instead of the smooth-bore tubes of earlier models. The projector developed out of a weapon which fired one single rocket filled with incendiary material. Boxes of four of these projectiles were then fitted up as primitive dischargers and following this came the introduction of adaptor rails so that a 28cm HE bomb could be fired from the same projector. The final adaptation was the 30cm HE Projector 42 which fired either incendiary or explosive rockets over a distance of 7,000 metres. In its final design the launcher was open-framed and made up of two rows of three launchers mounted on a two-wheel trailer.

There were several very interesting and apocryphal stories concerning the Nebelwerfer. One of these was that the rockets used in the first months of the war against the Soviet Union had been charged with liquid oxygen explosive. The presence of so many dead showing no external signs of injury seemed to support that theory. The truth was more prosaic. The rapid and successive detonations produced during a Nebelwerfer barrage produced such rapid variations in air pressure within the bombarded zone that many victims suffered extensive damage to their lungs which killed them.

The main types of ammunition fired from the various projectors

	15cm 41 HE or smoke	21cm 42 HE	28cm HE	32cm Incendiary	30cm HE
Projector weight	540kg	600kg	850kg		1,100kg
Weight of projectile	34.2kg, 35kg	110kg	83.7kg	79.2kg	126kg
Range	6,900, 6,800m	8,000m	1,800m	2,200m	4,500m
Length of projectile	92.5cm, 101.5cm	126cm	126cm	130cm	124.9cm
Thrust (approx.)	2,000kg	4,000kg		2,000kg	4,000kg
Speed after burn out	340m/sec	340m/sec	140m/sec	130m/sec	

A Red Army infantryman and his first encounter with the Nebelwerfer, spring 1942

The experience of one man who encountered the Nebelwerfer in the early spring of 1942 may be considered as typical. He was a Pole who joined the Red Army after the opening of Operation Barbarossa and who served in an infantry unit on the central front.

Our regiment formed up in a forest and moved out of cover to form the second wave of the attack. We had no special winter camouflage clothing – only the first line was that well equipped and there was a reason for this. It was their task to crawl forward without being seen until the line was within assault distance of the German positions, and then to rush them. We, in the second wave, were to consolidate the gains which the first line was to make. My battalion began to form line but here and there, there were still little groups of men gathered around the officers. They were chiefly HQ personnel, company officers and senior sergeants all getting last minute instructions. We were a young unit but most of us had already seen action and we were not green troops.

There was not much noise. The sound of voices and an occasional shot from a rifle. No artillery fire at all from our side for it was to be a shock assault. Then suddenly as we moved forward away from the trees we heard a whining sound which grew and then we saw smoke trails in the sky. I thought at first that these were markers showing our position to the Nazi artillery observers but my right-hand neighbour thought that these were aircraft which were crashing. The projectiles moved fast but were visible. Two of them exploded about twenty metres behind our line, two about the same distance in front and one each to left and right immediately in front of us. This number of explosions following immediately upon each other was like a six-gun battery firing salvo. The casualties were slight although the explosions were quite shattering. I noticed that the shell casing of one projectile peeled back like a banana as it flew through the air after detonating and as I watched it struck and nearly cut in half one of the men marching behind our wave.

We had not taken cover but continued marching and then suddenly we saw sheets of flames coming from behind the German lines, then smoke and then the howling again. This time the mass of smoke and flames roaring towards us seemed to cover the whole battalion front. The whole area in front of us and behind us as well as at intervals along the line was suddenly blotted out and what seemed to be hundreds of explosions occurred simultaneously. Snow and earth clods were flung up obscuring visibility and then came the cry for medical personnel to help the wounded. Under this first mass bombardment we had gone to ground and thus we were a stationary target. Within seconds, it seemed, of the first flight of missiles exploding the second wave had come down and then a third. After that I lost count – it just seemed as if the whole sky was raining noise and explosive on us. We lay there immobile with our senses numbed for what seemed a long time and then my right-hand man touched me on the shoulder and pointed to the groups of men who were streaming back towards the woods. We thought that the regiment had been ordered to withdraw and were rather pleased that we were going to be away from the shelling, but then as we ran I noticed that quite a lot of the men had flung their guns away and were screaming at the tops of their voices, throwing off their equipment so that they could run faster. Others had collapsed trembling and crying or were having spasms like epilepsy.

Even before we reached the safety of the woods the Nazis had increased the range and had also brought in conventional artillery so that the tree line suddenly disappeared in smoke and explosions catching the poor devils who had gathered there hoping to escape from the shelling. Even when we had penetrated deeper into the woods the smoke trails followed us and their bombs exploding in the tree tops had the effect of air burst shells.

When order had been restored we were sent in again to carry out the attack and this time we had barely emerged from the trees when the barrage came down again. The officers were desperate. If a unit did not reach its objective the commanders - in those days anyway - were held responsible and were either summarily executed or arrested, tried and then shot.

At the end of the third attempt we had shrunk to less than half strength and the attack was called off. The first attack wave had penetrated the German line in parts but being without support they had been driven back. Their regiment was very bitter at our cowardice, as they called it, and their survivors were sent back to rest behind the lines. I was one of a group told to collect the equipment which had been left lying on the battlefield and as a former artilleryman was interested enough to examine the shell fragments which were lying about. These were very large and it was clear that the purpose of the projectiles was not to produce shrapnel but to create a blast effect. The shallow craters indicated that the projectiles had an instantaneous fuse and the snow around the craters was yellow and black streaked. The pieces of casing which I found showed that the walls of the projectile were thin and the blast effect which I had felt and seen indicated that the explosive charge was quite heavy in relation to the weight of case.

It was a weapon which broke our regiment inside a quarter of an hour and as I have said before, we were not green troops.

A Nebelwerfer regiment in the German summer offensive towards Voronezh, 1942

The second of these narratives details the task of a Nebelwerfer regiment in the opening moves of the second summer campaign.

In the spring of 1942 the Nebelwerfer unit had taken part in the fighting on the southern wing of Army Group South and then, with regrouping completed, found itself as part of the forces assembled for the drive by the 4th Panzer Army on the northern wing. The initial drive by that army was to capture Voronezh. The thick, clinging mud of spring had passed, the summer sun had dried out the roads and now the hopes and expectations of Army Group South were that it would carry out the Führer's Directive No. 41 to defeat the Soviet armies in the bend of the Don and thereafter to capture the economic prizes of southern Russian and to seize the Caucasus.

One week after Midsummer day the leading elements of the 4th Panzer Army struck in the opening moves of the new offensive. Eight days later they had not only crossed the Don but were

attacking Voronezh, more than 120 kilometres from their start line.
The following account is the action of a regiment of heavy
Nebelwerfer mortars supporting the advance towards the Don,
across that river and into Voronezh.

The fanatical resistance of the Red Army at the approaches to
Voronezh can be attributed to two factors. The first of these was the
strategic importance of the town and the second the fact that the
Soviet rearguard was fighting hard to protect the movement of the
main body across the river and thus out of the trap which the
Germans had set. It was this bitter fighting for which the heavy
mortars were brought into action to collaborate with an infantry
regiment in attacks to clear the obstinate Soviet rearguard from off
the line of advance. One hour before the German grenadiers went
over the top at 02.30hrs the Nebelwerfers were to open a destructive
fire which would 'lift' the grenadiers on to their objective: a ridge of
high ground twenty or so kilometres west of the Don.

Throughout the preceding afternoon the batteries had been
moving forward across the sun-baked steppe, skirting where
possible the steep-sided *balkas* or ravines which cut up the terrain,
bucketing and bouncing behind the prime movers which towed them
into pre-selected positions from which their fire would breach the
Soviet front and thus allow the infantry advance to flow forward
once again.

The firing point was reached only half an hour before last light.
The ground was flat and open, being without cover of any sort. A few
burnt out wooden huts, decorated with Soviet propaganda placards
and aircraft identification posters showed that the site had been
used by the Red Air Force as a forward landing strip. The arrival of
the mortar regiment had not gone unnoticed by enemy artillery
observers and even as the gunners struggled to unlimber the
projectors and to bring them into readiness, shells from Soviet field
artillery began to fall around the airfield area. The regimental
commander went out to meet the grenadier officers and to coordinate
with them his fire plan and to key it in with their advance. Light
signals and timings were agreed and as the commander drove back
to his TAC headquarters he passed in the dark evening a long
column of lorries bringing up ammunition to his mortars. There
would be no shortage for this operation; its success was vital.

The night was dark but clear and without too much wind, ideal
conditions for observation by the Forward Observation Officer who
would accompany the grenadier assault. Punctually at 01.30hrs
three batteries of Nebelwerfers opened fire and for the grenadiers,
most of whom were seeing the new, heavier weapon in action for the
first time, the sight was as awe-inspiring as the sound was nerve-
shattering.

A low-pitched howling rose quickly to a screaming crescendo and
then huge gouts of flame erupted, firing the rockets and sending
them like huge comets hurtling through the air towards the Soviet

positions. Lines of flame escorted by trailing clouds of red-lined smoke marked their route as they streaked across the sky. They fell and exploded with such terrible detonations that the vibrations were felt as far back as regimental HQ, in whose dug-outs the walls shook, bringing down rivulets of sandy earth.

The initial discharge by the three batteries was followed by a mass bombardment fired by the entire regiment, the gunners working frenziedly, loading, running to their slit trenches, 'Fire' and then to reload. It will be appreciated that when the projector was loaded and ready to fire the gunners evacuated the area lest they be caught and burned by the long searing flames which poured from the rockets' bases. Firing in salvoes the mortars poured out upon the Soviet rearguard a bombardment against which there was no defence. Flames streaked in blocks as the whole regiment fired; lines of flame erupted as single batteries bombarded and then the six lights of a barrage by just a single mortar. The fire plan was intricate and designed to shatter the enemy's morale with unexpected pauses followed by crushing bombardment.

The explosions of the conventional artillery shellfire went unheard in this fierce thunder of noise; the flames from the gun muzzles unseen in the brighter glare of the Nebelwerfer's flames. Encouraged by the fury of the guns the grenadiers moved across their start line. Until now the Red rearguard in that sector had held firm. How would Ivan react to this new and frightful weapon? Soon the infantry had moved off the flat ground and had begun to ascend the slope which led to the crest and to their objective. Covered by the screaming mortar shells the advance pushed on until, at last, the leading groups came to the area which had been the first target for the mortars.

This was easily recognisable even though the moon was down, for extensive fires which the rockets had caused illuminated the whole scene. The ground was cruelly torn up. Wide, shallow craters overlapped each other. Bushes were alight, the few trees in the area had been torn up by their roots and everywhere there were bodies, killed or wounded alike, mutilated by the force of the concussions. From the number of casualties it seemed that the barrage must have caught two units in the process of relief and that, trapped by the box barrage, there had been no escape for them. But then, suddenly out of the smoke, there crashed a horse-drawn gun, without drivers or crew, the gun and limber being swung from side to side as if they had no weight. This sudden and unexpected emergence from the dark alarmed the leading grenadiers who opened fire and brought down the team kicking and dying in the traces.

To observers moving behind the infantry lines the scene was devilish as groups of grenadiers were seen silhouetted briefly against the flames and were then swallowed up by the billowing smoke clouds. And all the time the rockets stamped out on the ground their explosive prints as the barrage moved deeper into

Russian territory, bringing the infantry forward.

Dawn broke unseen in the rockets' glare but then as freshening wind blew the smoke away and as the light grew stronger it was clear for observers to see how effective had been the Nebelwerfer bombardment, for, like a black scar up the length of the green slope ran the breach which the rockets had blasted through the Soviet positions.

Puffs of smoke high on the ridge showed where Soviet artillery was bombarding the grenadier lines but onward and upward the infantry carried their attack, signalling by Very light their forward positions until there burst, at last, and hung momentarily motionless in the bright daylight, the white magnesium blaze which showed that they were on their objective. Opposition had been beaten down by the infantry; now the Soviets had to be crushed and this was the Luftwaffe's task. Punctual to the minute there then flew in the squadrons of Stukas and fighter bombers whose job it was to carry out the next phase of the operation. Their vertical descents, their screaming sirens and the deadly accuracy of their bombing destroyed the last Soviet resistance. Singly, then in pairs, then again in groups and, finally, in a khaki flood the Russians poured out of their positions and headed eastward, throwing away their weapons and covering their heads with their arms, oblivious to anything except the need to escape and scarcely aware that behind them roaring up the road were German personnel carriers bringing in fresh battalions of grenadiers to harry this broken rear guard. It was now a pursuit battle and with their immediate task completed the Nebelwerfer crews stood down and began the routine tasks of overhauling their weapons and servicing the vehicles, checking ammunition, tidying up the area and, generally, carrying out the thousand and one duties which keep a soldier employed when he is not actually fighting.

The rest from battle was a short one, for within days the leading troops of Hoth's 4th Panzer Army had bounced the Don and had begun to move into Voronezh, and the Nebelwerfer regiment was ordered to assist in the capture of this strategically important town.

In the heat of an early July afternoon the batteries, which had crossed the great wide river, were formed up, brought into position and were made ready to fire. Orders were passed by the gun commanders, the crews sheltered themselves in trenches, the electrical contacts were made and the first salvoes left the smooth-bore barrels, flying towards a complex of tall buildings which was their target. Soon this was hidden from view by the smoke clouds and dust from the explosions.

The grenadier assault which the mortars were to cover was to move off at 12.30hrs and five minutes before this the barrage stopped to allow the mortar men to change their firing positions. In the sudden quiet the grenadiers rose out of the shell holes, emerged from the ruined buildings and slit trenches and moved forward, shaking out their groups as they moved up the road into the smoke-enshrouded town. Some mortars had been selected to give the infantry close support and these limbered up and moved, with rigidly maintained distances, along the tarmac road which led into the centre of the town. The forward movement of the grenadiers was fluid and furious. Here a hand-grenade to wipe out a group of Red machine-gunners who were firing from a doorway; there a burst from a machine pistol to bring down a sniper. But not all the enemy soldiers were killed or captured and as the Nebelwerfers moved up behind the infantry they came under fire, from defenders still determined to resist.

Quickly the gun crews dismounted, took up their personal arms and entered the battle, advancing against one machine gun which had opened fire on them. From a second house another Russian machine-gun group began to fire and then a third. The situation was precarious. The mortars could not be left unguarded and yet the machine-gun nests had to be destroyed otherwise the advance would halt. Then into the battle rolled an SP gun. The young lieutenant commanding the vehicle jumped down; there was a hasty conference with the battery commander and a grenadier officer. The German troops vanished from the street upon a signal and concealed themselves in doorways. The SP rolled forward and the 7.5cm gun pointed at the first machine-gun post. A deafening explosion and then a rumbling sound as bricks and concrete crashed down upon the Red soldiers. The first nest was wiped out. A second shot from the SP and then a third. The resistance had been crushed and all that remained was to collect the dazed, bewildered Russian soldiers who staggered out to surrender, each of them bearing his 'passport', the white surrender leaflet which the Luftwaffe had dropped over their positions.

As the advance took the grenadiers and the Nebelwerfer crews deeper into Voronezh opposition became stronger and more determined. The grenadiers sprayed each window and door now, great gouts of bullets climbing up the outside walls and pouring through the smashed glass of the houses, holding down the Russians by the sheer weight of fire. Then out of a side street roared a T 34 tank and drove at a furious speed down the road pursued by streams of red and green tracer from German machine-guns. Menacingly its gun swung round to fire at the halted mortars but before the Russian gun had been laid on shells from the SP, which had emerged from behind the giant mortars, smashed the Soviet vehicle. It caught fire and then blew up with so great an explosion that the turret was hurled hundreds of metres, cartwheeling its way through the air and trailing a plume of sable smoke.

Soon the infantry could make no more headway against the fanatical Soviet resistance and then it was time for the close support mortar crews to go in and to blast the Red defenders out of the way. On open streets, strewn with rubble and the litter of destruction, the

Nebelwerfers went into action. The first salvoes produced a dust storm as the recoil flames, hemmed in within the tall buildings, streamed along the road surface, whirling dust and pieces of brick into the air. Visibility was cut to almost nothing as this miniature, man-produced dust storm whirled about hiding the sun with its density. The street, the projectors, the target all had vanished from sight but the gunners kept firing for they knew that wherever their projectiles landed was an enemy target whose destruction would bring the fall of Voronezh nearer.

At the next street corner the scene was repeated, the gunners hiding in the same doorways and cellars as those within which frightened civilians cowered, overawed by the flames, smoke and destructive powers of the mortars. The discharge of the rockets in this narrower street had an even more devastating effect than the first salvoes and brought plaster crashing down from the ceilings. Slowly the Nebelwerfer and grenadier groups made their way towards the centre of Voronezh, tumbling houses into ruin and beating down the resistance of Red Army snipers and machine-gunners.

The air was full of hot ashes blown from the burning buildings and the scene resembled that of a volcanic eruption of immense proportions. Everywhere there were houses and buildings in flames and above their roofs rose high into the sky the black trails of Nebelwerfer rockets. Suddenly as the grenadiers, the Nebelwerfer and the SP gun turned from one small and narrow street there lay before them a large and imposing square from which bursts of machine-gun bullets and salvoes of mortar bombs were being fired. One Nebelwerfer was all that could be put into action but after only two flights of rockets prisoners began to leave the houses and move down to surrender, eyeing the rocket launcher which had been their downfall with wonder and fear. Then it seemed as if the whole of that great open place was filled with German troops and the rocket men stood down. They and the grenadiers whom they had been escorting had reached their objectives. The capture of the rest of the town could be left to other troops.

At last orders came for the Nebelwerfer regiment to move out of town and into reserve positions. The single projectors rejoined their parent units, batteries formed up in rubble-strewn side roads waiting until the regiment had assembled. As the first battalion pulled out the weapons, vehicles and gunners of the other battalions swung from their side streets and joined the main column heading south-westwards out of Voronezh and towards the Don.

The light projectors swayed and bumped their way across craters, along streets through which the regiment had fought its way into the centre of the town. The tired gunners were flung about as the lorries bumped in and out of holes in the damaged roads.

The journey back down the line was as difficult as the journey forward had been. The whole of 4th Panzer Army's guns and armour seemed to be massed on this single road inching a way forward, bumper to bumper as its units advanced upon Voronezh. What little space there was on the down route was a chaos of ammunition lorries heading for the dumps, ambulances bucketing along with their loads of wounded, or plodding columns of infantry. Tracks and wheels had churned the road surface so that above the highway hung a white dust, a thick chalk fog which concealed the vehicles and men going up or down the line and covered them all with a heavy layer of white powder.

A left turn into a secondary road brought the Nebelwerfer column on to a ridge overlooking Voronezh. The heavy smoke cloud which had hung above the town had begun to disperse and as visibility improved the whole of the ground towards and past Voronezh was laid suddenly open. The town lay there; distance concealing not only the ugliness of the buildings but also the damage which these had sustained in the fighting. But not one gunner looked down upon the town on the Don. They were all asleep, in that deep unconsciousness of exhaustion which is brought about by days of bitter fighting. Voronezh lay at their feet but the gunners who had helped to bring about its fall were oblivious. They were dead to the world. It had been a hard battle.

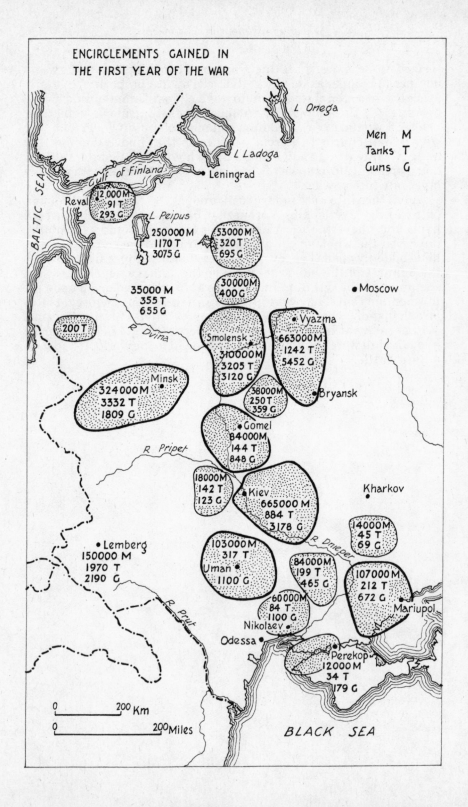

ENCIRCLEMENTS GAINED IN
THE FIRST YEAR OF THE WAR

L Onega

L Ladoga

L Peipus

• Leningrad

Men   M
Tanks T
Guns   G

Reval •
12,000 M
91 T
293 G

250000 M
1170 T
3075 G

53000 M
320 T
695 G

30000 M
400 G

35000 M
355 T
655 G

200 T

R. Dvina

• Moscow

• Vyazma

Smolensk •
310000 M
3205 T
3120 G

663000 M
1242 T
5452 G

Minsk •
324000 M
3332 T
1809 G

38000 M
250 T
359 G

• Bryansk

R. Pripet

L Gomel
84000 M
144 T
848 G

18000 M
142 T
123 G

Kiev •
665000 M
884 T
3178 G

• Kharkov

14000 M
45 T
69 G

• Lemberg
150000 M
1970 T
2190 G

103000 M
317 T
1100 G

Uman •

R. Dnieper

84000 M
199 T
465 G

107000 M
212 T
672 G

• Mariupol

R. Prut

60000 M
84 T
1100 G

Nikolaev •

Odessa •

Perekop
12000 M
34 T
179 G

0   200 Km

0   200 Miles

BLACK SEA

BALTIC SEA

Gulf of Finland

26

A phenomenon of the Eastern Front: encirclement

"It is the duty of the troops to maintain their position without concerning themselves whether the enemy has broken through on their flanks or in their rear."

Hitler's Order
16 DECEMBER 1941

In the days when linear warfare was the standard method of disposing troops in battle, a unit encircled and cut off by the enemy was considered lost, for its surrender through starvation, lack of ammunition or sickness could be only a matter of time. The classic concept of a successful military operation was to outflank the enemy, roll up his line, thereby encircle his force and thereafter destroy it.

By a strange paradox the mass use of motor engines during the Second World War allowed on the one hand a more rapid encirclement operation to be undertaken but on the other hand, simultaneously, supplied the weapons and tactics to negate the theory that encirclement equalled destruction. The aeroplane and the air drop could now nourish troops beleaguered miles behind the enemy lines.

The fast advances by German panzer forces in the early months of the new war against the Soviet Union, allied to a stiffness of intellect on the Russian side, was responsible for the fact that during the first years of that conflict whole armies of Soviet troops were encircled. At the same time manpower shortages on the German side forced them to leave unmanned and unprotected whole sectors of the front and through these Red troops were able to advance to bypass and then encircle German units. Thus it can be claimed that encirclement became a standard feature of military life on the Eastern Front and was a situation in which troops of both sides were liable to be placed. Indeed, towards the end of the war, Hitler ordered the garrisons of some towns to allow themselves to be cut off in a deliberate attempt to deny certain strategic areas to the advancing Soviets. It is significant that, certainly in the early campaigns, Soviet troops caught in encirclement operations were nearly always destroyed, whereas German units were usually able to escape or as a rule suffered destruction only as the consequence of orders expressly forbidding them to break out.

A brief study of the war on the Eastern Front will show that in its early stages rapid and virile thrusts by German armour created pockets within which the Soviet forces were contained and then smashed. The great battles at Minsk, Kiev and Uman are familiar to all and in these and other encirclements millions of Red Army men were killed or taken prisoner.

Quick to adapt and able to apply the bitter lessons it had had to learn, the Red Army High Command was eventually to use, with consummate skill, the same flair in operations and combat tactics which had given the Wehrmacht such success in the great envelopment battles of 1941 and 1942. Thus, by the middle years of the war and with increasing success thereafter, the German Army was bled to death in the East as Soviet forces advanced westward, cut off, surrounded and destroyed whole German armies. Two battles stand out – Stalingrad and Berlin.

The difference in approach by the staffs of each of the two armies to the problem of encirclement are of interest. It must be said at the outset that neither had considered it as a situation worthy of detailed note in the pre-war training manuals and that, therefore, both armies began their considerations from the same start line.

Within months the experience of German commanders and men had been collated and assessed. A rough but ready guide was produced whose basic tenets, with slight refinement, have since become military practice. The Soviets, with their overwhelming manpower and their insistence upon attack as the best form of defence, seem to have produced no regulations other than that of invested units fighting through an encircling ring as a body or filtering through as individuals. Since we are here dealing with the German view of warfare on the Eastern Front then, we shall deal firstly with the successful encirclement of autumn 1941, in which the German forces killed or captured nearly a million Red Army men and then go on to describe an envelopment operation undertaken by Soviet forces against German units.

Before going on to describe these actions reference must be made to the guidelines drawn up by the German Army for units which were encircled.

Three types of situation were catered for: the one where encircled troops stayed in position until a relieving force rescued them; the second, where they undertook a break out operation using just their own forces, or, thirdly, where the whole encircled body rolled, as a sort of mobile pocket, through enemy lines to regain their own main force.

The tactics governing each of these types of operation differed but two tenets were fundamental to each; firstly the maintenance of morale and the second a strong command. Taking morale first: the Germans appreciated that men surrounded by enemy forces are subject to neurosis, a so-called *Kesselfieber* (encirclement fever), wherein are exhibited the two great fears of beleaguered garrisons. These are the loss of links with home and medical treatment or evacuation of the wounded. The question of adequate food supplies was found to be of a less concern than that of ammunition. Thus, the successful pocket was one which had an air strip on to which planes could land with supplies, fresh troops, ammunition and mail and from which wounded could be evacuated to the main line. Failing an air strip, regular and frequent air drops, especially where the supplies included little luxuries, maintained morale at a high pitch. Propaganda was another important factor and the realisation that Red Army men deserted to encircled German troops helped to maintain the spirits of the invested army. Particularly was their morale high if they could know that their defence was causing the enemy huge losses and that its morale was suffering as a result. The bringing in, wherever possible, of fallen German dead and their formal interment was in direct contrast to the heaps of fallen Russian whom their comrades did not bother to remove and bury. Then, too, the growing mounds of Soviet dead were a reminder of how successful was the defence.

Strong command was vital and, depending upon the size of the pocket, the commanding general had a number of staffs directly responsible to him for various services within the invested area. Also, it was important, indeed essential, that the ordinary soldier should be aware that the staff and the senior commanders were undergoing the same privations that he himself was expected to bear. The presence of the senior commander in the front line had to be a common occurrence. Indeed the participation of very senior commanders became a feature of such operations and at Stalingrad it was accepted that general and field officers would take up machine pistols or rifles and act as infantry soldiers once their own commands had been destroyed or amalgamated.

Unnecessary road traffic and movement by motor vehicles was avoided; the staff walked and did not ride in cars. It was, in any case, vital that traffic regulations be introduced and strictly enforced if for no other reason than the need to conserve fuel. The absence of traffic also allowed the more rapid movement of troops across the perimeter from one threatened point to another, for encircled units worked on interior lines.

Regarding food and ammunition, it was vital that a rationing system be introduced and adhered to. On special occasions an increase of food or an issue of alcohol had almost the effect of a holiday. Clothing supplies were important, particularly in cold weather periods or during the time of the thaw. Felt boots, which were essential during the winter, soaked through and fell to pieces during the rainy season. During all periods shirts and underwear changes were needed to prevent infestation by lice and thus the likelihood or spread of typhus.

Given that all these points were carried out, the German High Command saw no reason why encircled troops should not be able to either regain their own lines or be brought out. Then to the basic guidelines others were introduced dealing with the conduct by units which found themselves in such conditions.

The primary task of any self-contained unit which found itself encircled was to sit tight and maintain its defence until a higher command had decided whether it was to wait for relief, to break out or whether it was to make its way as a mobile pocket to reach the German lines.

A unit in the first situation – that of waiting for relief – had certain tasks, including the seizure or recapture of tactically important ground, particularly dominating heights. With his troops in tactically secure positions the commander of the encircled troops could coordinate plans with the commander of the relief force. It was for the garrison commander to decide these, particularly the tactics which the relief operation was to use and the direction from which it would strike. This seemingly unusual situation was logical because only he was in a position to know to what extent his own forces could collaborate in helping to smash the ring around them. The duties of the commander of the relieving troops included the need to plan for the reception of the relieved garrison, particularly in the matter of swift evacuation of wounded, supplies of food, clothing, arms and ammunition. In winter conditions it was also essential that the relieved force be given warm and dry billets in which they could be rested before being reformed into fighting units.

In the second of the three situations, an encircled unit whose commander had decided to break out had first to ensure that the main force could receive it and that preparation for the arrival of his troops would not weaken those forces engaged in fighting the enemy. Once assured of this, then the break-out followed a pattern which became almost a battle drill. The most important decision was which was to be the direction in which the attempt was to be made. In contrast to the Russian tactic, in which escapes were made in a number of directions, the German principle was to select one point and to channel every force to that place. This is not to deny that feint attacks would attempt to deceive the enemy as to the point of the actual break-out. Extensive cannibalisation was then resorted to, to produce only absolutely roadworthy vehicles, and this weeding out also had the effect of producing sufficient fuel should the route be longer than expected or the fighting more intense.

The main burden of the break-out fell upon the infantry, whose task it was to reconnoitre and to clear the road ahead, to patrol on either flank and to attack the enemy forces which might obstruct the escape operation. If opposition was met then the armour was called forward to smash the obstruction, after which control of operations reverted to the infantry.

The 'mobile pocket' was another matter, however. In this, speed was more important, for such operations usually were undertaken when the beleaguered garrison was too far from its own main lines to be brought out by a relief force or to make a single thrust to gain that objective.

In 'mobile pocket' actions armour formed both the advance and the rear-guard while armoured reconnaissance detachments swept the flank. The infantry component was held in readiness to undertake operations to destroy Soviet infantry or armour which impeded the advance.

Circumstances, of course, alter plans, however carefully-laid down, and the basic tactics were amended to meet changing circumstances. This was particularly true during the final stages of the war when, particularly in March, April and May 1945, a main German battle line in the East had ceased to exist and during that period a number of 'mobile pockets' wandered about trying to find a larger body with which they could amalgamate.

We have dealt, thus far, with the encirclement of German units by the Soviets. However, throughout the war, but particularly in the first two years, the Germans had considerable success in massive encirclement battles: and their fast moving panzer forces were one reason for those successes. A second was the obstinate refusal of Stalin and the senior Russian military commanders to withdraw their forces in time to escape encirclement.

For the conduct of encirclement operations the Germans drew upon experience already gained, and worked out complex battle drills for the successful prosecution of such battles. It was obvious that, except in those cases where an unequivocal stand-fast order to the Soviet forces had been issued, attempts to break out would be made and the problems of containing large, active, not to say aggressive Red Army units created problems for the German commanders. They were well aware that at any point the encircling German troops would be inferior in number to the Soviets and would be too thin on the ground to oppose concerted efforts by the trapped forces to escape. The regulations stressed good positions from which to observe Russian movements as well as the need to seize well-sited defensive areas, for it was further appreciated that, in the face of superior numbers, the German forces might have to go, albeit temporarily, on to the defensive. It was found that in many cases 'Chinese attacks' and sudden diversionary thrusts were made by Soviet units to conceal the true direction of escape attempts or the movement of vehicle columns. Many of these Soviet deceptions were cleverly designed and skilfully executed, but a great number were infantry assaults where mass was used to conceal the real break-out point and where Red troops were to save guns and tanks.

The German forces found that it was not sufficient to merely block roads or railway tracks. Soviet troops and their equipment, particularly armour and guns, moved across country and thus evaded German blocks. Intensive, wide-ranging sweeps by reconnaissance battalions or lightly armoured battle groups were the only way in which they could be contained. Then, too, where aerial reconnaissance discovered a Soviet attempt to escape encirclement, dive-bombing to split the group or at least to slow its movement would enable the faster moving German recce or infantry groups to close the gap or intercept the fleeing Russians. In this context it is as well to draw attention to the incredible marching ability of the German infantry. Marches of forty to sixty kilometres per day were not uncommon and were repeated week in and week out. Often the infantry would be taken straight from a long march and put into an attack. Guderian's thesis "In movement lies victory" was proved by the German Army in the vast battles which were fought out during the first and second summer offensives.

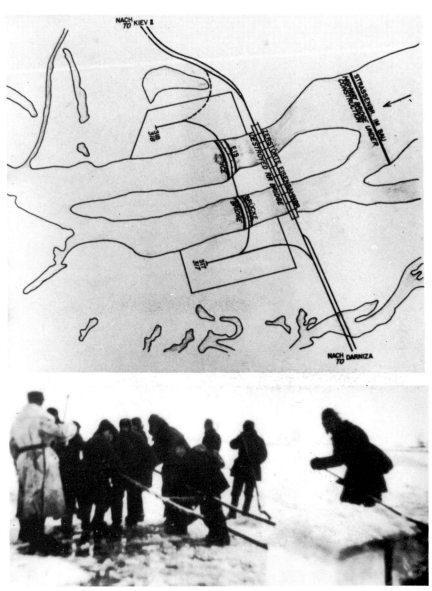

Top: View of the ice bridge across the Dnieper showing the railway spur lines (317 and 318) and the island in the middle of the river. *Centre:* Removing the ice blocks from the ice-wells using tongs and special equipment. *Below:* The permanent way with the supporting beams upon which the rails were laid.

A Nebelwerfer being loaded.

Left: "Bring up the assault artillery."

The ten-barrelled Nebelwerfer mounted on a half-tracked vehicle. The rocket's long tail of flame and smoke can be clearly seen.

Men of a German Army anti-tank team with their single shot projectors, the Panzerfaust.

The Nebelwerfer at night. The flames of the discharge pin-pointed the position of the projector and this ten-barrelled mortar was mounted on a half-tracked vehicle for greater mobility.

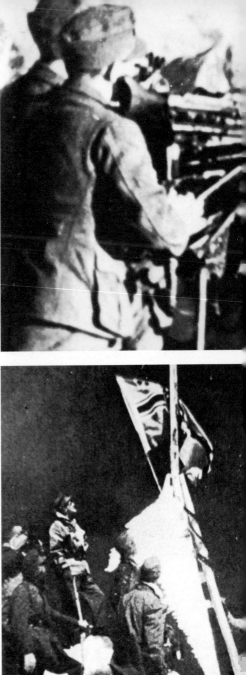

Above: Anti-tank gunners of an SS unit firing upon advancing Soviet armour; central front, summer 1943.

Centre top: During the ascent of the main body of the high-Alpine detachment towards the summit of Mount Elbrus, machine gun groups of the Gebirgsjäger were sent out to cover the advance and to dominate the Soviet troops in the mountain-top hotel.

Right: Men of the specially picked high-Alpine detachment of the Gebirgsjäger, fighting in the Caucasus, raise the German war flag on the summit of Mount Elbrus during the campaign in southern Russia in autumn 1942.

Far right: Ivan. The eternal Russian infantryman. It was the courage and determination of men like this which won the war on the Eastern Front.

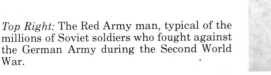

Top Right: The Red Army man, typical of the millions of Soviet soldiers who fought against the German Army during the Second World War.

A Soviet anti-tank rifle team, concealed by the hulk of a German tank, await a new onslaught during the fighting for Kursk in the summer of 1943.

Soviet infantry clearing the German defenders from a village on the northern front.

Well equipped Soviet partisans carrying out an operation to cut the railway line in Byelo-Russia in the summer of 1943.

Red Army tanks in Königsberg, East Prussia, in April 1945.

By the middle of 1943 the Soviet partisan organisation was strong enough to engage the German Army in military operations. This group, here seen carrying a wounded comrade on a stretcher, are returning from an operation in the Pripet Marsh area.

Berlin 1945. Soviet troops at the Brandenburger Tor being addressed by their commanding officer shortly after the capture of the capital city of the Third Reich in May 1945.

Columns of captured German soldiers passing through the streets of Berlin; the symbols of Soviet power, ISU SP-guns, wait ready to move forward again.

27

The destruction of the encircled Soviet forces in the fighting around Kiev

AUTUMN 1941

Assessing the situation at the end of the first phase of 'Operation Barbarossa', OKH, commanding the ground forces on the Eastern Front, could be pleased with the results gained and confident that these would be maintained for the next stage of operations. Complete satisfaction was, however, qualified by the knowledge that the time-table for the war against Russia was running late.

Instrumental to the successes which the Germans achieved had been the gaining of air superiority from the first day of the campaign and flexibility in the use of armour en masse. These two factors had brought the Germans, covered by an air umbrella, deep into Russian territory where their wide-ranging panzer sweeps had time after time encircled Soviet forces still tied to the concepts of linear warfare. Army Group Centre had enveloped large Russian forces in two giant pockets around Bialystok and Minsk, while a third, even larger, grouping was caught fast in and around Smolensk. For its part Army Group South was initiating moves which would eventually enclose great numbers of Red Army men around Uman.

Reflecting upon the losses which the Red Army had suffered, the planners at OKH could believe that they were well on the road to victory. At least eighty-nine Soviet divisions had been destroyed and this number, according to their own estimate of Russian strength, meant that the Red Army had already lost over fifty per cent of its effectiveness. But if OKH felt satisfaction at the number of Soviet formations which had been destroyed, Halder of OKW saw the other side of the coin and calculated that the German Army had, up to 23 July, lost twenty per cent of its effective strength and no less than fifty per cent of its panzer force.

Late in July, however, the Germans had the feeling of men who had made a terrible gamble and who had succeeded. Now that the operations connected with the opening of the campaign were at an end it was time to prepare for and to undertake the next stage. Once again this question brought dissension and bitter disagreement.

In the view of OKH any new offensive must set out to capture Moscow, having first destroyed the Red Army mass drawn up in front of and protecting the capital city. Hitler, ignoring logic and obsessed politically with the need either to take out Leningrad or to obtain the agricultural and economic riches of the Ukraine, wavered between those two options, indecisive, until he received a

memorandum from OKH urging him in the strongest possible terms
to drive for Moscow. In a critically worded reply he castigated the
High Command in general and von Brauchitsch, its chief, in
particular for a lack of ability and, having now decided to strike
southwards, insisted that his plans be followed. The Army High
Command surrendered and allowed Hitler's ideas for achieving a
tactical success in the south to override their strategic plans for
gaining total victory over the Soviets.

Let us recall the situation facing Army Groups Centre and South
during the middle weeks of August 1941. A combination of terrain
difficulties in the Pripet Marsh and the determined resistance of the
5th Red Army on the southern side of that obstacle, was obstructing
the advance of the inner wings of both Army Groups. Whereas the
central and outer wing corps of both Army Groups had forged
steadily eastwards these restraining factors on the inner flanks had
led to the creation of a 300 kilometre long salient which separated
one Army Group from the other and prevented an effective junction.
This was a situation which Hitler would no longer permit to
continue. He had already noted that German spearheads were
already deep behind the Soviet front in the north and calculated that
if he could destroy the 5th Red Army during an advance into the
Ukraine he would have flung a northern pincer around the Red
armies echeloned eastwards from Kiev. Then he would drive part of
Army Group South along the Dnieper until it too outflanked the Red
armies around Kiev and thus formed the southern pincer. The 2nd
Army on the northern flank would descend to meet the upstriking
17th Army and these two would form the infantry inner pincer jaws.
East of that encirclement would take place the panzer encirclement
when Guderian's Panzer Group 2, coming down from the north
would link with von Kleist's Panzer Group 1. While these
manoeuvrings and advances were taking place the attention of the
Soviet Command would be held by the German 6th Army which
would make moves as if to threaten Kiev itself.

Other sections of this book have stressed the importance of the
few metalled roads and the railways in the German-Russian War
and of the need to hold road junctions and crossings. So far as the
battle of the Kiev pocket is concerned, the most vital route of
communication was the railway line which ran from Moscow via
Konotop to Kiev, for this nourished the Red armies of the south-west
front. The rail junction of Konotop was, thus, the initial focus of
German intentions, for if that town could be taken then the rail link
would be cut and the unnourished south-west front would starve and
die.

To Guderian's Panzer Group was given the primary task of
advancing rapidly eastwards and of seizing that vital city.
Thereupon his armour would wheel southwards towards Romny.
When that place had also been taken and the northern pincer had
begun to form behind the Soviet forces then Army Group South

would make its move. Von Kleist, by that time, would have established and built up a bridgehead at Kremenchug out of which he would strike northwards. Between the inner, infantry pincers and the outer panzer arms the Red forces in the vast pocket, which extended in length for over 130 kilometres, would be contained, divided and destroyed piecemeal.

The second volume of the *History of the Great Fatherland War of the Soviet Union* in its treatment of the Kiev encirclement records an introductory battle whose outcome led almost directly into that great defeat for the tactics and principles of Stalin and his Chief of Staff, Shaposhnikov.

The Soviet official history records that to meet the thrust by the German 3rd Motorised Corps locally-raised militia units were flung in as sacrificial battalions to buy time while the defences around Kiev were made strong but admits that in carrying out this course of action the Soviet Command was following the dictates of OKH and allowing their forces in front of Kiev to be held fast. Meanwhile German armies had begun to outflank the Russian Front and the 17th Army, having found the junction of the south and south-west fronts, exploited that weakly-held seam, thereby helping to lift the 11th Army across the Dnieper. To evade another outflanking of the 6th, 12th and 18th Red Armies the Front commander launched the 26th Red Army into gallant but hopeless assaults to hold back the German drive.

When these desperate attempts failed, the Red forces in Uman had been encircled and even before the pocket had been destroyed, Army Group South had begun to sweep south-eastwards along the Dnieper, preparing to take up position ready to form the southern pincer of a newer, greater investment at Kiev.

STAVKA pulled back its troops, regrouped and raised more new units to hold back the enemy, but the raw levies which each successive comb-out produced were no match for the trained, experienced and aggressive German armies flushed with victory. Even the *Soviet History* admits that the troops of the south and south-west fronts were in a difficult situation which grew rapidly more serious as the pocket began to take shape.

To the west, around Kiev, the German 6th Army was exerting pressure while eastwards and southwards across the Soviet lines of communication ranged von Kleist's panzer units still thrusting eastwards against the fierce but futile opposition of the 26th Red Army. Meanwhile, to the north Guderian's Panzer Group 2 and the infantry mass of the 2nd Army, having completed their own eastward drive, halted for regrouping before they recommenced their thrusts on 8 August.

Wrongly assessing the German intention, STAVKA massed its troops in the Briansk sector, was caught off guard and could not deploy its forces when Guderian's Panzer Group smashed like a giant steel fist through the fronts of the 3rd and 21st Red Armies and penetrated deep into the Soviet rear area. Of his two panzer corps, Guderian selected the 24th to be the cutting edge to the drive that he was now about to undertake and delegated to the 47th Panzer Corps the less glamorous but more vital role of protecting the outer flank against Red Army assault. By 16 August his reconnaissance units had reached Starodub while advanced elements of the 2nd Army had begun their move on Gomel. The eastward drive for Konotop – the first, vital objective – was gaining ground against the most fanatic resistance and even the raising of a 40th Red Army and its insertion into the Russian battle line could not halt the German advance which now forced the main body of the south-west front to retreat in wild disorder.

During 17 August the 24th Panzer Corps was within striking distance of the Desna, a 1,000 kilometre long tributary of the Dnieper, whose natural strength had been reinforced by defensive lines of field fortifications, which had been built to supplement the already-strong existing defences, hastily constructed by the local civil population under military direction.

The German drive to 'bounce' the Desna gathered pace, and to concentrate the maximum force at the vital point Geyr von Schweppenburg, the 24th Corps Commander, selected the 3rd Panzer under Model and gave to that unit the task of forcing a crossing of the river at Novgorod-Seversk. Model grouped his division into two commands. One would strike for the town and draw the Soviet forces to that point while a second and more mobile battle group carried out a *coup de main* against the giant bridge which spanned the 400-metre wide river at that point. If that bridge could be seized and held, the 3rd Panzer Division would have formed a bridgehead dryshod and from this could then begin the drive southwards which would bring them into Konotop. D-Day for the assault was 24 August.

Model's time-table for the main assault on Seversk could not be kept. The poor roads, the sandy rutted paths along which the main column moved, slowed its advance but this delay served to convince the Soviet Command, persuaded by the size of the force that Model's main thrust was being made against the town and they committed their reserves to the battle at that point. The main body of the 3rd Panzer Division was involved in fierce fighting against Soviet infantry, artillery and armour whose counter-attacks slowed the impetus of the assault.

Meanwhile, the column whose task it was to seize the bridge had moved at dawn, 03.45hrs, and despite having had to fight its way through severe opposition had by 10.00hrs reached the approaches to the 700-metre long bridge, halted, concentrated and prepared to charge across the giant steel erection which stood on river banks as sheer as cliffs and which were 300 metres high.

The first German troops on to the bridge were men of an assault engineer detachment who began removing the green-packeted detonating charges under fire, sweeping for mines and clearing the road forward for the panzer company whose task it would then be to rush the defenders. A crossing made at the fastest speed which could now be got from tank engines overstrained with use, lacking proper maintenance and worn out with the strain of combat, would take in excess of three minutes. Three minutes of tension and fear during which one Soviet anti-tank shell could not only smash the first panzer but would block the bridge and stop any further advance, leaving the Soviet defenders to carry out a demolition of the bridge at a time of their own selection.

Soviet reaction to the German assault was surprisingly slow and within an hour of reaching the approaches to the bridge, German troops had crossed it and had established a bridgehead on the cliffs. Model flung his panzer columns across in unbroken line determined to build up his forces on the Desna's eastern bank before the full weight of Soviet counter-attacks came in against him. He was only just in time. Drawing upon reserves of armour, guns and infantry taken from the Briansk and Reserve Fronts Budyenny launched part of his south-west front against Model's Division, whose armour he now realised was part of a pincer that was beginning to encircle him.

A confused, desperate battle then ensued. Model's bridgehead at Seversk needed to be held so that he could pass fresh forces across the Desna, through the bridgehead and into the salient to the south which his armoured drive was creating. For the Soviets the destruction of the Seversk bridgehead was imperative for through it were being channelled the forces which would encircle them. Both sides put into battle all the forces and the skills which they possessed but of the two military commanders it was Model who was the more able and who handled his forces with the greater skill.

He flung out a battle group to capture Shostka to cut the Moscow–Kiev railway line at that point and in the fury of his advance the newly-formed 40th Red Army was badly mauled and driven back. On the right flank of Guderian's panzers a thrust by the 2nd Army broke through the Briansk Front and that of the 21st Red Army, driving these back towards lower reaches of the Desna river along whose eastern bank STAVKA hoped a cohesive battle line would be formed. The town of Chernigov, which it had been ordered to be held to the last, was abandoned and then Reichenau's 6th Army entered the battle in front of Kiev, to carry out its part of the encirclement plan. It struck forward and had reached the Dnieper by 22 August.

Although neither the Red Army infantry nor its tank masses had been able to hold back the German panzer advances the Red Air Force had been more successful and during one particularly fortunate day had destroyed practically the whole of a panzer regiment, leaving it, when the last Soviet machines had climbed away, with only ten vehicles as runners.

STAVKA then decided to launch the 21st Red Army across the lines of communication of the 3rd and 4th Panzer Divisions by attacking the Seversk bridgehead but even its most determined assaults were driven back, for by this time there was almost no liaison or cooperation between the Soviet fronts and little could be achieved. In some areas the Soviet line had begun to fracture and troops of the 13th Army had begun a retreat against orders from their positions. The fear of encirclement was spreading fast through the Red units still holding the walls of the salient.

The advance by the German forces was not without periods of great anxiety for the rank and file as well as for the commanders but these were caused less by the action of the Soviet forces or their reaction to German moves. The two greatest inhibitors to the smooth flowing forward movement by the panzers were shortage of fuel and tenacious mud. One particular crisis occurred when petrol columns failed to reach the panzer spearhead and left the vehicles of the 3rd and 4th Panzer Divisions stranded and isolated across the steppes, prey to the tank counter-attacks which then came in against the immobile vehicles. Only the stubborn defence of German infantry units helped to prevent the total destruction of Geyr von Schweppenburg's corps, but losses to the German armoured regiments during that engagement were severe and the 6th Panzer Regiment was reduced to the strength of a panzer company at the end of one day's battle.

The capture of Konotop was now unnecessary, for with Guderian's seizure of Shostka the railway life-line had been cut and the time had now come for Army Group South to set its own offensive in motion. On 31 August the 17th Army stormed across the Dnieper, a thousand metres wide at that point, and striking along the boundary between south-west and south front established a bridge-head south-east of Kremenchug. This was quickly consolidated and within a day a bridge had been erected, across which reinforcements poured. Von Kleist and his panzer group could begin the build up to form the second armour pincer. With the fall of Kremenchug on 12 September, the strategic road and rail network which that city controlled passed into German hands. All the prerequisites had been completed; von Kleist's group could begin its upward stroke.

For the task of bursting out of the Kremenchug bridgehead he chose two of the best panzer divisions in the German Army, the 16th and the 9th, even though the latter at that time had suffered such heavy casualties that it had had to be organised into two weak battle groups. Despite this weakness and the glutinous mud which held the AFVs fast for nearly a whole day, the 9th Panzer in a sudden thrust captured a bridge across the Senchas river, and had soon established a defensive perimeter. From there the move would begin towards the strategic high ground at Lubny and Lokvitsa and the sealing of the panzer ring.

The sister division, 16th Panzer, also had had to battle its way forward against opposition so strong that the War Diary on 13 September recorded that Red aircraft concentrated upon individual vehicles of the division. Despite these attacks and delayed by thrusts into its flank, the 16th Panzer Division nevertheless was able to bring the advance northwards.

In the north Guderian's leading troops reached the Seym river by 2 September and had located, from a set of captured Russian maps, the boundary between the Red armies facing them. To exploit the weakness along this seam the 3rd Panzer Division drove forward, smashed the inner wings of its opponents and not only drove them back in disorder, but threatened the rear of the 5th Red Army. The position of the Soviet troops in front of Model had now reached crisis point, but the strain of campaigning was also having its effect upon the men and machines of the 3rd Panzer Division. Lack of fuel, shortage of spares, the bad roads and Soviet opposition were a constant drain upon the vehicles which still kept up their careering advance southwards. On more than one occasion his point force was reduced to the strength of a single panzer battalion. Nevertheless, it continued to smash its way forward.

The German infantry armies, too, were making ground and under their continual pressure there were signs of dissolution in the Red Army units. Kirponos, South-West Front Commander, reported the critical situation to Budyenny, his superior, and demanded reinforcements if he was to hold the German thrusts. None were available. Budyenny's own request for a partial withdrawal to close the gap between the 40th and 21st Armies was rejected by STAVKA as premature, but two infantry divisions were released and sent forward to hold the jaws open.

The ring was almost tight-drawn around the Soviet troops, but neither Stalin nor the High Command would countenance a withdrawal of the forces from the salient and dismissed repeated appeals by Kirponos as expressions of panic. On 14 September central control in the pocket broke down and the troops as well as their commanders were to battle henceforth without properly formulated orders regarding the future course of action, particularly escape attempts.

That is not to say that the Soviet Supreme Command had abandoned the men in the salient. Far from it. On 14 September the GOC South-West Front ordered his troops east of the German pincer to strike at the panzer ring and to force a corridor through which an escape might be made. Remnants of the 40th Army, of 245th Cavalry Corps belonging to the 38th Army, as well as a number of independent divisions and other reinforcements were flung against the left flank of Guderian's panzer groups and the right flank of von Kleist's.

By this time Model had advanced southwards far and fast. He formed a small battle group whose task it was to increase the pace of the drive south. The immediate objective was the small town of

Romny, at which place it had first been planned that the pincer arms would meet but Red opposition had slowed von Kleist. To carry out Model's orders and to bring the armoured fighting vehicles forward through the liquid mud which pouring rain had produced, the tank men used torn-down fences, tree branches and straw bundles to help the panzer tracks get a purchase in the clinging slime. This all proved of no avail and vehicles which found firm ground had to winch out those machines still trapped. The battle through the mud lasted for much of the day and retarded the pace of the advance to Romny.

When, at last, all the panzer group's vehicles were on firm ground, one armoured group roared towards the town, fighting down the Red Army units and civilians who sought to impede them, while a second swung past Romny. This latter column cut the railway line and then took charge of the bridgehead which the main column had gained across the Sula river.

It took two whole days for 3rd Panzer Division to battle its way through Romny, for it encountered the most desperate defence of Soviet infantry and tank men as well as bombing from the Soviet Air Force whose commanders seemed prepared to burn the town to the ground rather than see it fall to the Germans.

The South-West Front Commander poured men of the 40th, 21st and 5th Armies into the battle, but all the many and furious assaults of his forces had been beaten back by Geyr's corps. Still the German panzers advanced. Model then sent out a smaller battle group with orders to fight its way through to Lokvitsa, a town deep inside territory which Army Group South detachments, by that time, should have reached. But the spearhead of Kleist's Panzer Group had reached only as far as Chorol and Lubny.

In the south fighting had been bitter and protracted, for the Soviet troops were battling with desperate fanaticism to hold open the pincer jaws. At Lubny during the height of the street battle Hube, the divisional commander, flung out a battle group of tanks to effect a link with a similar group from Model's 3rd Panzer Division which had, by that time, reached the heights at Luka.

The corridor separating the spearheads of the two panzer groups had now been narrowed to a funnel less than thirty to forty kilometres wide between Lokvitsa and Lubny and the Soviet troops were too few in number to hold open the pincer jaws or to smash the rapidly closing ring by attacks either from within or without the encirclement.

The two panzer groups joined hands in the Lokvitsa-Lubny sector and sealed the ring. Four whole armies – less the casualties – as well as elements from others were caught fast. The perimeter, starting from the west, was held by the 37th Red Army which, surrounded on three sides by German forces, was holding the area in front of Kiev. The battle front then followed the line of the Dnieper as far as Cherkassy, at which point it swung north to Lubny then westwards to Lokvitsa and ran back towards Kiev, where it ended some thirty kilometres north of the town on the Dnieper river. Within its confines there was growing confusion, for STAVKA could give no orders regarding the breakout for it was out of wireless touch with the senior formations.

According to the *Soviet History* it was Khruschev, a political officer, who ordered that Kiev be given up. This decision he forced through against the inclinations of Kirponos, the military commander, who stood by Stalin's order to fight to the last.

Late in the evening of 17–18 September, Kirponos ordered the trapped units to break out. The plan was for the 21st Red Army to make its attempt at Romny towards which point 2nd Red Cavalry Corps would strike from the east. The 5th Red Army was to drive on Lokvitsa and the 26th Red Army was to escape via Lubny. The one army within the pocket which received no order to break out was the 37th holding post at Kiev. Without orders to evacuate it stood and fought until 19 September when it began its own evacuation of Kiev. Budyenny, the failed commander and who had been described as 'an anachronism on horseback' was replaced by Timoshenko, another relic from the old Bolshevik days and another friend of Stalin.

The link had been made at 18.00hrs on 15 September, and to the first thin and broken line which the meeting of the two German battle groups effected, reinforcements came up to thicken the investing troops around the Soviets and to prepare to fragment these and to destroy them piecemeal. At tactically important points, road or rail junctions, for example, the German ring was made up of a double layer of units fighting in a back-to-back situation. One line faced eastwards ready to battle against the Soviet troops outside the encirclement who would seek to smash through and to liberate their comrades, while troops of the inner German line faced westwards and their units advanced like beaters in a drive, overrunning and destroying the Red Army troops which they met.

To conclude this account of the Kiev encirclement let us draw upon the impressions and recollections of German soldiers who fought in it. The first is that of a battery commander in a field artillery regiment which helped to split up and destroy the unit within the encirclement.

> The battery was told that it was being pulled out of the line as there were signs that the enemy's resistance was weakening. A break would have given us a chance to service the vehicles and to check the guns, but our rest period lasted less than half a day. Just after first light on the next morning a DR came roaring up. How I hated DRs: they always brought bad news. First it was 'Officers to O Group' and then 'Forty minutes notice to move'.
> According to the IO large enemy forces were trying to break out eastwards. An infantry battalion was placed under command to give us protection as the location of both enemy and friendly units was unknown. We reached our destination, a collection of huts shot to pieces during the fighting of the past few days, past masses of dead,

shot up Red tanks, hundreds of steel helmets which had been thrown away, dead horses, burnt out vehicles and a few German graves with birch wood crosses. The passage of our vehicles threw up clouds of dust which coated our faces like masks. Stukas flew overhead to give us cover and a few MEs came roaring over.

Russian civilians were still there wandering about trying to rescue their pitiful few bits and pieces from the shattered houses. We tried to get some of our recently taken prisoners-of-war to help the civilians but they were not keen – there seems to be no spirit of community in this country.

Orders came for us to move further forward, but the bridge ahead was destroyed and we had to find our way up the line through a night lit up like a firework display. The horizon flickered with light; tracer sent out strings of multi-coloured pearls through the darkness. Here and there Very lights climbed into the night sky. At 01.00hrs we finally reached our positions. We had to be ready to open fire at first light . . . Just before dawn we were ready and as it grew lighter we could see that our guns were in an area devoid of almost every bit of cover except for a few small bushes and we were only then informed that small groups of Bolsheviks were trying to escape along the road which ran past the battery positions. Even with our infantry battalion all round us we did not feel that safe.

A low ridge in front of us I took to be part of our front line for there was a mass of transport moving about and other vehicles standing on the high ground camouflaged under trees. We could see soldiers, horses and all the paraphernalia of an army. We thought they must be from another of our divisions, otherwise they would not be moving about quite so openly.

Suddenly the troop next to mine opened fire and shells began to explode on the ridge. Then back came the reply. Shells began to fall around us and we flung ourselves to the ground. As soon as there was a pause in the firing, I got my guns into action even though they were standing uncamouflaged and in the open. We could see our shells setting fire to the houses and lorries. An enemy battery was blown apart; one of its guns limbered up and began to race downhill in an attempt to escape, but a direct hit halted and destroyed it.

This was a gunners' dream. My men could not believe their eyes. They were firing and could actually see the effect their fire was having; they could see their shells exploding in the enemy positions. This was for gunners a most unusual experience.

Prisoners began to come in. The Bolsheviks still fought up there on the ridge even though they were surrounded on all sides. Their machine-gun fire swept across our gun positions and their mortars dropped bombs near our guns. Then suddenly, their resistance weakened and they began to come over to us with the strain of the past weeks' fighting imprinted on their faces and showing in their eyes. They seemed to be pleased that the war is over for them. Some of them are quite old men and others are boys scarcely old enough to be out of school. In the next few days our infantry battalion and our artillery patrols took nearly 400 captives. The enemy in this part of the cauldron was crumbling fast.

The soldiers holding the eastern wall had as hard a task to hold off the attacking Soviets who were trying to break into the pocket as those other German formations had who were fighting to destroy the entrapped Soviet units. The account given here is by a grenadier who, in the desperate weeks of battle before the pocket was finally destroyed helped to hold off the attacks by Timoshenko's armies.

Behind a low hill are our mortars. The ground at the foot of the hill on the forward slope is broken with small ravines and we have dug our defensive positions into the wall of one of these. We've been here two weeks now and it is not only my cave, but also my home. One can get used to anything. Of course our first slit trenches on this sector were a bit primitive. We had dug them under fire using only our entrenching tools, but when the Bolsheviks sent in attack after attack the line was moved back to this little ravine which is better ground from a tactical point of view, and is a ready-made trench system.

I am safe in my little hole in Russia. Safe from the heavy shells which roar over us like express trains as well as from the smaller shells from the field artillery; even from the Rata aircraft which fly over us at night and drop their little anti-personnel bombs on us. Our mortars are quite close at hand and our MGs are always at instant readiness. We have to be alert. It is our task to form part of the corps which is to hold off the Bolsheviks who are trying to break through the panzer wall which we have put around most of their army. Their attacks are quite desperate and quite hopeless. As I have said, you can become accustomed to anything; even to their attacks. Whether they come in with tanks or whether the infantry comes in without support; whether their Cossacks charge in on horses or whether they come rolling forward in motor lorries, the end is always the same. They are driven back with such losses that one wonders how they can find the courage and the men to keep coming on. Some of the dead have been out there for weeks and are badly decomposed. The sights and smells are bad enough for us, but they have to attack across this carpet of their own dead comrades. Do they have no feeling of fear? It certainly seems not for they attack regularly and charge forward without hesitation. Some of my comrades think that the Bolsheviks must be either drugged or drunk to keep coming in like that. But we do have also a constant stream of their soldiers coming over to us surrendering; not always after a heavy attack, but often during a lull. The Bolshevik soldiers are a strange mixture of fanaticism and oriental despair.

Clearing the pocket was not always a matter of flushing out and capturing the soldiers of a defeated army, for many Soviet troops did not consider themselves beaten and their units fought literally to the death.

The dead stretched for miles, [recorded a German soldier]. Here there would be one or two. Farther away a small group, some piled upon each other. We lost men too, for it must not be believed that this was an easy victory. But their dead, particularly where there had been a fierce battle, formed a carpet.

The efforts to break out like the break-in attempts, by and large, were unsuccessful and have gone unrecorded. No Soviet personal accounts written by junior ranks and dealing with that period seem to have been written nor have Soviet regimental histories appeared in the West. Lacking these, one has to rely upon German accounts. Their wireless intercept service was excellent and their reports recorded in war diaries, together with the official archives and unit histories, are available, but must be considered subjective. The only counter-balance to the German record of those days is the *Soviet Official History*, but this is heavily shot through with propaganda.

Nevertheless, that history describes the break out attempts as disorganised. German accounts are less charitable. The truth was that with the encirclement complete the German forces then began to split the Soviet forces within the perimeter into small groups. The 37th and 26th Armies were cut up into three smaller pockets and destroyed. With their annihilation all cohesive attempts seem to have collapsed and there was a general uncoordinated struggle to escape. The *Soviet History*, describing in some detail the escape attempts of South-West Front HQ, states that when the Command Group arrived in Goroditche during the morning of 18 September, there were no aircraft to fly them out of the pocket. The HQ Group was then intercepted and surrounded in the woods of Shumaikovo and involved in a battle which lasted until 22 September. It was during this battle that General Kirponos was mortally wounded. In whatever direction the Soviet troops turned there were German panzer and grenadier groups ready to engage them. On the Sula river the Germans held the only crossing points and a mass escape was out of the question. Individuals and small groups passed silently and stealthily through the German ring, but many were intercepted, others were driven back into the encirclement. At other points the extensive marshes of the region helped to conceal the escaping Red Army men, but less than 500 of 21st Army headquarters managed to get away. Weeks later German patrols sweeping the area still encountered small groups of ragged and exhausted Red Army soldiers determined to fight through to reach the main Soviet battle line.

The Red armies in the Kiev pocket had been destroyed; in a sense they had been sacrificed. It is questionable whether Stalin's determination to reinforce the salient around Kiev was due to a fore-knowledge of Hitler's plans, a premonition, a desire to draw the German forces away from Moscow, or whether his decision to hold Kiev was a military blunder which had accidently turned out to have been the correct solution. As far as most German military writers are concerned, it was Hitler's insistence on fighting that particular battle which lost Germany the war with Russia. Obsessed as he was with propaganda he was determined to give the German people a victory – the greatest military encirclement of all time – and in pursuit of that tactical success he cast away the chance to win the strategical prize: total victory. Hoffman in his work *Die Schlacht von Moskau 1941* had no doubt when he wrote, "Set against this victory was the time which had been lost as a result of the operation. Two valuable months spent in the encirclement battles went by before Army Group Centre could resume the attack on Moscow". The virtual standstill at the approaches to Moscow during August and September gave the Red Army a respite as well as a chance to bring in strong forces and to construct deep defences in front of the capital. Which, if either, of the two dictators was correct cannot now be determined. The only facts are that as a result of this battle of encirclement nearly 655,000 Red Army men had been killed or taken prisoner, as well as 884 armoured fighting vehicles and 3,178 pieces of artillery.

The causes of this Soviet defeat are many and varied, but the most important factors must be attributed to a lack of planning and this may well have resulted from the fear which at that time obsessed all Soviet commanders at every level of command. To admit failure in those early days was to suffer degradation at least, but more often failure meant death before a firing squad of NKVD men. The communications problem within units and between senior commands was not resolved until much later in the war, and it is true to say that never at any time did the Red Army have a communications network as sophisticated as that of the Germans.

In any case for the Soviet troops the problem and the tactics involved in breaking out of encirclement became academic ones after 1943, for in that year and for the remainder of the war it was, generally, the German Army whose forces were invested and who had to fight their way out of pockets in which they were caught as a result of their inferior equipment and the stubbornness of the Supreme Commander and his docile OKW.

28

The Cholm pocket

Winter 1941–1942

"On the northern sector of the Eastern Front German troops ... gained contact with men surrounded in a (strategically) important position. The garrison, under the command of Major General Scherer, had been fighting a battle since 21 January 1942...."

OKW COMMUNIQUÉ, 6 MAY 1942

During the night of 6 October 1941 the first snows fell upon German soldiers fighting in an offensive intended to capture Moscow. That this snow soon thawed and turned to slushy mud could not hide the fact that the period of campaigning weather remaining was now reduced to only weeks. By 2 December the German offensive had ground to a halt and almost immediately the Soviet forces went over to a counter-offensive.

Four Red armies first struck the 3rd Panzer and 4th Panzer Army and flung those back. Then along the rest of the frozen Eastern Front other major German groupings were also forced to withdraw as their under-equipped and inadequately-clothed soldiers fought an overwhelmingly strong enemy who was determined to drive them back from the approaches to Moscow.

These withdrawals turned into a retreat and then threatened to degenerate into a rout as losses increased to enormous scale. Nearly a million German soldiers had been killed, wounded or were missing, and, seeing this at unit level, the 6th Panzer Division, for example, was soon without any armoured fighting vehicles, had only ten per cent of its artillery strength and had lost most of its lorries.

Aware of the weakness of his battle line Hitler ordered his troops to form 'hedgehogs' around strategic towns and areas, planning to use these to slow and then halt the Soviet drive. The chess board pattern of strong points did cause the Russian drive to lose its first impetus but during January 1942 this picked up again. Germany's 135 divisions grouped into twelve armies then came once again under the pressure of the 328 Soviet divisions which had been massed into forty-two Red armies. Soviet thrusts forced salients in the German line, seized bridgeheads and trapped German troops in pockets of men cut off from their own lines.

One of the greatest of these was that containing nearly 100,000 men and 20,000 horses of 2nd and 10th Corps in the area of Demyansk, but it is not with that great encirclement that we are dealing. The description given here is of a smaller encirclement; of a garrison of less than 4,000 men but who, without artillery, armour or heavy weapons, demonstrated the principles and characteristics required in the successful defence of a pocket.

The little town of Cholm lies at the confluence of the Lovat and Kunya rivers in an area of marsh and swamp south of Lake Ilmen. Cholm and the area around it was the only solid ground between Veliki Luki and Demyansk. Thus it was a land bridge and this militarily-important consideration was underlined by the fact that the town of 12,000 inhabitants was located at a crossroads where the roads north-south and east-west met. Thus, for the Germans as well as for the Soviets, the possession of Cholm was essential to the success of their future battle plans. It was this compulsion to possess the Cholm springboard that produced the battles which raged during the winter of 1941–42 around this hitherto insignificant town.

As a result of the Soviet offensive, by 13 January the 3rd Red Assault Army (five infantry divisions, five infantry brigades, a tank brigade and a ski-brigade), forming part of the Kalinin Front, had smashed part of the southern wing of Army Group North, had crossed the Waldai plateau and reached the banks of the Lovat river. Under the pressure of their advance the main body of the 39th Corps was forced back; Cholm itself, garrisoned by 3,500 men of a variety of different units, was quickly surrounded and cut off from the mass of the 39th Corps which took up positions to the south-west of the town.

The Corps mounted local counter-attacks in an attempt to pass armour through to strengthen the defence but the vehicles could not advance along the icy roads. Only the infantry could move, wading through the deep drifts to join the little garrison which had met, held and driven out of Cholm the first attacks launched by ski troops of the Soviet Assault Army.

The Corps commander was determined to do everything in his power to support the Cholm troops and organised convoys to bring up rations, clothing, fodder for the animals and great amounts of ammunition. The first of these reached their destination, but within hours Russian ski troops had swung past the town and had cut the road. The convoys were halted. Nothing could reach Cholm by road. This situation prevailed for the following 105 days and the only links to the outside world were the wireless morse key, and the aircraft which brought in arms and ammunition.

The principal task of Major-General Scherer, the fortress commander, was to deny the town to the Soviets. When the former commander of 281st Sicherungs Division contemplated his force he may well have been dismayed, for it was made up of fragments of 123rd Infantry Division, 218th Infantry Division, from two other infantry regiments, elements of a Luftwaffe field regiment, men from 65th Reserve Police Battalion and some drivers from a naval detachment. Among this sprinkling of miscellaneous units there were also artillerymen who were without guns, but who had skill as Forward Observation Officers which was to make them invaluable during the months of the coming siege. By the force of his personality Scherer was able to weld together these remnants and to convert them into a homogeneous whole determined to stand fast until relieved.

Being so quickly and so completely isolated from the German main line and lacking a road link, the only solution was for the pocket to be supplied by air. Within the two-kilometre square area into which it was compressed the garrison constructed an airstrip seventy metres long and twenty-five metres wide, on to which it was intended that Ju 52 transport aircraft would land with supplies and take off again carrying wounded. Under fire and shuddering along such a primitive runway it is not surprising to learn that the loss-rate was so high (twenty-five Ju 52s during the period of the siege) that glider landings had to be introduced. Eighty of those aircraft were lost. Parachute drops were also used but to land supplies with accuracy upon such a small perimeter – a perimeter which shrank at one time to only a kilometre square – proved impossible.

The situation facing Scherer was depressing. Cut off and surrounded, with no firm supply link, with a shortage of trained infantry, lacking field artillery, anti-tank guns or armour he was expected to hold, with a force numbering only a few thousand a strategically vital area, and his orders were to hold out to the end or until relieved. The prospect was grim.

Talking later of the time spent in the pocket, General Scherer recalled that the first heavy attacks came in during 23 January, and produced serious crises as the Soviet tank assaults nibbled away at the defences; first to the west, then to the east, subsequently from the south and, finally, from the north. "Soviet tanks shot everything to pieces. They smashed everything. My men had no respite, no rest; could not even warm themselves. Enemy artillery smashed the last remaining houses in which my men were sheltering, but they held out and fought, defending themselves like lions." Without anti-tank guns there was little that the defenders could hope to do against the Russian armour, but two barricades were erected across a street and on the second of these an explosive charge was laid. Coolly an infantryman watched the approach of the tanks and as these began to push aside the flimsy barrier a fuse was lit, fire ran along the cable and with a shattering detonation one of the tanks was destroyed. The other machines turned back; for the moment the danger was averted.

During that day there was a welcome addition to the strength of the garrison when a detachment of mountain troops, 200 men of the 10th Machine Gun Battalion, fought their way through the encircling Soviets and into the perimeter. This accretion of strength was the morale boost which the garrison needed and on the following day a counter-attack drove the Red troops out of the north-western part of the city into which they had penetrated.

A lieutenant writing about Scherer's garrison described the positions they held, "Positions – What positions? The ground was frozen hard and the snow was breast deep. Within a short time the town itself was a heap of ruins. Within these ruins or in the cellars which still remained Scherer's soldiers were quartered. In these primitive conditions it was almost impossible for them to get warm when they were released from sentry duty or came back after long hours of fighting. Simple stoves were made from milk churns and petrol drums. Explosive charges blew holes in the frozen earth to make the first defensive positions inside which machine-guns were positioned. The Scherer battle group not only fought the enemy but also the Russian winter with its unimaginable cold. Without proper quarters, with no prepared defences, crouched in holes and behind walls of snow those men undertook the battle of Cholm."

Behind these parapets of snow and ice, day and night, the small garrison withstood attacks by Soviet armour and infantry. As usual the Russian assaults came in punctually and according to a precisely-maintained timetable. This rigidity was a defect enabling General Scherer to move his men from one threatened sector to another, secure in the fact that the area from which they had been taken would be unattacked until its turn came round again.

The area in which the troops were confined was so small that much of the air-drop ammunition, food and supplies either fell into Soviet areas or into no-man's-land. In this latter case rescue attempts were made. From vantage points within the perimeter eyes watched to see that the Soviets did not remove the container with its precious freight and during the hours of darkness small commandos of men moved out into the ground in front of their trenches to recover the canisters. The amounts parachuted in, particularly of food, were never sufficient and the group was on reduced rations from the first day of encirclement.

The commanders within and without the pocket had not been idle and plans had been made to mount a relief operation. For its part in this the garrison formed two assault groups in company strength and placed these on the western side of the town ready to advance to contact the relief force. To prepare a jumping off point for this two company battle groups, a fighting patrol of Alpine troops, first attacked the Soviets and drove them from a vital height. It was from that hill that the battle groups would strike westwards towards the relief columns, but first the jumping-off point had to be built up.

This was no easy task for the weather had deteriorated. Hour-long blizzards, bitter cold and biting winds which drove particles of freezing ice into unprotected faces made this a superhuman task. Each round of ammunition, each weapon had to man-ported through waist high snow and then defensive positions had to be cut out of the snow and thickened with ice blocks.

The appalling conditions had also affected the efforts of the relief column, only a dozen miles away. Snow, blizzard and icy roads halted all movement except sledges drawn by Russian horses accustomed to the intense cold. The relief column infantry struggled forward against an implacable enemy who were growing in strength with each passing day. One attack cleared Soviet blocks from the Cholm road but the attempt failed to seize the strategic Point 72.7. The cold had now reached forty degrees below zero and the winds were of a power sufficient to knock a man down. The grenadiers went in again and again to capture the high ground, wading through snow so deep that they had to hold their rifles and machine-guns above their heads to prevent the action from being fouled by snow and thus frozen solid. Every attack failed. The last one reached a plateau, an area of flat and open ground 300 metres long, across which the grenadiers would have to pass to reach the crest. Each attempt they made was beaten back; was renewed and beaten back again. Then the Soviet troops waded slowly through the snow into their counter-attacks and they in turn were crushed. For hours the battle raged to and fro without result until the Russians committed their last reserves and this was sufficient. They drove back the German grenadiers.

There was then an unexpected advantage. The efforts that the relief column had made for their advance had created a salient in the Russian line at whose point was massed the field artillery of the 218th Division. The fire from those guns could now support the beleaguered garrison.

With the failure of the relieving forces to break through, the Cholm battle group waiting in the jump-off area was stood down but the position itself was still held despite the most appalling conditions. So great had been the deterioration in the weather that the journey from the last houses in the town to the exposed positions on the high ground consumed the greater part of the night, and the porters arrived at the outpost trenches in a state of complete exhaustion. Soviet artillery fire and Siberian snipers caused casualties which were an added strain, reducing front-line strengths. Supplies of protective cream began to run out and more and more cases of frostbite and sickness withdrew men from the front. Illness and casualties now meant that there were insufficient troops to man the extended perimeter and a withdrawal had to be made to a shorter one based on the original front line. At some points the battle zone ran along the main east-west street of the town of Cholm.

Night after night the Red infantry attacked at regular and precise intervals but without success. Then came a pause in their assaults. Then, clearly through the night air, could be heard the sound of lorry engines. The Soviets were building up their forces and provisioning themselves for a new offensive. This opened with a barrage of shells from a battery of 17.2cm howitzers under whose crushing bombardment the Soviet commanders expected to destroy the obstinate Germans who were obstructing the advance. When the barrage failed to blast a way through, a longer and more concentrated bombardment by lighter guns began destroying systematically the houses in which the garrison was sheltering. For two days and nights the barrage continued and then behind it the Soviet armour came in against men without proper anti-tank guns. The German anti-tank rifles were ineffective against the case-hardened plates of the Soviet tanks and it was, once again, upon the hard pressed infantry that the task fell of fighting the T 34s at close quarters.

Smothered in the rubble of a cellar there was found a 3.7cm German anti-tank gun – called the 'door knocker' because of its inability to destroy the Russian tanks. This was cleaned and wheeled out to engage the Soviet vehicles. The weapon had no proper sights but, using it at point-blank range, the German gunners fired and with four shots destroyed first one T 34 and then a second. A third Russian tank bombarded the single gun but this was then driven off by the persistent shelling of the 3.7. This single gun time and again held back the Soviet tanks as they struck forward towards the town.

Contact between German batteries in the main battle line and Forward Observation Officers in the garrison then enabled the artillery to direct their fire not only upon Russian artillery positions and troop emplacements but to go on to lay down defensive barrages around the German strong points. Such was the degree of cooperation that the guns served as long range anti-tank guns, picking off individual tanks of an assault wave.

The force of the Soviet attacks then began to fade and become less persistent, allowing the garrison to form Alarm Companies whose task it was to carry out immediate counter-attacks should a Soviet thrust obtain a foothold in some part of the town. Despite the length of time that the siege had now lasted the Soviet commanders had still not learnt flexibility and the stubborn rigidity of their assaults still allowed the Germans, fighting a battle on interior lines, to switch troops rapidly from one threatened point to another.

As the days of investment lengthened into weeks the garrison began to establish a routine. The unit war diary was written up daily and sent out by morse to Corps HQ. Cellars were strengthened, improved and made proof against the bitter weather and the incessant snowstorms. Outside the perimeter the main German force was able to send greater support.

On one occasion while Stukas dive-bombed Soviet infantry and armour concentrations, dispersing or dominating them, three Ju 52s landed and unloaded three anti-tank guns, a mortar and badly-needed medical supplies. The garrison was still under-armed, but at least it could now fight back with more than one PAK.

In the corner of a cellar six anti-tank mines were found, not much

under normal conditions but worth their weight in gold to men short
of tank-busting weapons. Russian weapons captured during their
frustrated assaults, found in the rubble or damaged and abandoned,
were rescued by special squads of men, repaired, refurbished and put
back into use against their former owners. Towards the end of the
encirclement even a Soviet tank was repaired and used. Everything
was pressed into service.

For their part the Soviets were not inactive and infiltrated
snipers right forward to the very edge of the German positions.
Camouflaged, often completely buried in snow, they waited
patiently for the chance to achieve a kill. The garrison concealed its
trenches and hid its communications routes from observation by the
extensive use of the white supply drop parachutes. Day followed day,
night followed night, sometimes with long periods of silence in
which every sound could be heard and at other times in shattering
noise when the earth shuddered with the concussion of explosions of
hour-long barrages and bombardments of savage proportions. Very
lights would uncover in their harsh white light a Soviet infantry
attack moving towards the town and then the troops in the
threatened sector, brought to instant readiness, would man the line
of icy trenches and fire into the masses charging towards them.

Deserters from the Red Army reported that for 23 February, Red
Army Day, a major assault was being built up and on that day an
entire Soviet infantry division advanced to the assault behind a
wave of tanks. Only the armour reached the outskirts of the town;
the infantry waves were driven back with heavy loss. They reformed
and came on again only to be smashed a second time in the fire of the
German machine-guns. Again and again they tried and eventually
they had forced a way into and had penetrated the eastern outskirts
of the little town. Their broken formation was hastily regrouped to
exploit the situation and then the Red infantry mass charged
forward, shoulder to shoulder, attempting to crush the defenders.
The grenadiers cut down the advancing infantry, but were
themselves forced to withdraw under the great pressure. Immediately the Alarm Companies were brought forward and went
into action to stem and to thrust back the Russian incursions.

Throughout that day and for the following two days and nights
the Russians poured forward in eighteen separate attacks, with or
without tank support, covered by savage bombardments of artillery
or by the Soviet Air Force which strafed the German perimeter. This
activity brought the Luftwaffe back into the battle and under the
cover of the Messerschmitts and Focke Wulf fighters Stukas dive
bombed the Soviet transport columns, tank and infantry concentrations.

While this battle raged more Ju 52 transports flew in, unloaded
infantry reinforcements and evacuated some of the many wounded.
Those who could not be got away were given the few luxuries which
were brought in – a little cognac, a few cigarettes, some sweets. It was

little enough and could not compensate for having to stay behind in Cholm, but now there was a certain pride in being there even though the situation of those who still manned the crumbling positions was a serious one. Clothing was becoming threadbare through continual use and none was being received. There had in any case been no proper winter clothing issued and the temperature at times had touched forty-two degrees below zero. So many men had been wounded or were sick that every available soldier was in the line and there was little relief from sentry duty. Then came typhus. "It was now a matter of refusing to give in, for thereby the sacrifices of our dead comrades would have been in vain. We could not let them down."

Russian attempts to approach the German front line were to dig tunnels in the snow through which small groups would crawl to emerge almost on top of the defenders and to try to destroy them with explosive charges. These assaults were driven back with heavy loss. Round the perimeter there now lay thousands upon thousands of unburied Russian dead, the more recently killed showing black against the snow and others merely snow-covered mounds.

More Soviet troops were brought up and, aware that another time of testing was approaching, a bastion of wrecked and damaged vehicles was formed on the eastern side of the town. Russian patrols and snipers infiltrated into this little fortress and miniature battles were fought as the grenadiers struck back with hand grenade, machine pistol and entrenching tool against the defiant Red Army men. The object of these constant attacks was to force back the German line and to gain the higher east bank of the Lovat River. Then the Soviets would dominate the lower western ground. The Red attacks came and were repulsed, but each gained a few yards until at the end of one furious assault less than a hundred metres separated the Soviet infantry from the eastern bank. The Alarm Companies were alerted and swung forward into action once again, driving back in close combat assault the enemy from the advanced positions which he had reached. There was bitter fighting in the brick-built GPU (secret police) headquarters, and in room to room battles. In the building, according to General Scherer, more than 900 hand grenades were used in just a few hours.

Under continuing Soviet pressure the perimeter shrank until the drop zone was no larger than 200 by 500 metres and of the daylight consignment of up to 200 canisters, an increasing proportion was lost to the enemy or fell into no-man's-land. Nevertheless, the supply position did improve even if there was still too little fodder for the horses which towed the anti-tank guns. The greatest deprivation was that, for the whole length of the siege, no mail was received; a serious blow to the morale, this, although eggs were dropped at Easter to let the garrison know that it had not been forgotten.

The days began to lengthen, winter was passing, the air was becoming warmer and the thaw was setting in. A combination of air warmth and cold earth produced thick fogs in which battle patrols from both sides met, clashed and vanished again. Soviet pressures began to increase once again as the time of campaigning approached and STAVKA, needing Cholm as a springboard, demanded its capture.

The thaw brought with it not only the promise of warmth, but also certain inconvenience and danger to the garrison. Water from the melting snow poured into cellars and underground dugouts, driving the occupants into the open where they were vulnerable to shell-fire. The ice walls which had for so many weeks served as trenches and parapets began to diminish, exposing the defenders to Russian fire.

During March the corps' relief columns began fighting their way up the west-east highway, making only slow progress in the bad going and against tenacious Russian defence. Only slowly did von Arnim's men advance and within the perimeter a certain anxiety manifested itself as May Day approached, for it was almost certain on that day a major assault would be launched against the town. The garrison prepared itself to meet the new thrusts and when the first of these came in on May Day gunners knocked out five tanks in quick succession. The defence still stood firm, heartened by the knowledge that relief was not too far away. During 2 May, four more Russian tanks were destroyed.

On the following day a relief column made up of a panzer and grenadiers set off at 11.50hrs to smash their way through to Cholm. The first efforts failed and the assault was renewed on the 4th. The German barrage opened just before dawn and the SPs thrust forward but, unsupported by the grenadiers who had been involved in bitter fighting with Red Army infantry, the advance was halted only a kilometre from Cholm. Reveille for the battle group was at 03.45hrs on 5 May, and to keep the exact time of the attack hidden from the Soviets the battle group commander ordered that only one vehicle engine at a time could be started. The point SPs went over their start line at 05.20hrs and not long after that time Stukas began to bomb Soviet positions. Dazed by the artillery and dive-bomb barrage the Red troops were quickly overrun and at 06.20hrs the garrison of Cholm linked up with grenadiers and SPs of the relief column. This advance-guard was followed by more troops and the garrison, depleted, worn, tired but jubilant, was taken out of the line for a rest. A force of less than 4,000 determined men had held off an enemy whose numbers rose during the siege to six infantry divisions, six infantry brigades and two tank brigades. The losses which the garrison had sustained, 1,550 dead and 2,200 wounded, were a minute fraction of the 1,107,830, all ranks which had been suffered by the German forces from the first day of 'Operation Barbarossa'; but those from Cholm were comrades, men who had fought, suffered and endured together.

Statistically the garrison had repulsed 128 Soviet assaults, forty-two of which had been made with tanks and infantry. By rifle and machine-gun fire the men of Cholm had shot down two Soviet aircraft and had destroyed forty-two Red tanks. They themselves had carried out ten infantry attacks and had mounted forty-three counter-attacks. Two hundred of their wounded had been evacuated by air and on the day on which they were relieved there were only 1,200 men still fit for action.

The outward and visible sign of the comradeship which had been forged in the battles since January was the Cholm arm shield; that and the East Front medal which showed that its wearer had served during that first, terrible winter of 1941–42.

One military result was that the line around Cholm stayed immobile until late in 1944, when Russian offensives drove the last Germans from Soviet soil. It may be perhaps that the defence which the small garrison put up in the first winter battles influenced the STAVKA decision not to attack in force again at that part of the line.

Epilogue

"Since midnight the guns have been silent ..."

THE LAST OKW COMMUNIQUÉ, MAY 1945

In May 1945 the gunfire died away in Europe as the war ended. It was over. The men of the German Army who had stood facing eastward on that June morning in 1941 were, for the greater part, dead, wounded or missing. What had been achieved, what gained for a blood toll of millions and for the misery inflicted upon tens of millions?

Politically and geographically the German attempt to move her frontier eastwards to the line of the Volga had failed. Instead the borders of the Soviet Union had been advanced westward and the status of that country raised to a super power. The frontiers of Soviet-dominated lands were no longer on the Bug but were within striking distance of the Rhine. The political structure and the shape of Europe had been changed. The Soviet system, which the dead Hitler had thought could be brought crashing down by a single kick, was now determining the fate of a great part of his Thousand Year Reich.

The consequences of war can been seen in many countries in the memorials to the fallen or in the cemeteries which mark the passage of armies. The traveller crossing Soviet territory today will find no evidence of the passing of Hitler's army. Determined that there would be no mark, no sign to commemorate those whom the Soviets considered to be invaders and criminals, all traces of the German military cemeteries on Soviet soil were effaced. The plots in which German units had once interred their honoured dead were laid waste. The inscriptions above the wooden gateways were cast down and even the birch wood crosses which marked the final resting place of so many German soldiers were overturned and removed. There would be no part of Soviet territory to which Germans might come to mourn their fallen. All was ploughed up and resown. Within a few years the silver grey steppe grass had recovered the sites, crops grew again in soil made more fruitful by the fruit which it held. The forests reclaimed their own and nothing now recalls that across the wide and open steppe there was fire and movement, death and destruction on a massive scale, elation for a victory gained or elation for having survived at all.

But across the eastern parts of Europe in areas where the Red Army advanced to victory, there stand the monuments to its fallen. These imposing memorials have a common design. They show, either singly or in groups, Russian soldiers in heroic pose, their calm and resolute gaze directed westwards. Some weapon of war decorates the granite bases of these structures: an anti-tank gun, a field gun, a T 34 from the unit which liberated the town. Each of these memorials is a statement of the strength of the Red Army.

At one of them even today Russian guards goose step into position, swinging their arms across the body in German fashion, as they move, the well-drilled representatives of the Soviet military, to their places at the war memorial in West Berlin. There they stand, khaki, immobile, immaculate in the heart of the capital city from which the orders went out, so many years ago, to open that great war in the East whose passage ran for forty-six months.

The Reichstag building is gone; the Führer bunker is a ruin. The grandiose buildings in which the officers of the services planned and executed the campaigns of the Second World War have long since vanished. All is gone and forgotten – but not quite all. Still in the columns of German Old Comrades' Association magazines there appear the lists of those who are still missing, lost on steppe or tundra, in a freezing hell or in liquid mud, screaming alone and frightened as they died crushed to a bloody pulp under tank tracks or were incinerated in the petrol blaze of a burning panzer. There are hundreds of thousands still missing, whose fate is either unknown or uncertain. In many German homes there are those who still hope to hear that the one whom they thought long dead has returned from prison camp, for although the Soviet government has declared officially that no more German prisoners-of-war are held in camps, this statement is disbelieved by Germans who are convinced that still behind the Iron Curtain are men who more than thirty years ago passed into a captivity from which they have not yet been, nor perhaps ever will be, released.

The scale of losses on the Eastern Front worried deeply the leaders of Nazi Germany, but there were many men in more humble circumstances who were also deeply concerned at the loss of so many future fathers, future leaders of their country. One of these was a padre in a Styrian Gebirgsjäger unit who had fought alongside his men throughout the long years of war. Let his words of worry and concern be the epitaph to this war on the Eastern Front. He wrote these in the autumn of 1941, shortly after the battle of Uman. "Today I buried some more of my former parishioners, Gebirgsjäger, who have died in this frightful land. Three more letters to write to add to the total of all those which I have written already in this war. The deleted names of the fallen are now more numerous in my pocket diary than the names of the living. My parish is bleeding to death on the plains of this country. We shall all die out here."

Bibliography

BÜHLMANN, G.: *Die Versorgung fremder Heere*. Huber & Co., 1949.

BRAUN, J.: *Enzian und Edelweiss*. Podzun Verlag, 1955.

COOPER, M. & LUCAS, J.: *Panzer. The Armoured Force of the Third Reich*. Macdonald & Jane's 1976; St. Martin's Press, USA, 1978.

COOPER, M.: *The German Army 1933-1945*. Macdonald & Jane's, 1978; Stein & Day, USA, 1978.

DWINGER, E.: *Wiedershen mit Sowjet-Russland*. Diederiche Verlag, 1942.

GEYER, H.: *Das IX A. K. im Ostfeldzug. 1941*. Vowinckel Verlag, 1969.

GORDON, G.: *Soviet Partisan Warfare, 1941-1944. The German Perspective*. University of Iowa, USA, 1972.

GROSSMANN, H.: *Geschichte der 6ten Infantrie Division*. Podzun Verlag, 1958.

HESSE, E.: *Der sowjetischen Partisan Krieg*. Musterschmidt, 1969.

HILLGRUBER, A. (Ed): *K. T. B. der O K W*. Bernhard & Graefe, 1963.

KERN, E.: *General von Pannwitz und seine Kosaken*. Schulz, 1971.

KÖHLER (Pub).: *Heereskalendar 1943*. Köhler, 1943.

LEACH, B.: *German Strategy in Russia*. Oxford University Press, London and New York, 1973.

LEDERREY, E.: *Germany's Defeat in the East*. War Office, London, 1955.

MIDDELDORF, E.: *Taktik im Russlandfeldzug*. Mittler, 1956.

MUNZEL, O.: *Panzer Taktik*. Vowinckel, 1959.

NEKRITSCH, A. & GRIGORENKO, P.: *Genickschuss. Die Rote Armee am 22.6.1941*. Europa Verlag, 1969.

O A K II: Partisanen Meldungen. Anlageband zu Tätigkeitsbericht. 15/11/41—1/9/42. Unpublished typescript.

O K H: *Jahrbuch des deutschen Heeres 1942*. Breitkopf, 1942.

O K H: *Taschenbuch für den Winterkrieg*. O K H, 1942.

PAUL, W.: *Geschichte der 18 Panzer Division*. Kameradschaftskreis der Division.

PHILLIPI, A.: *Das Pripjetproblem. Beiheft 2 to Wehrwissenschaftliche Rundschau*. Mittler, 1956.

PHILLIPI, A. & HEISE, F.: *Der Feldzug gegen Sowjet Russland*. Kohlhammer, 1962.

PIEKALKIEWICZ, J.: *Pferd und Reiter im Zweiten Weltkrieg*. Südwest Verlag, 1977.

SCHMIDT, A.: *Geschichte der 10 Division*. Podzun Verlag, 1968.

SENGER u ETTERLIN, F. M. Von: *Die 24 Panzer Division*. Vowinckel, 1962.

SIMON, M.: Experiences Gained in Combat Against Russian Infantry. Unpublished typescript, 1949.

TESSIN, G.: *Verbände und Truppen der deutschen Wehrmacht und Waffen SS 1939/45*. Biblio Verlag, 1975.

WESTHEN, W.: *Geschichte der 16 Panzer Division*. Podzun Verlag, 1958.

WILLMEYER, W.: Die Eisbrücke über den Dnieper. Unpublished typescript. Das Verhalten der roten Armee im besetzten Gebieten Deutschlands. Unpublished typescript. 1945.

Personal diaries, war diaries, letters and interviews.

Index